The Oxford Library of Italian Classics
GENERAL EDITOR: ARCHIBALD COLQUHOUN

USELESS MEMOIRS
OF
CARLO GOZZI

Useless Memoirs

of

CARLO GOZZI

The translation of
JOHN ADDINGTON SYMONDS

Edited, Revised, and Abridged by
PHILIP HORNE

With an Introduction by
HAROLD ACTON

LONDON
OXFORD UNIVERSITY PRESS
NEW YORK TORONTO
1962

Oxford University Press, Amen House, London E.C.4

GLASGOW NEW YORK TORONTO MELBOURNE WELLINGTON
BOMBAY CALCUTTA MADRAS KARACHI LAHORE DACCA
CAPE TOWN SALISBURY NAIROBI IBADAN ACCRA
KUALA LUMPUR HONG KONG

Printed in Great Britain
by Richard Clay and Company, Ltd., Bungay, Suffolk

CONTENTS

INTRODUCTION

Tout Venise, son ancien gouvernement, son bavardage dans les *Memorie inutili di Carlo Gozzi*, 3 vol.

Stendhal (1818)

Realism, surrealism, existentialism, neo-realism—somewhere the battle is raging even now, albeit with flagging energy. It started long ago, and it was fought with surprising vigour in Venice, of all placid places, plumb in the middle of the eighteenth century. Eventually realism seemed to triumph but pure fantasy still wins an occasional victory, apart from *Peter Pan* and the perennial Christmas pantomimes. The gaps left by Rostand and Maeterlinck are filled, however ephemerally, by M. Cocteau and Mr. Beckett.

Count Carlo Gozzi was the paladin of fantasy, which had been kept alive in the theatre by the improvisations of the aptly styled *Commedia dell'arte*. His profound distaste for what he called 'those vulgar scenes from life', with which Carlo Goldoni was trying to reform the Venetian stage, impelled him to lead the assault against the new realism. Time has vindicated Goldoni's comedies, which continue to draw large audiences, whereas the fairy dramas of Gozzi have only survived in operatic versions which are seldom performed.

Naturalism or realism is still going strong in most theatres though some of us may feel that it is gyrating in a vicious circle and that for sheer momentum of monotony it will soon go gurgling down the kitchen sink. Goldoni's charm endures less on account of his realism than because he has become a synonym for eighteenth-century Venice. He portrays a Carnival period, as it were, and appeals to our nostalgia for that happier day before 'the kissing had to stop'. Pietro Longhi was, as he recognized, his parallel in painting: he depicted similar aspects of Venetian life with the same rosy cheerfulness and meticulous observation. There is no intensity of feeling in either. The socially engaged, self-conscious realist of today is less rosy than blood-stained.

Those who seek escape from the butcher's shop and the kitchen sink will find Carlo Gozzi sympathetic for all his grumbling and sneering. The wry smile is less tedious than the golden grin. While Goldoni was the type of beaming Rotarian, Gozzi was a Daumieresque Don Quixote tilting at windmills. He laughed at his misadventures and took his successes with many a grain of salt. His theatrical frescoes were to crumble with the dissolution of Sacchi's company, but what frantic applause greeted them in their heyday while the plaster was still wet! In order to evoke their long-departed glory we should consult the contemporary critic Giuseppe Baretti, who was carried away by his enthusiasm.

In the years 1764 and 1765, [wrote Dr. Johnson's crony[1]] I have seen acted in Venice ten or twelve of Gozzi's plays, and had even the perusal of two or three of them in manuscript; and no works of this kind ever pleased me so much : so that, when I saw Mr. Garrick there, I lamented that he did not come in carnival-time, that he might have seen some of them acted; and I am confident he would have admired the originality of Gozzi's genius, the most wonderful, in my opinion, next Shakespeare, that ever any age or country produced. The cast of Gozzi's mind leads him to strike out many characters and beings not to be found in nature, like that of Caliban in *The Tempest*; and yet most natural and true like Caliban's.

To his astonishing power of invention, so rare among modern poets, Gozzi joins great purity and force of language, harmony of versification, intricacy of plot, multiplicity of incidents, probability of catastrophe, variety of decoration, and many other excellencies expected in the modern drama. It is a pity that this author could never be prevailed upon to publish his plays. He has resisted the strongest solicitations of his friends, without giving any satisfactory reason for his aversion to such a publication. Some attribute it to his partiality for an actress, to whom he leaves the profits arising from their exhibition : but this I can scarcely believe, as her profits from such a publication would be much more considerable than those which she reaps by her acting. I rather think that having no great value for his audience, Gozzi sets likewise but little value on the things that please them : and perhaps it was a similar reason, that kept Shakespeare from publishing a correct and complete edition of his plays while he lived. May the good genius of the Italian stage befriend Gozzi's compositions, and not suffer it to be robbed of them. . . .

[1] *An Account of the Manners and Customs of Italy*, by Joseph Baretti, London, 1768.

Had his *fiabe* never been printed Gozzi's reputation might have remained fabulous. As soon as they were published, in 1772, they lost their mysterious magic. Not that their author staked any great claim for them. Goldoni and Chiari having attacked the *Commedia dell'arte*, he set out to prove that the Venetian public would desert their plays for a nursery tale dramatized in the tradition they despised. This he accomplished with such effect that Goldoni and Chiari soon retired from Venice. Between 1761 and 1765 ten *fiabe* were produced with preponderant success. Some critics will share Vernon Lee's predilection for *L'augellin Belverde* ('The Little Bird Fair Green'); others may share Schiller's preference for *Turandot*: each has its individual appeal which defies any detailed synopsis. John Addington Symonds, with his habitual acumen, remarked that they are admirable 'not as finished literature, but as the raw material of dramatic presentation. They need the life of action, the adjuncts of scenery, the illusion of the stage.' And he concluded that they 'might furnish excellent *libretti* to composers of opera'. In fact the composers had been swift to take note. Wagner had based one of his earliest operas, *Die Feen*, on *La donna serpente* in 1833; Busoni and Puccini both seized upon *Turandot*; Sergei Prokofiev's operatic version of *The Love of the Three Oranges* was first produced in Chicago in 1921; and Hans Werner Henze's version of *Il re Cervo* ('The King Turned Stag') was performed only recently, almost two centuries after its first production.

The German romantics mistook Carlo Gozzi for a precursor but he was no more romantic than the author of *Candide*, for his fantasy was combined with the earthy common sense of the *Commedia dell'arte*. The real Carlo Gozzi has revealed himself in his *Memorie inutili*, of which Symonds has provided such a skilful translation. He was a caustic moralist of conservative bent who considered that he had been born under an evil star to struggle against a hostile world. 'A good fellow at bottom, but splenetic', he said of Goldoni, which applied more exactly to himself. Just as his *fiabe* owed their origin to his quarrels with Goldoni and Chiari, his *Memoirs* were inspired by his dispute with Pietro Antonio Gratarol. If the former succumbed to the comedy of manners, the latter have every reason to survive Goldoni's, which are dull and prosaic. The crotchety bachelor offers us a more varied and particularized panorama of Venetian manners in the eighteenth century, no student of which should ignore it. Unlike his famous rival he spent most of his long life—1720–1806—on Venetian land and water.

An impoverished scion of the burgher aristocracy and the sixth of eleven children, he was mainly self-educated. Like his elder brother Gasparo, he was a precocious writer and an omnivorous reader. All the Gozzi children indulged frequently in amateur theatricals and improvised farces in which their parents and neighbours were caricatured. These must have planted the seeds of his future plays and trained that talent for female impersonation which delighted his military comrades in Dalmatia. His anecdote about the sonnet he composed for a midwife at the age of nine shows that he was sophisticated as well as precocious, and it is not surprising that he caught the eye of Metastasio's distinguished predecessor Apostolo Zeno, who encouraged his juvenile efforts. But his father became paralysed and speechless as the result of a stroke, and his foolishly extravagant mother made life at home intolerable. After three years of roughing it in Dalmatia, then a Venetian colony, he realized that he had no military vocation. His account of his return to the decaying family mansion is none the less pathetic for its humorous detachment.

Amid the hurly-burly of a chaotic household he managed to devote six hours a day to writing, practising verbal scales until he could master a technique of his own. The rest of his time was spent studying cranks and oddities, for which he had a flair, in local coffee-houses and theatres. Aristocrat though he was, he enjoyed the company of shop-keepers and artisans who 'carried the art of getting the maximum of pleasure at a minimum outlay to perfection'. His attempts to

restore the family fortune after his father's death only resulted in bickering and litigation. His ancestral estates having
been divided, he left his uncongenial home and made up his
mind to remain a bachelor : 'First, because I abhorred indissoluble ties of any sort. Secondly, because my brothers were
married, with large families, and I could not stomach the
prospect of charging our estate with jointures, and of procreating a brood of little Gozzis, all paupers.'

The satirist in him was stimulated by a long series of lawsuits, but his health suffered from the strain. He was warned to
avoid raw milk like poison, and indeed he would have turned
any milk sour. Friendship he shunned as well as matrimony,
'being of opinion that a man of many friends is the real friend
of none'. Literary controversy seems to have been his absorb-
ing passion until he took to writing plays in middle age. He
joined one of those typical academies, half-serious, half-
facetious, more sociable than literary, which pullulated
throughout Italy at that time. This was called *Granelleschi*
from a word meaning testicles : an owl clutching two balls
was adopted as its crest, and its avowed aim was 'to promote
the study of our best old authors, the simplicity and harmony
of chastened style, and above all the purity of the Italian
tongue'. But the tone of its sporadic publications was more
scurrilous than chaste. Carlo Gozzi led the vanguard against
Goldoni and Chiari with his satirical almanac *La Tartana
degl' influssi* ('The Tartane of Influxes') for the leap-year 1756.
To follow the details of this campaign would be tedious. Goldoni challenged his assailant to compete with him on his own
ground in these words :

> He who proves not both theme and argument
> Acts like the dog who barks against the moon.

Gozzi riposted by offering his first play, *The Love of the
Three Oranges*, partly written and partly improvised, to
Antonio Sacchi's *Commedia dell'arte* company in 1761, when
it was threatened with ruin by the vogue of Chiari's and
Goldoni's plays, and especially by the latter's propaganda.

By refusing payment he strengthened his position as the company's mentor-patron and prolonged its lease of life.

It is the narrative of this close collaboration which gives his *Memoirs* a special value for students of the eighteenth-century theatre in Italy. Sacchi's company became a second family to him. He examined their characteristics and exploited their mutual rivalry 'for their own advantage, the profit of the company, and the success of his dramatic writings'. But, as in his own domestic circle, he had to cope with bickerings and intrigues, backbiting and slander. The leading ladies were very pernickety about precedence, etiquette, and salary. Compared with other theatrical troupes in Venice Sacchi's was quite respectable. Having fanned its dying embers to a cheerful blaze he sat down to enjoy the warmth and sniff the incense. But in consorting with actresses he risked burning his fingers for, as he was soon to realize: 'Let no man deceive himself by supposing that it is possible to converse with actresses without love-making. You must make it, or pretend to make it. This is the only way to guide them to their own advantage. . . . Among actresses, the term friendship is something fabulous and visionary. They immediately substitute the word love, and do not attend to distinctions.' He fancied himself incombustible, but fifty is a dangerous age for bachelors though he tried to conceal it.

When Teodora Ricci joined Sacchi's company in 1771 Carlo Gozzi was caught off his guard. His description of this actress was penned long after his infatuation for her had cooled: it was far from flattering. His first impression must have been different. Perhaps she was a *jolie laide*; perhaps he had a hair fetish. For she was pregnant and pitted with smallpox. 'The abundance of her beautiful blond hair made up for some defects of feature. . . . One incurable fault she had; this was the movement of her lips, which often amounted to what is called making a wry face.' Her habitual expression was one of disgust.

Gozzi promptly became the official protector and Pygmalion of this pock-marked Galatea. He urged the reluctant

Sacchi to engage her. The failure of her Venetian début would have discouraged others, yet he wrote plays expressly for her and coached her for the title-rôle of his *Principessa filosofa*, in which she won her first applause. He fails to convince us that his connexion with her was platonic. As she was a typical product of her age and profession it is unlikely that he took such pains to launch her without submitting to some elusive magnetism. He also became the godfather—some said the father—of one of her children; and he introduced her into polite society. Her husband, a seedy journalist and mummer, felt honoured by this relationship. Gozzi on his side had no objection to her intimacy with a young actor called Coralli: he only drew the line at 'gentlemen callers' of his own class.

This Bohemian liaison lasted six years, and it seems to have been an agreeable substitute for matrimony. Gozzi was a creature of habit: he was proud of being regarded as the tutelary genius of Sacchi's company. But his creative talent, which had galloped gaily under the spur of literary controversy, slowed down to a humdrum trot under the influence of Teodora Ricci. He was evidently more gifted as a hater than as a lover. No doubt the plays he wrote for Teodora displayed her qualities to advantage but they were definitely inferior to his *fiabe*. Most of them were adapted from Spanish models.

Inevitably the actress grew tired of her elderly protector. She longed for Paris, where she imagined she would captivate a more glittering public and perhaps soar to the rank of a royal mistress. While Gozzi was prostrated by rheumatism she met Pietro Antonio Gratarol, a Paduan grandee, distributing sugar-plums among the ladies of Sacchi's troupe. Her appreciation of these dainties was so touchingly expressed that Gratarol promised to send her a fresh supply. Thus started another liaison which was soon the talk of the town, for Teodora's relations with the playwright were notorious and Gratarol was a flamboyant public figure. As a secretary to the Venetian Senate Gratarol was eligible for various diplomatic appointments, which in his case proved disappointments. Recently he had been appointed resident in Turin and had spent lavishly on his equipage, retinue, silver, and porcelain in advance. Then the King of Sardinia recalled his resident from Venice and Gratarol was forced to unpack. After all the pomp and publicity of his preparations the Venetians were maliciously amused. He was expecting to be sent to Naples when he became infatuated with Teodora Ricci in 1776, and the storm followed which wrecked his career. This was the background of Carlo Gozzi's *Memoirs*, which are haunted by the Malvolio-like ghost of Gratarol.

Gozzi's account of these events should be weighed against Gratarol's *Narrazione apologetica*. Racked with rheumatism and jilted by Teodora, he had cause for provocation. He was about to discard a comedy adapted from Tirso de Molina when he had a flash of inspiration: he would enliven it with a caricature of his rival. A fatuous Don Adonis was introduced into the plot. After reading it aloud to a few friends, however, he was still opposed to its performance. But Sacchi had a nose for novelty: he scented a sensation. Gozzi's title *Le droghe d'amore* ('The Love-Potions') should titillate the public; Don Adonis would do the rest. The author's statement is not entirely persuasive: 'Pestered by perpetual applications for this comedy, in an evil moment I drew it from its sepulchre and tossed it over to the *capocomico*. I told him that he might take the manuscript as a gift, but that if the play failed before the public, as I thought it would, I should never exercise my pen again on compositions for the stage.'

Teodora Ricci warned Gratarol that he was to be pilloried and he tried to stop the play. But it had already been passed by the censor and Gratarol had made enemies in high places. To the most influential of these, Caterina Dolfin Tron, married to the Procurator of St. Mark, Sacchi entrusted the manuscript for safety. Would he have done this without prompting from Gozzi, whose brother Gasparo was one of her oldest cronies? The *doyenne* of Venetian hostesses was enchanted: by reading and discussing the comedy in her salon she gave it the widest publicity. One and all declared that they could see no personal satire in the character of Don Adonis and blamed Gratarol for trying to spoil their fun.

Caterina Dolfin Tron bore the so-called 'resident' a grudge. Having made use of her to curry favour with her husband, his attentions had noticeably dwindled. He was all puffed up with the importance of his diplomatic status. His wife, whom he had deserted after twenty years of marriage, had appealed to Caterina for protection. Either for her sake or for that of Carlo Gozzi (whom she nicknamed 'The Bear' on account of his aloofness) Caterina had urged Gratarol to break with the actress. His blunt refusal increased her resentment. At this juncture the manuscript of *The Love-Potions* fell into her lap. Owing to Gratarol's position in the government Gozzi lost his nerve. He pleaded with Caterina to stop the production but she told him not to be silly. The censor thereupon informed him that the comedy had passed beyond his control and that the magistracy which he served was infallible.

Both the outraged dramatist and his rival in love were anxious to avoid a scandal. Had Gratarol kept quiet the affair might have evaporated, but his hysterical conduct inflated it. Caterina Tron induced Sacchi to give the rôle of Don Adonis to an actor resembling 'the resident', who studied his mannerisms and wore identical garb. The rumour had spread and the theatre was crammed in consequence : hundreds were turned away on the first night.

Gozzi pretends to deplore the liberty taken with his text, but a tell-tale gusto creeps into his narrative all the same. Sacchi shrugged his shoulders : he was only interested in his box-office receipts. The appearance of Don Adonis brought the house down. Gozzi felt ill at ease but Gratarol writhed under the very eyes of his cast-off spouse. Caterina Tron led the applause.

The comedy was repeated for four nights running with Don Adonis as the principal attraction. The wretched Gratarol, as he duly recorded, was dogged by a swarm of 'lackeys, barbers, players, spies, pimps, and baser beings, if such there be,' who 'compared notes with each other as to my resemblance to the

B

vile actor travestied to mimic me'. This shower of mockery brought on persecution mania.

Albeit against the grain, Teodora Ricci had been obliged to perform in *The Love-Potions*. After its initial success she sent a messenger to the theatre to announce that she had hurt her leg and could not move. This caused a riot among the incredulous audience. The surgeons sent to examine her confirmed that she was malingering. An officer of the Council of Ten was ordered to escort her to the theatre and see that she fulfilled her contract. In the meantime Gratarol petitioned the State Inquisitors and insisted that Gozzi could and should suppress the play 'tomorrow and in perpetuity'. Gozzi promised to do his best and failed, but not through lack of effort. He was reminded once more that his comedy was the property of the public and the magistrates of State.

The play went on and on. In his impotent rage Gratarol sent Gozzi an insulting letter which he consigned to Signora Tron, complaining that her pique against a madman had subjected him to this. The lady forwarded it to the State Inquisitors and Gozzi added a petition to vindicate his honour. Gratarol had to send him a written apology as an alternative to arrest. Copies of these letters were circulated, and one must agree with Symonds that so much official pother about a comedy and a pock-marked actress was a symptom of the proud Republic's decadence.

The Love-Potions enjoyed another triumph in spite of Teodora Ricci's atrocious acting. Gratarol hibernated until a new play was billed at the Rialto. His fury was concentrated against Signora Tron, whom he blamed not only for his own misfortunes but also for those of the Republic. He posed as the advocate of morality against the corruption of Caterina and her husband. Months went by and his promotion to Naples was suspended: he was advised to return discreetly to his secretarial post. But the cause of his distress lay primarily in himself. After a visit to Vienna he was still the butt of gossip. The actor impersonating Don Adonis in Milan had had a bottle of ink thrown at him. Fortunately it had missed his face, but the incident was attributed to Gratarol's revenge.

By Venetian law no secretary of the Senate could resign unless he entered the Church. It was mortifying to linger on the lagoon when he might have been preening himself in the bay of Naples. He was tired of Teodora. In September 1777 he planned to escape—like the 'Missing Diplomats' in our own day. For a civil servant to leave the Republic surreptitiously was considered an act of treason. A proclamation was issued setting a price upon his head and confiscating his property. He published his *Narrazione apologetica* in Stockholm and it reached Venice during the summer of 1779, when Paolo Renier had been elected Doge instead of Andrea Tron. This was a diatribe against his enemies, and the laws and abuses of the Republic of Saint Mark. Carlo Gozzi was called a lying hypocrite and much else, but the worst shafts were reserved for Caterina Tron and her husband : 'in her youth she had passed through all the different stages of womanhood and had gone down into the mud in order to rise above the rooftop'; she had enslaved Andrea Tron before marrying him; she paid brisk young men to satisfy her lusts, etc. Clandestinely the pamphlet was soon sold out.

Gozzi replied with an elaborate *Confutation*; he also wrote or dictated his *Useless Memoirs*. But the State Inquisitors would not allow him to print either : they preferred to draw a veil over the scandal since the pamphlet contained too many unpalatable truths.

After devious wanderings and misadventures the outlaw died miserably at Madagascar in 1785. His *Narrazione apologetica* was reprinted by his friends in 1797 when the ancient Republic had collapsed and its citizens had more serious concerns. Anachronistically, Carlo Gozzi availed himself of the new freedom of the press to publish his *Memoirs* together with his *Confutation* and additional pages bringing the former up to date (March 1798).

'With the Sacchi company at his command, Carlo Gozzi appeared a genius;' wrote Vernon Lee,[1] 'as soon as the Sacchi

---

[1] *Studies of the Eighteenth Century in Italy*, London, 1880.

company broke up he was forgotten.' His *Memoirs* end fittingly with the dissolution of the last great *Commedia dell' arte* troupe in Italy. The aged Sacchi bade him farewell before leaving Venice furtively in 1782, and they parted in tears. Their association had continued for a quarter of a century. After that moment Gozzi gave up writing for the theatre. He must have realized that the comedy of masks was as doomed as the Republic of Saint Mark.

The translation of this long-neglected document was undertaken by John Addington Symonds after the merited success of his translation of Cellini's *Autobiography*. From Davos Platz he wrote to his friend Horatio Brown on 15 November 1887: 'Nimmo [the publisher] proposes that I should translate Gozzi's "Life". Do you know anything of Gozzi? I fancy it would be a pleasant book to do.' And on 21 December: 'The great difficulty is to get a copy of the *Memorie inutili*. I feel rather indignant with myself for going in for lucrative literature, as I am doing. I should not have thought of Cellini except for the £210 . . . or of Gozzi except for the £210 to come.'

No sooner had he embarked on this work than he expressed his misgivings to Brown on 21 January 1888:

Excellent to read through rapidly for a student of *roba italiana*, his *Memoirs* are hardly worth translating, and their interest depends upon such trivialities—the decadence of Venetian society in a putrid mass of political corruption, Brummagem French philosophy aped by Italians with no revolutionary force inside them, prostitution, literary cabals, vain efforts to rehabilitate Dante in the city of Casanova, Baffo, and the Doge Renier, bad style, bad morals, effeminacy, hypocrisy, sloth, *dappocaggine* of every sort—with an odd unsympathetic bastard between Don Quixote and a pettifogging attorney, a man of cramped genius and of respectable sentiments turned sour, to serve as a central figure—all this is so irrelevant to the main current of world-history, so bizarre, so involved in masses of petty details which have lost the accent of humanity, that I despair of making anything out of my work. And yet I am engaged.

Symonds toiled with prodigious speed in spite of his acute lung trouble and on 17 July 1888 he wrote that he had finished the translation. Whereupon his publisher had qualms:

Nimmo writes to say that he cannot venture on publishing the love-stories in Gozzi's *Memoirs*, and that he agrees with me about the impossibility of leaving them out. In this case he wants me to consent to a 'privately printed' edition. He says that the Vigilance Society is prosecuting two publishers for translations which it thinks improper. I have replied to Nimmo that I will not evade the peril of prosecution by 'privately printing', the result of which would be to throw the whole odium and responsibility of Gozzi upon me.

Accordingly the two stout volumes were published in 1889 in a luxurious limited edition which was sold out immediately. 'I never did anything with less spontaneous sympathy, and with a greater sense of merely mechanical dexterity', Symonds told Horatio Brown. But Brown was bored by the eighteenth century like most Victorians, whereas 'the picturesque aspects of Venetian decadence' appealed to Symonds, who justly appreciated the historical and psychological value of genuine autobiographies.

Owing to his immense facility, productivity, and geniality, Symonds has not been given his due as a writer. The seven tomes of his *Renaissance in Italy* are still invaluable to students of that period, and his translations are masterly though somewhat handicapped by Victorian prudery. Today no translator would dream of omitting Gozzi's account of his amorous adventures, but then his frankness and cynical humour were, as Symonds wrote, 'out of tune with modern taste'. His sensible retort to those who raised objections was that 'the debated passages are good in literature, true to nature, and sound in moral feeling'. He felt justified, however, in removing sentences and phrases which might have caused offence to his readers. We are less squeamish now, and Mr. Philip Horne has done much to restore verisimilitude in this new edition. In other respects Symonds improved the original text by condensing certain chapters and omitting prolix redundancies, for Gozzi was in a hurry to vindicate himself as he was getting on in years.

Like Gozzi, Symonds was also a genius *manqué*, a highly intelligent scholar and prolific versifier, dreaming of an unattainable perfection. Gozzi's awareness of failure made him misanthropic, whereas Symonds had a warmer, more artistic temperament. 'I am nothing if not cultivated,' he confessed, 'or, at least, the world only expects culture from me. But in my heart of hearts I do not believe in culture, except as an adjunct to life. "Life is more than literature," I say.' But he was a chronic invalid with 'the curious fretful energy of someone tormented by a persistent drain on his vitality'. He was only 52 when he died in 1893 after finishing his *Life* of Michelangelo : his *Study of Walt Whitman* was published on the day of his death.

Symonds was an inspired amateur, a literary *viveur* as he called it, in contrast with Walter Pater and such wholly dedicated writers as Flaubert. Not the least of his contributions to the history of literature is his resurrection of these far from useless *Memoirs*, now so ably edited by Mr. Philip Horne.

HAROLD ACTON

A NOTE ON THE TEXT

In abridging Symonds's translation, I have tried to retain everything in Gozzi's Memoirs that has a strong narrative interest or that throws some light on the personality of the writer or on the times in which he lived. The parts omitted are, in the main, whole chapters of relatively small interest, whose contents are summarized in connecting passages, printed in italic type to distinguish them from the text of the translation itself. This procedure preserves the continuity of the narrative, and readers can feel that nothing of any importance has been withheld from them. Some individual paragraphs have been eliminated too, and the contents of these, when they are of sufficient interest, are summarized in a note at the foot of the page. As indicated by the footnotes on pp. 178, 200, and 216, these omissions constitute in effect, not a first, but a second abridgement of Gozzi's text; for Symonds himself skilfully condensed the contents of the later chapters of the Memoirs into about a third of their original length.

It has been a guiding principle, in view of the excellence of the translation by Symonds, not to meddle too much with his version in a mistaken attempt to modernize an idiom which in many ways conveys the flavour of the eighteenth-century text more successfully than a twentieth-century idiom could ever do. One or two obsolete expressions, such as 'savagery' and 'mud-honey', have been dropped in favour of equivalents —'unsociability', 'darling'—that will be more easily understood today. Readers will doubtless be grateful to have been spared the 'thee'-ing and 'thou'-ing of parts of the intimate dialogue in its original form; and they will find 'Signora Ricci', 'Teodora Ricci', more natural forms of address than 'Mme Ricci', 'the Ricci', as used by Symonds. Otherwise I have intervened only where it was absolutely necessary in order to rectify the occasional (very rare) mistranslation, misspelling, or wrong date. I have also altered the spelling of some of the proper names used by Gozzi in favour of the more familiar spellings in general use at the present time : for example, Innocenzo, Loredan, Vendramin, in preference to Innocenzio, Loredano, and Vendramini.

Those who are curious to find out the extent to which Symonds toned down Gozzi's account of his love-affairs by omitting any allusion likely to be considered in bad taste by his Victorian readers, may compare the old version with the new, which faithfully records each palpitation and sigh. I hope that anyone who does not make such a careful comparison of the two versions will not so readily detect that the additions are the work of a different hand. The largest single addition to the text is the new translation of the Proem, without which the Memoirs had an incomplete appearance. Now for the first time Gozzi is allowed to make a preliminary bow to his English public, instead of plunging directly into a recital of the intimate details of his life without any introduction. A number of shorter passages—in some cases merely single phrases—which Symonds omitted, though their contents are of some interest (e.g. Gozzi's reference to his translation of Marivaux's novel *Pharsamond* on p. 21; his complimentary allusion to Boileau on p. 167), have also been restored in the new edition.

The footnotes composed by Symonds admirably complemented his translation. It seemed to me, as I was testing their accuracy against the historical sources, that to discard them would be a senseless waste of the labour and care which went into their compilation. I am glad, therefore, that it has been possible to retain a very substantial part of them, dispensing only with those that do not directly elucidate or illustrate the text. The sign (S) indicates that a footnote is entirely—or with insignificant modifications—the work of Symonds. The sign (S; Ed.) means that the original footnote has been enlarged or altered in some material respect. The other footnotes are new.

PHILIP HORNE

PROEM

If I thought that I was a man whose life contained such remarkable feats as might be expected of a great saint or of a great soldier, of a great jurist, philosopher, or man of letters, I should certainly not have the crazy ambition to write and publish my own memoirs. I should leave the task either to the romancers, whose aim is to astonish the reader, or else to those earnest persons desirous of passing on to posterity some edifying instances of exemplary behaviour.

I have seen too many men—and men not wholly devoid of good qualities to boot—render themselves ridiculous, forfeit every merit, and bring down misfortunes upon their own heads as a result of the foolishly inflated opinion which they have of themselves. Men of this sort, blinded by pride, assume a comical 'Touch me not' air of superiority, which makes them as quick to shy as fractious colts. Should they deign to think that they are under an obligation to apologize for themselves, they can do so only by portraying themselves as demigods, while accusing the rest of the world of begrudging them the fame to which they aspire. Poisonous invectives and scurrilous libels pour from their over-heated imaginations, which misrepresent to them as an adversary anyone who does not fall on his face and humble himself before their ridiculous air of self-importance. They rarely condescend to praise other people, because they rarely find anyone worthy of their panegyrics. Such praise as they do give is almost always accorded to simpletons who have admired them, and to milksops who have flattered them.

My greatest and constant concern has been to examine myself as rigorously as if I were conducting my own trial. In this way I have sought to dull the impatient prickings of that vaingloriousness which is to be observed in the gait, mien, and glance of many people. 'Look at me,' they seem to say, 'watch me closely, admire me, worship me, and fear me.' I profited greatly from this exercise, and it is purely from motives of humility that I offer the reader some account of my domestic life, my character, my travels, and my modest literary production. Those who are prepared to endure the tedium of reading these memoirs will discover that the course of my life up to the present merits neither the eulogies of those who wish me well, nor the vile calumnies of those who do not. I shall always be grateful to the former for the honour which they have been pleased to show me, but I shall never bear any ill-will towards the latter because they would fain have discredited me.

Every man living has friends and enemies. These sometimes result, not from consideration of a man's morals and behaviour, but simply from the feeling of attraction or repulsion that a person experiences in respect of a face or a portrait, a temperament like or unlike his own, or a particular manner of speech—rapid or phlegmatic, prolix or laconic, as the case may be. For this reason alone the laws were necessary which forbid us to injure our fellow-men and threaten to castigate the offender. It could be that some people have been prejudiced against me from such innocent causes as these. Therefore I shall paint an accurate portrait of my external appearance, so that anyone wishing to amuse himself by forming an opinion about it can form a correct one. I shall also paint a true picture of the workings of my heart, my manner of thinking, and my temperament, so that those people with subtle and venomous minds who wish to indulge in malicious portraiture at my expense, may do so without departing from the truth. In any case I do not wish to be accused of misrepresentation.

We all carry in our minds a sort of philosophic lens through which we view the objects of this world. Granted that I do indeed possess some grains of philosophy, I may say that the rays which filter through my particular lens incline me more to the outlook of Democritus than to that of Heraclitus. I have never singled out anyone for attack, apart from those who have directed their attacks at me, and even then I have always used pleasantries of a moderate kind, not hurtful to their reputations. On the other hand, I have always laughed indiscriminately, and made others laugh with me, at the infinite number of impressions that my brain received through the aforementioned lens; and since fraud and hypocrisy were, among other things, the principal targets of my humour, I may have acquired many enemies on that account. With all my jesting and laughter I have not forgotten the aphorism of a wise philosopher who said: 'Jokes and satirical quips excite laughter, but they do not win hearts.'

The hostility of enemies created in this way is most unreasonable. Equally unreasonable is the man whose hatred is founded on nothing else but suspicion. I am under no delusion that such adversaries will be disarmed when they see that I treat even my own misfortunes as subjects for laughter and ridicule, but I do not concern myself about them. I offer them a sincere account of my life, just so that they may laugh at me to their hearts' delight.

I

My pedigree and birth

There are people foolish enough to make every family history the object of their ridicule and satire. For the sake of wits of this sort I shall give a short but truthful account of my ancestry, in order that they may have something to quiz.

Our stock springs in the fourteenth century from a certain Pezòlo de' Gozzi. This is proved by an authentic genealogy, which we possess; the authority of which has never been disputed, and which has been accepted as evidence in law-courts, although it is but a dusty document, worm-eaten and be-cobwebbed, not framed in gold or hung against the wall. Since I am no Spaniard, I never applied to any genealogist to discover a more ancient origin for our race. There are historical works, however, which derive us from the family de' Gozze, extant at the present epoch in Ragusa, and original settlers of that venerable republic. The chronicles of Bergamo relate that the aforesaid Pezòlo de' Gozzi was a man of weight and substance in the district of Alzano, and that he won the gratitude of the most serene Republic of Venice for having imperilled his property and person against the Milanese in order to preserve that district for her invincible and clement rule. His descendants held office as ambassadors and podestàs for the city of Bergamo, which proves that they were members of its Council; while two privileges of the sixteenth century show that two separate branches of the family obtained admission to the citizenship of Venice.[1] They erected houses

[1] Thus Gozzi belonged to the class of the *cittadini originari* of Venice, that is to say to the class of those who had been born legitimately in the city, who exercised no 'mechanical' trade, and whose fathers and grandfathers had been citizens. Citizenship was also

for the living and provided tombs for their dead in the quarter and the Church of S. Cassiano, as may be seen at the present day.[1] One of these branches was honoured with adoption into the patrician families of Venice in the seventeenth century,[2] and afterwards expired. The branch from which I am descended remained in the class of Cittadini Originari, on which they certainly brought no discredit whatsoever.

None of my ancestors aspired to the honourable and lucrative posts which are open to Venetian citizens.[3] They were for the most part men of peaceful unambitious temper, contented with their lot in life, or perhaps averse from the disturbances of competition. Had they entered upon a political career, I am quite sure that they would have served their Prince faithfully, without pride and without vain ostentation.

About two centuries ago, my great-great-grandfather pur-

---

granted by privilege, as it had been originally in the case of the Gozzi family. In his 'Lettera confutatoria' (Memorie inutili, Bari, Laterza, 1910, ii. 270) Gozzi asserts that this privilege was given to his ancestors by the Doge Pasquale Cicogna (1585–95). The cittadini took no part in the actual government of the State, but they could serve as secretaries to various magistracies, and also filled the position of Grand Chancellor. In Alessandro Zilioli's chronicles of the famiglie cittadinesche of Venice, compiled in the seventeenth century, the Gozzi arms are described as consisting of a green olive-tree on a field of gold. In the topmost branches of the tree is a dove bearing an olive-branch (omitted in some copies of the work). Round the trunk of the tree is a white scroll inscribed 'Signum Pacis'. See Le due corone della nobiltà veneziana; Corona seconda (Venice, Museo Correr, Cod. Cicogna 2459, p. 179). (S; Ed.)

[1] The arca, or family sepulture, can no longer be traced in the church. It was at the foot of the altar in the Chapel of the Madonna. Here Carlo Gozzi was buried. (S)

[2] During the Turkish war of 1645–68, many cittadini were admitted to the ranks of the nobility in recognition of the financial assistance which they had given. This privilege was granted in 1646 to Alberto Gozzi in exchange for 60,000 ducats 'in libero dono' and a further loan of 40,000 ducats (Venice, Museo Correr, Cod. Correr 1448, fo. 163 v).

[3] The Grand Chancellor, the Ducal Notaries, and the Secretaries of many Magistracies, were chosen from the cittadini, who were also sent, after holding such posts, as ambassadors of the second class, or Residents, to foreign Courts. (S)

chased some six hundred acres of land,[1] together with buildings, in Friuli, at the distance of five miles from Pordenone. A large portion of these estates consists of meadowland, and is held by feudal tenure. All the heirs-male are bound to renew investiture, which costs some ducats. Upon this point the officials of the Camera de' Feudi at Udine are extremely vigilant. If the fine is not paid immediately after the death of the last feudatory, they confiscate the crops derived from the meadows subject to this tenure. That happened to me after my father's decease. A few months' negligence cost me a considerable sum in excess of the customary fine. It is probably by right of some old parchment that we own the title of Count, conceded to our family in public acts in the addresses of letters.[2] I should feel no resentment, if this title were refused me; but it would anger me extremely if my hay were withheld.

My father was Jacopo Antonio Gozzi; a man possessed of a delicate sense of humour, of fine and penetrative intellect, of susceptible temper, resolute, and sometimes even formidable. His father Gasparo died while he was yet a child, leaving this only son to the guardianship of his mother, the Contessa Emilia Grompo, a noble woman of Padua. The estate was sufficient to sustain his dignity with credit; but he indulged dreams of magnificence. Sole heir, and educated by a tender mother, who humoured every fancy of her son, he early acquired the habit of following his own inclinations. These led him into lordly extravagances—stables full of horses; kennels of hounds; hunting-parties; splendid banquets—nor did he reflect upon the consequences of a marriage, which he made with-

---

[1] The word, which I have translated acre, is *campo*. Now the *campo* differed in different provinces of Lombardy. But the *campo padovano* corresponded pretty nearly to an English acre; and from another passage in Gozzi (*Memorie*, ed. cit., ii. 236) it appears that he was in the habit of using the Paduan standard. (S)

[2] The Gozzi were what are called in Venice *Conti di Terra Ferma*, and their title seems to have been dependent upon these feudal tenures. (S)

out deliberation in his early manhood, to indulge a whim of the heart. My mother was Angela Tiepolo, the daughter of one branch of that patrician house, which expired in her brother Almorò Cesare.[1] He died, a Senator of the Republic, about the year 1749.

I shall perhaps have wearied my readers with these facts about my pedigree and birth. Satirists will not, however, find in them anything to excite ambition in myself or to wing their pen with ridicule. Social ranks have always been regarded by me as accidental, though necessary for the proper subordination on which our institutions depend. As for my birth, I think less of whence I came than of whither I am going. Conduct unworthy of a decent origin might cause sorrow to my deceased parents, whose memory I hold in honour, and might cover myself and all my posterity with shame.

My name is Carlo. I was the sixth child born by my mother into the light, or shall I say the shadows of this world. I am writing on the last day of April in the year 1780. I have passed fifty, and not yet reached the age of sixty.[2] I shall not put

---

[1] At the time when Gozzi wrote, this was the eldest branch, called Di San Fantin. Two remote branches, of S. Apollinare and S. Polo, survived. They descended from a collateral ancestor, Girolamo Tiepolo, who died in 1516. The branch of S. Polo expired in 1820. See Litta, *Famiglie celebri*. The Tiepolo family was one of the oldest and most illustrious among the patrician houses. It ranked with the *Case vecchie*, as distinguished from the *Case nuove*. These *Case vecchie* were also called *tribunizie*, from having exercised the highest offices of the State at the time when Venice was still governed by tribunes, and before the foundation of the Dogeship. Of these oldest and purest noble houses there were twenty-four . . . I may add to this note that the Gozzi had previously intermarried with the Corner, Zuccato, Donà, and Morosini, patrician houses of high respectability. (S)

[2] Carlo Gozzi was born 13 December 1720. He probably knew that he was in his sixtieth year; and this passage enables us to measure the exact amount of duplicity which he thought venial in composing his Memoirs. It was Gozzi's object to extenuate the fact that his *liaison* with Teodora Ricci had been carried on when he was past the age of fifty. When he asserts that he had 'not yet reached the age of sixty', he was just within the bounds of veracity; for he wanted more than seven months to complete his sixtieth year. (S)

the sacristan to trouble in order to view the register of my
baptism, being quite sure that I was christened, and not having
the stupid vanity to pass for a curled dandy. That is obvious,
and has been always obvious, from the fashion of my clothes
and the way I dress my hair. Besides, I set no value on the age
of men. Human beings die at all ages; and I have seen boys
who are adult, while grown-up men or grey-beards are often
nothing better than peevish and ridiculous children.

2

*My education and circumstances down to the age of
sixteen—Concerning the art of improvisation, and my
literary studies*

Our family consisted of eleven children, male and female. I
could record nothing but what is creditable of my brothers
and sisters, had I proposed to write their memoirs. But this
is not my thought; and they are capable of writing their own,
if the whim should take them; for the epidemic of literature
was always chronic in our household.

A succession of priests with little learning were our domestic pedagogues up to a certain age. I say a succession
advisedly; each in turn having earned his dismissal by impertinent behaviour and intrigues with the serving-maids.

From early childhood I was always a silent observer of men
and things, by no means insolent, of imperturbable serenity,
and extremely attentive to my lessons. My brothers used my
taciturn and peaceable temper to their own advantage. They
accused me to our common tutor of all the naughtinesses of
which they had been guilty. I did not condescend to excuse
myself or to accuse them, but bore my unjust punishments
with stoicism. I venture to affirm that no boy was ever more
supremely indifferent than I was to the terrible penalty of being sent away from table just as we were sitting down to

C

dinner. Smiling obedience was my only self-defence. Enemies may conclude from these traits of character that I was a stupid lout, and friends that I was a philosopher in embryo. Nothing is rarer than the eye of equal justice. Yet anyone who takes the trouble to inquire of my acquaintances and servants, will learn that my taciturnity, my tolerance, my stoical endurance, have not changed with years—that I continue to view the events of this life with a smile, and that only those have nettled me which touched my honour.

The growing disorder in our family affairs did not at first deprive us boys of a sound education. My two elder brothers, Gasparo and Francesco, went to public schools,[1] and were in time to drink at all the fountains of the regular curriculum. Extravagant expenditure, however, combined with the needs of a numerous progeny, soon rendered anything like an adequate course of studies impossible for the younger children. I was intrusted for some years to a learned country-parson, and then to a priest in Venice, of decent acquirements and excellent morality. After this I entered the academy of two Genoese priests, who supplied instruction to some youths of noble birth, and to some of no nobility whatever. There were about twenty-five pupils in this academy. We pursued the same studies, with some difference according to our classes. Here I had the opportunity of observing that teachers are very valuable guides to youths who love learning, and mere images of ineffectual deities to such as hate it. For my part, being fond of books and eager for information, I imbibed my fill of such instruction as a boy can acquire before the age of fourteen. But sloth and vicious habits extirpate the seeds of learning planted by preceptors in the minds of ill-conditioned lads. Therefore I saw, and still see, more than two-thirds of my fellow-pupils sunk in a slough of baseness. Grammar, the classics, and rhetoric only taught them to get drunk in taverns, to carry sacks for hire upon their shoulders, and to cry 'Baked apples, plums, and chestnuts!' about the streets with a

[1] *Collegi.* Gasparo was educated in the Somaschan establishment at S. Cipriano on the island of Murano. (S)

basket on their heads and a pair of scales slung round their waists. Wretched fate to be a father!

When I became aware that our domestic difficulties would prove an obstacle to my remaining long at school, I determined to utilize the little I had already learned, and to carry on my education by myself. My elder brother Gasparo's example, whose passion for study had won public recognition, and my own good-will, kept me nailed to books of all sorts; nor could I imagine any pleasure worth a thought, beyond reading, meditating, and writing.

Poetry, choice Italian, and correct style were then in vogue. The young men of Venice met to discuss these three topics, which have now been utterly forgotten—possibly for the greater advantage and convenience of our citizens. I see crowds of young people hare-brained, conceited, idle, frivolous, presumptuous, and harmful to society. Heaven knows what their studies are! Not poetry, not the niceties of the Italian language, not correct style. And then, forsooth, I am to admire a hurly-burly of well-born persons, who claim in their foolhardiness to be omniscient, who produce nothing whatsoever, who cannot write three lines of a letter which shall express their sentiments, and which shall not swarm with revolting faults of grammar and of spelling!

I will omit to observe that respect for nobles in a state is necessary; but that the respect shown simply for their birth and wealth is not respect but false feigned adulation. I will refrain from asserting that a daily correspondence, maintained with a large variety of persons—people who may not perhaps be scientific, but who understand whether a letter is well written or ridiculous—may be capable of securing a large part of the regard, or of occasioning a large part of the contempt, bestowed on nobles. I make no mention of the rich man in Signor Mercier's comedy of Indigence, who found it impossible to write a letter of the utmost importance because his secretary was away from home. I will say nothing to those scientific tutors of the scions of our aristocracy, who instil derision and disdain for polite literature and the art of elegance in diction into the brains of their pupils, moulding them into geometricians, mathematicians, philosophers, physicists, astronomers, algebraical professors, naturalists, a whole deluge of sciences, but who cannot after all their labour express in writing what they have taught or what the common business of life requires.

All these things, and everything which imposture has presented to my senses and impressed upon my mind, must remain unwritten in my pen. I have no wish to make enemies.

Yet we cannot prevent drops of ink from falling sometimes from the pen and making blots upon our papers. Just so, while I am dictating these memoirs of my life, I shall not be able to avoid splutterings, however out of place and inconvenient.

I am almost ashamed to confess the intense assiduity with which I applied myself to those frivolous literary studies of which I have been speaking. They brought on a hæmorrhage from the nostrils, so violent and so frequent, that I was more than once or twice given up for dead in the manner of Seneca.[1] In the anxiety about my health, my friends hid away all my books, and deprived me of paper and inkstand; but I was the cleverest of thieves in searching for them, and went on doggedly reading and writing by stealth in the uninhabited attics of our mansion. After relating this fact about my boyhood, malicious people may think that I am claiming to be considered worthy of a panegyric. They are quite mistaken. I fix them with my eye-glass, and assure them that it is rather my intention to provide them with another good reason for quizzing me. The famous Doctor Tissot angrily rebukes excessive application to those studies which are universally esteemed as useless. He reserves his praise for folk who ruin their health in pursuits considered beneficial to humanity; and such, I do not doubt, are the studies affected by himself and his admirers.

The Abbé Giovan Antonio Verdani, keeper of the select and

[1] Casanova, in the first chapter of his Memoirs, says that he suffered during his boyhood from the same violent hæmorrhages. (S)

extensive library of the patrician family Soranzo, was a man
of vast literary erudition. He felt compassion for my weakness, which coincided with his own, and directed my reading
by lending me the rarest books, masterpieces of pure Italian
diction in prose and poetry. To estimate the quantities of
paper which I covered with my thoughts in verse and prose,
would be beyond my powers. I tried to imitate the style of
all the early Tuscan writers who are most admired. Assuredly
I never approached the perfection of their language; but I
am none the less sure that the diligent and attentive perusal
of a mass of the best works, treating of a vast variety of subjects, cannot fail to furnish a better head than mine with
instruction and ideas, with the power of making just reflections and probable conjectures, and with the principles of
sound morality. I am also convinced that the imitation of
style in writing, pursued methodically, enables a man to express his own thoughts with facility, propriety of colouring,
exactitude of phrase and term, according to the variety of
images, grave or gay, familiar or dignified, which we desire
to develop and to communicate under their true aspect in
prose or poetry.

Without attaining to the mastery of style at which I aimed,
I acquired the miserable satisfaction of finding myself in the
very select group of persons who know this truth. I also
earned the wretchedness of being forced to read with insuperable aversion and disgust the works of many modern Italian
authors, which are full of false fancies and sophisms, the
rhetoric and diction of which never vary however the sub-
ject-matter changes, which are defiled by all manner of gibberish, bombast, nonsense, with periods involved in unintelligible
vortices, and with preposterous phraseology. The sciences,
the discoveries, the branches of new knowledge which are
now so loudly vaunted, may well be useful and worthy of respect. For this reason it is wrong to profane them and to
render them contemptible by barbarous impurity and impropriety of diction. Francesco Redi, that great man, great
philosopher, great physician, great naturalist, confirms my

doctrine by his written works.[1] As regards the literature of art and wit and fancy, it is obvious that without correctness of style this is absolutely worthless and condemned to merited oblivion. No one could count the fine and ample sentiments which perish, smothered in the mire of inartistic writing. Not less numerous, on the other hand, are the small but brilliant thoughts, duly coloured with appropriate terms, and placed at the right point of view by a master-hand, which sparkle before the eyes of every reader, be he learned or simple.

There is no disputing about tastes. Yet I think it could be easily maintained that our century has lapsed into a shameful torpor with regard to these things. I have written and printed quite enough upon the subject; without effect, however; and now I see no reason why I should not utter a last funeral lament over the mastery of art I longed to possess. That mastery, which nowadays is reckoned among the inutilities of existence, has been freely conceded to me by the verdict of contemporaries—blind judges, governed not by intelligence but by ignorant assumption—so that their opinion does not sustain me with the sure conviction of having attained my purpose. Nevertheless I am grateful even to the blind and deaf, who see and hear what gives them pleasure in my writings.

My pursuit of culture advanced on the lines I have described, whether for my happiness or my misfortune it is worthless to inquire. I read continually, and wasted enormous quantities of ink; paid close attention to men and manners; profited by the encouragement of the Abbé Verdani and Antonio Federigo Seghezzi; walked in the steps of my brother Gasparo; and frequented a literary society which met daily at our house. From a Piedmontese, who knew how to read and nothing more, I learned the first rudiments of French; not that I wished to talk French in Italy, an affectation which I loathed; but because it was my desire, by the help of grammar

---

[1] Gozzi might have cited Galileo, whose style, formed by the study of the 'divine' Ariosto, is a model of exquisite and urbane Italian diction. (S)

and dictionary, to study the books, most excellent in part, in part injurious to society, which issue daily from the French press. It was thus that I formed those literary tastes, to which I have always clung for innocent and disinterested amusement, and which, now that my hairs are grey, will be my solace till the hour of death. The giants of science, to whom I dare not raise my quizzing-glass for fear of committing an unpardonable sin, will perceive that in describing the scanty sources of my education, I am only painting the portrait of a literary pigmy in all humility.

As regards my moral training, it is only necessary to observe that the family of which I was a member has always cherished a deep and fervent reverence for the august image of religion, and that my father, careless as he was in matters of economy, never neglected religious duties or the good example of honourable conduct. He was a bitter enemy of falsehood. His delicate susceptibility detected a lie by the inflection of the voice, and he punished it upon the spot with sounding boxes on the ears of his offspring.

Being a bold rider and passionately fond of horses, he taught us to ride, and liked to see us every day on horseback during our summer visits to the country. It was useless to plead timidity, or to shrink from the snortings and jibbings of some half-broken beast he wanted us to back. Up we went; a cut or two of the switch across our legs set us off at a gallop; and there we were in full career, without a thought for broken shins or necks. Some horse-dealers, who came to break in vicious colts, put me up to tricks for mastering a hard-mouthed bolting animal. One of these tricks stood me in good stead upon an occasion I shall afterwards relate. Indeed, I may say that I owe my life to a trader in horses.[1]

We had a little theatre of no great architectural pretensions in our country-house; and here we children used to

[1] The trick was for the rider to push his fingers into the horse's eyes. Gozzi used it once when he was soldiering in Dalmatia. The incident, described in Part I, chap. 8 of the Memoirs, is here omitted.

act.[1] Brothers and sisters alike were gifted with some talent for comedy; and all of us, before a crowd of rustic spectators, passed for players of the first quality. Besides tragic and comic pieces learned by heart, we frequently improvised farces with a slight plot upon some laughable motive. My sister Marina and I had the knack of imitating certain married couples notorious in the village for their burlesque humours. We used to interpolate our farces with scenes and dialogues in which the famous quarrels of these women with their drunken husbands were reproduced to the life. Our clothes were copied from the originals; and the imitation was so exact that our bucolic audience hailed it with Homeric peals of laughter, measuring their applause by the delight it afforded their coarse natures. My father and mother took a fancy to see themselves represented in this way. My sister and I were shy at first, but we had to obey our parents. Finally, we regaled them with a perfect reproduction of their costume, their gestures, their way of talking, and some of their familiar household bickerings. Their astonishment was great, and their laughter was the only punishment of our dutiful temerity.

I learned to twang the guitar with a certain amount of skill, and vied with my brother Gasparo in improvising rhymed verses, which I sang to music in our hours of recreation. This was done with all the foolhardiness inseparable from a display which the vulgar are only too apt to regard as miraculous. Since I have touched upon the point, I will digress a little on this so-called miracle. In my opinion, the immense crowds of people hanging with open mouths upon the lips of an *improvvisatore* only prove that, in spite of the

[1] Compare what Goldoni says about the marionette theatre at his grandfather's country-seat. In some of the great villas of the Venetian nobility these private stages were built on an enormous scale. The account of Marco Contarini's theatre at Piazzola near Padua, and of the sumptuous dramatic performances which took place there, reads like a passage from the *Arabian Nights*. See Romanin's *Storia documentata di Venezia*, Venice, 1853–61, vii. 550. (S)

contempt into which poetry has fallen, it still possesses that power over the minds and the brains of men which their tongues deny it. Cristoforo Altissimo, a poet of the fifteenth century, is said to have publicly improvised his epic in octave stanzas on the Reali di Francia; the words were taken down from his lips, just as he composed them at the moment. The book was published; and though it is extremely rare, I have read it through the kindness of the Abbé Verdani. Only a few stanzas, out of all that ocean of verse, are worthy of the name of poetry; and yet we may believe that before the work was given to the press, some pains had been bestowed upon it. I have listened to many extempore versifiers, male and female, the most famous of our century. It has always struck me that if the deluge of verses which they spout forth with face on fire, to the applause of frantic multitudes, were written down, they would have very little poetical value, and that nobody would have the patience to read the twentieth part of them. Padre Zucchi, of the Olivetan Order, whom I heard in my youth, surpassed his rivals; now and then he produced sensible stanzas; but he improvised so slowly that reflection may have had some part in the result. I do not deny that these extempore rhymesters may be people of culture and learning, qualified to discourse well upon the themes proposed to them. Yet they would not be listened to, if they spoke ever so divinely in prose. In order to draw a crowd, they are forced to express their thoughts and images, just as they come, with voluble rapidity, in bad rhymed verses, which often are no better than a gabble of words without sense. This throws their audience into a trance of astonishment. Humanity has always quested after the marvellous like a hound. If a painter sought to depict foolhardiness or imposture wearing the mask of poetry, I could recommend nothing better than the portrait of an *improvvisatore*, with goggle-eyes and arms in air, and a multitude staring up at him in stupid dumb amazement. These being my sentiments, I am willing, out of mere politeness and good manners, to approve the coronation of a Cavaliere Perfetti or a Corilla on the Capitol. But I can only accept with

cordial and serious enthusiasm the honours of that sort paid
to a Virgil, a Petrarch, and a Tasso.

The Arcadians will laugh when I proceed to speak about an
improvvisatore, whom I knew and whom I have listened to a
hundred times. Yet I should be committing an injustice if I did
not mention him, and declare my opinion that he was the
single really wonder-worthy artist in this kind, with whom I
ever came in contact. He used to pour forth anacreontics,
octave stanzas, any and every metre, extempore, to the music
of a well-touched guitar. His verses rhymed, but had no *Clio,
Euterpe, plettro, Parnaso, Aganippe, ruscelletto, zefiretto*, and
such stuff, in them. They composed a well-developed discourse, flowing evenly, not soaring, but with abundance of
well-connected images and natural, lively, graceful thoughts.
He invariably used either the Venetian or the Paduan dialect;
which will augment the derisive laughter of Arcadia, and
make the Campidoglio ring. On one occasion, while he was
improvising on the theme : *diligite inimicos vestros*, it
happened that two enemies were present. At another time, he
dilated on his own grief for a cavaliere[1] who had been kind to
him, and who was then dying, given over by the doctors. Not
only did the audience hang upon his lips with rapt attention;
but in the former case, the enemies were reconciled, while in
the latter tears were freely shed for the poet's expiring bene-
factor. Such influence over the passions of the heart reveals a
true poet; for such a man I reserve the laurel crown upon my
Campidoglio. His name was Giovanni Sibiliato, brother of
the celebrated professor of literature in the University of
Padua.

Returning from this digression, I will resume the narrative
of my boyhood. I learned to fence and to dance; but books
and composition were my chief pastime. Before a numerous
audience in our literary assemblies I felt no shyness. In private
visits, among people new to me, the reserve of my demeanour

[1] I may here say that the title of cavaliere, or knight, was commonly
given to members of patrician families at Venice, irrespective of their
being laymen or in orders. (S)

often passed for unsociability. My first sonnet of passable quality was written at the age of nine. Besides the applause it won me, I was rewarded with a box of comfits; and for this reason I have never forgotten it. The occasion of its composition was as follows. A certain Signora Angela Armano, midwife by trade, had a friend at Padua whose pet dog died and left her inconsolable. Signora Angela wished to comfort her friend; indulged in condolements for her loss; and sent a little spaniel of her own, called Delina, to replace the defunct pet. Delina was to be given as a present, and a sonnet was to accompany the gift, expressing all the sentiments which a lady of Signora Angela's profession might entertain in a circumstance of such importance. Though our family was a veritable lunatic asylum of poets, no one cared to translate the good creature's gossiping garrulity into verse. Moved by her entreaties, I undertook the task; and the following Bernesque sonnet was the result:

> Madama, io vi vorrei pur confortare
> Con qualche graziosa diceria;
> Ma la sciagura vuole, e vostra e mia,
> Che in un sonetto la non vi può stare.
> Non vi state, mia cara, a disperare,
> Chè la sarebbe una poltroneria
> L'entrar per un can morto in frenesia;
> Chi nasce muor, convien moralizzare.
> Vi sovvenite ch' egli avrà pisciato
> Alcuna volta in camera o in cucina,
> Che in quell' istante lo avreste ammazzato.
> Io vi spedisco intanto la Delina,
> Che più d'un cane ha d'essa innamorato,
> E può farvi di cani una dezina.
>   È bella e picciolina;
> Di lei non voglio più nuova o risposta;
> Servitevi per razza, o di supposta.[1]

[1] 'Madame, I should like to console you with an elegant effusion, but unhappily for us both there is no room for that in a sonnet. Do not continue to despair, my dear; it would be a stupid waste of time to

Two years later, a new edition of the poems of Gaspara Stampa appeared in Venice, at the expense of Count Antonio Ramboldo di Collalto of Vienna, a prince distinguished for his birth and writings. Scholars know that this sixteenth-century Sappho sighed her soul forth in love-laments to a certain Count Collaltino di Collalto, doughty warrior and polished versifier, and that she was reputed to have died of hopeless passion in her youth.[1] The ladies of our century will hardly believe her story; for Cupid has changed tempers since those days, and kills his victims with far different and less honourable weapons. Some verses by contemporary writers in praise of our literary heroine were to be appended to this edition of her works. I dared to enter the lists, and wrote a sonnet in the style of the earliest Tuscan poets. Such as it is, the sonnet may be found printed in the book which I have indicated. It appears from the juvenile production that I already acknowledged a mistress of my heart; compliance with fashion was alone responsible for my precocity.

This trifling composition was read by the famous Apostolo Zeno. He deigned to inquire for the author, who had reproduced the antique simplicity of Cino da Pistoia, Dante da Maiano, Guittone d'Arezzo, and Guido Cavalcanti. On my presenting myself, Signor Zeno politely expressed surprise at discovering a mere boy in the learned writer of the sonnet,

---

work yourself up into a state of frenzy over a dead dog. Think rather of the wise saying: Whatever is born must die. Remember, your pet must have left a puddle in the bed-room or the kitchen more than once, and then you could have killed him on the spot. I am sending you Delina, who has several dogs courting her and can provide you with ten or more offspring. She is a pretty little thing. I do not want you to give me any news of her, or to send me a reply. Use her to breed from, or as a substitute.' The last word of the poem conceals a vulgar pun, *supposta* meaning either a substitute or a suppository.

[1] Gaspara Stampa was born at Padua, but was a gentlewoman of Milan by descent. She died in 1554, at about the age of thirty. If this edition of Gaspara Stampa's *Rime* is the one prepared for publication by Luisa Bergalli (Gozzi's sister-in-law), there is the same confusion of dates here as I have noticed above. It was published when Gozzi had reached his seventeenth year. (S)

treated me with kind attention, and placed his choice library at my disposal.[1] The encouragement of this distinguished poet, true lover of pure style, and foe to seventeenth-century conceits, added fuel to the fire of my literary passion. From that day forward not one of those collections of verses appeared, in which marriages, the entrance of young ladies into convents, the election of noblemen to offices of state, the deaths of people, cats, dogs, parrots, and such events, are celebrated in Venice and other towns of Italy, but that it contained some specimen of my Muse in grave or playful verse.

Books, paper, pens, and ink formed the staple of my existence. I was always pregnant, always in labour, giving birth to monsters in remote corners of our mansion. I scribbled furiously, God knows how, up to my seventeenth year. Besides innumerable essays in prose and multitudes of fugitive verses, I wrote four long poems, entitled *Berlinghieri, Don Quixote, Moral Philosophy* (based upon the talking animals of Firenzuola), and *Gonella* in twelve cantos. The Abbé Verdani took a fancy to this last, and wished to see it printed. Signor Giulio Cesare Beccelli, however, had published a poem at Verona on the same subject, which robbed my work of novelty; and though mine was richer in facts drawn from good old sources, I did not venture to enter into competition with him. The three years' absence from home, which I shall presently relate, and the revolution in our domestic affairs which surprised me on my return, exposed these boyish literary labours to ruin and dispersion. It is probable that pork-butchers and fruit-vendors exercised condign justice on the children of my Muse. There was one of these children, however, which I saw on my return home had somehow or other found its way into print: a translation of Marivaux's *Pharsa-*

---

[1] A tablet over the entrance to no. 782, Fondamenta de le Zatare (next to Ruskin's house by the Ponte della Calcina), records that Apostolo Zeno dwelt there. It was, perhaps, to this house that young Gozzi paid his visit. Zeno (b. 1668, d. 1750) exercised considerable influence over the Italian drama. He wrote plays for music and oratorios. For some years he held the post of Cesarean poet at Vienna, which he resigned to the more celebrated Metastasio. (S; Ed.)

mond (the first in Italian) which I had made with the help of a French grammar and dictionary in order to familiarize myself with the language. I glanced over this translation, recognized it as my own, and had to confess with shame that it was very badly done.

3

The situation of my family, and my reasons for leaving home

In the course of these years, the early deaths of a brother and a sister had reduced our number from eleven to nine. Meanwhile, our annual expenditure exceeded the resources at our command, and left but little for the needs of a numerous offspring, too old to be contented with a toy or plaything. Some lawsuits, which we lost, diminished the estate. Clouds of doubt and care began to obscure the horizon, and in a few years the family was plunged in pecuniary embarrassment.

My brother Gasparo had taken a wife in a fit of genial poetical abstraction. Even poetry has its dangers. This man, who was really singular in his absolute self-dedication to books, in his indefatigable labours as an author, and in a certain philosophical temper or indolence, which made him indifferent to everything which was not literary, learned to fall in love from Petrarch. A young lady, ten years older than himself, named Luigia Bergalli,[1] better known among the shepherdesses of Arcady as Irminda Partenide, a poetess of

[1] Luisa Bergalli was born at Venice in 1703. She commenced her literary carrer at the age of twenty-two with a musical drama *Agide, re di Sparta*, which earned her the praise and encouragement of Apostolo Zeno. She wrote various other plays for music, as well as a number of tragedies and a comedy in blank verse entitled *Le avventure del poeta*, which she dedicated to her future father-in-law. She published a blank-verse translation of Terence's comedies (1730) and a prose translation of the tragedies of Racine (1736–37). She was thirty-five and Gasparo Gozzi was twenty-five when they married (1738).

romantic fancy, as her published works evince, was my brother's Laura. Not being a canon, like Petrarch, he married her in Petrarch's spirit, but with due legal formalities. This woman, of fervent and soaring imagination, which fitted her for high poetic flights, undertook to regulate the disorder in our affairs. Impelled by the instincts of a good nature, with something of ambition and a flattering belief in her own practical ability, she did the best that in her lay. Yet all her projects and administrative measures revolved within a circle of romantic raptures and Pindaric ecstasies. Thirsting with soul-passion after an ideal realm, she found herself the sovereign of a state in decadence. It was the desire of her heart to make us all happy, in the most disinterested way. Yet she accomplished nothing beyond involving every one, and herself to boot, in the meshes of still greater misfortune. Her husband, poring perpetually upon his books, could only oppose her at the sacrifice of ease and quiet. This he was incapable of doing. But in order to judge people equitably, it is necessary that character, temperament, and circumstances should be thoroughly explained.

I know how unphilosophical it is to ascribe the discords of a family to malignant planetary influences. Our domestic circle consisted of a father, a mother, four brothers, and five sisters, all of them good-hearted, honourable, mutually well-inclined; and yet it became the very mirror of infelicity at every moment and in each of the persons who composed it. Minute investigation into the causes of this painful fact would probably reveal them. But it is better to adopt the language of the vulgar, and to say that a bad star pursued our family. Otherwise, analysis might lead one into acts of unkindness, and involve one in hatred.

The confusion in which we lived at that period, and the bitter discomforts we had to bear, were augmented by expenses due to my brother's increasing progeny. Our worst disaster, however (and this wound I carry in my heart even to the present day), was a cruel stroke of apoplexy which laid my beloved father low. He continued to exist, an invalid, for about seven years after the sad event; dumb and paralytic, but in possession of all his mental faculties—a circumstance which rendered his deplorable condition almost unbearable to a man of my father's extreme sensibility.

The tears of five sisters, the births of nephews and nieces, a house swarming with female go-betweens, brokers, and the Hebrew ministers of our decaying realm—all this whirlpool of economical extravagance and folly, to utter one word against which was reckoned mutiny, drove my second brother, Francesco, into exile. He went into the Levant with the Provveditore Generale di Mare,[1] his Excellency the Cavaliere Antonio Loredan, of happy memory. At that period I was about thirteen.

Letters written from Corfu by this brother describing the kindness shown him by his Provveditore, and the rank of ensign to which he soon attained, awoke in me a burning desire to escape like him from those domestic turmoils, the gravity of which I felt in experience and measured by anticipation, but which my state of boyhood rendered me unable to remedy. Our uncle on the mother's side, Almorò Cesare Tiepolo, recommended me to his Excellency Girolamo Querini, Provveditore Generale elect for Dalmatia and Albania. Furnished with a modest outfit, in which my book-box and guitar were not forgotten, I bade farewell to my parents at the age of seventeen,[2] and went across seas as volunteer into those provinces, to study the ways and manners of my fellow-soldiers, and of the peoples among whom we were quartered.

[1] The title *Provveditore Generale di Mare* was given to the supreme head of the Venetian naval and military forces in the Levant. He resided at Corfu, where he maintained a princely court, and ruled like a sovereign, being only responsible for his actions to the Senate. Next in importance to this functionary was the *Provveditore Generale in Dalmazia e Albania*, of whose Court we shall hear much in Gozzi's Memoirs. Casanova gives an excellent account of the Court of the Provveditore Generale at Corfu, its military, naval, and civil establishment. (S; Ed.) See J. Casanova, *Histoire de ma vie*, ed. Brockhaus, Wiesbaden-Paris, 1960, vol. ii, chaps. 3–6.

[2] Not at seventeen, but at twenty. Gozzi was born in 1720, and Querini took the government of Dalmatia in 1741. (S)

4

I embark upon a galley, and cross the seas to Zara

I was not slow to perceive that I had adopted a career by no means suited to my character, the proper motto for which was always the following line from Berni:

> *'Voleva far da sè, non comandato.'*

My natural dislike of changeableness kept me, however, from showing by outward signs of any sort that I repented of my choice; and I reflected that abundant opportunities were now at least offered for observations on the men of a world new to me. This thought sufficed to keep me in good spirits and a cheerful humour through all the vicissitudes of my three years' sojourn in Illyria.

According to orders received from his Excellency, the Provveditore Generale Querini, I embarked before him on a galley called *Generalizia*, which was riding at the port of Malamocco. There I was to wait for his arrival. A band of military officers received me with glances of courtesy and some curiosity. In a Court where all the members are seeking fortune, each newcomer is regarded with suspicion. Whether he has to be reckoned with or may be disregarded on occasions of promotion, concerns the whole crew of officials who, like him, are dependent on the will of the Provveditore. It was perhaps insensibility which made me indifferent to these preoccupations; this the sequel of my narrative will show; and yet such thoughts are very wood-worms in the hearts of courtiers.

I had to swallow a great quantity of questions, to which I replied with the laconic brevity of an inexperienced lad upon his guard. Some of those gentlemen had known my brother Francesco at Corfu. When they discovered who I was, they

D

seemed to be relieved of all anxiety on my account, and welcomed me with noisy demonstrations of soldierly comradeship. I expressed my thanks in modest, almost monosyllabic phrases. They set me down for an awkward young fellow, unobliging, and proud. This was a mistake, as they freely confessed a few months later on. I had retired into myself, with the view of studying their characters and sketching my line of action. The quick and penetrative intuition with which I was endowed at birth by God, together with the faculty of imperturbable reserve, enabled me in the course of a few hours to recognize in that little group some men of noble birth and liberal culture, some nobles ruined by the worst of educations, and some plebeians who owed their position to powerful protection.

Gaming, intemperance, and unbridled sensuality were deeply rooted in the whole company. I laid my plans of conduct, and found them useful in the future. My intimacies were few, but durable. The vices I have named clung like ineradicable cancers to the men with whom I associated. Sound principles engrafted on me in my early years, regard for health, and the slenderness of my purse helped me to avoid their seductions. At the same time, I saw no reason why I should proclaim a crusade against them. Holding a middle course, I succeeded in winning the affection of my comrades. They invited me to take part in their orgies. I did not play the prude. Without yielding myself to the transports of brutal appetite, I proved the gayest reveller at all those lawless meetings.[1] Some of my seniors, on whom a career of facile pleasure had left its inevitable stigma, used to twit me with being a reserved young simpleton. I did not heed their raillery, but laughed at the inebriation of my comrades, studied the bent of divers characters, observed the animal brutality of men, and used our uproarious debauches as a school for fathoming the depths of human frailty.

[1] Symonds abridges the Italian text slightly at this point. Later in the chapter he omits some paragraphs of slight importance from Gozzi's account of the voyage to Zara.

Now I will return to the point of my embarkation on the galley *Generalizia* in the port of Malamocco. While awaiting the arrival of the Provveditore, I had two whole days and nights to spend in sad reflections on humanity. These were suggested by the spectacle of some three hundred scoundrels, loaded with chains, condemned to drag their life out in a sea of miseries and torments, each of which was sufficient by itself to kill a man. An epidemic of malignant fever raged among these men, carrying away its victims daily from the bread and water, the irons, and the whips of the slavemasters. Attended in their last passage by a gaunt black Franciscan friar, with thundering voice and jovial mien, these wretches took their flight—I hope and think—for Paradise.

The Provveditore's arrival amid the din of instruments and roar of cannon roused me from my dismal reveries. I had visited this gentleman ten times at least in his own palace, and had always been received with that playful welcome and confidential sweetness which distinguished the patricians of Venice. He made his appearance now in crimson—crimson mantle, cap, and shoes—with an air of haughtiness unknown to me, and fierceness stamped upon his features. The other officers informed me that when he donned this uniform of state, he had to be addressed with profound and silent salaams, different indeed from the reverence one pays at Venice to a patrician in his civil gown.[1] He boarded the galley, and seemed to take no notice whatever of the crowd around him, bowing till their noses rubbed their toes. The affability with which he touched our hands in Venice had disappeared; he looked at none of us; and sentenced the young captain of the guard, called Combat, to arrest in chains, because he had omitted some trifle of the military salute. My comrades stood dumbfounded, staring at one another with open eyes. This singular change from friendliness to severity set my brains at

---

[1] *Togato.* The State dignitaries of Venice wore robes of various colours and forms, according to their office. A simple nobleman was bound to go abroad in a flowing robe of sik, or toga, ample enough to conceal whatever costume he may have worn beneath it. (S)

work. By the light of my boyish philosophy I seemed to comprehend why the noble of a great republic, elected general of an armament[1] and governor of two wide provinces, on his first appearance in that office felt bound to assume a totally different aspect from what was natural to him in his private capacity. He had to inspire fear and a spirit of submission into his subordinates. Otherwise they might have taken liberties upon the strength of former courtesy displayed by him, being for the most part presumptuous young fellows, apt to boast about their favour with the general. For my own part, since I was firmly bent on doing my duty without ambitious plans or dreams of fortune, this formidable attitude and the harsh commands of the great man made a less disheartening impression on me than on my companions. I whispered to myself: 'He certainly inspires me with a kind of dread; but he has taken immense trouble to transform his nature in order to produce this effect; I am sure the irksomeness which he is suffering now must be greater than any discomfort he can cause me.'

The general retired to his cabin in the bowels of our floating hell, and sent Lieutenant-Colonel Micheli, his major in the province, to make out a list of all the officers and volunteers on board, together with the names of their protectors. Nobody expected this; for we had been personally presented to the general at Venice, and had explained our affairs in frequent conversations. Once more I reflected that this was his way of damping the expectations which might have been bred in scheming brains before he exchanged the politenesses of private life for the austerities of office. The Maggiore della Provincia Micheli—a most excellent person and very fat—bustled about his business, sweating, and scribbling with a pencil on a sheet of paper, as though the matter was one of life or death. Everybody began to shy and grumble and chafe with indignation at passing under review in this way. When my turn came, I answered frankly that I was called Carlo Gozzi, and that I had been recommended by the patrician

[1] *Armata*, composed of naval and military forces, to act equally on sea and shore. (S)

Almorò Cesare Tiepolo. I withheld his title of senator and the fact that he was my maternal uncle, deeming it prudent not to seem ambitious.

The *Generalizia*, convoyed by another galley named *Conserva* and a few light vessels of war, got under way for the Adriatic;[1] and the night fell very dark upon the waters. I shall not easily forget that night, because of a little incident which happened to me, and which shows what a curious place of refuge a galley is for young men leaving their homes for the first time. A natural necessity made me seek some corner for retirement. I was directed to the bowsprit; on approaching it, an Illyrian sentinel, with scowling visage, bushy whiskers, and levelled musket, howled his '*Who goes there?*' in a tremendous voice. When he understood my business, he let me pass. My next step lighted on a soft and yielding mass, which gave forth a kind of gurgling sound, like the stifled breath of an asthmatic patient, into the dark silent night. Retracing my path, I asked the sentinel what the thing was, which responded with its inarticulate gurgling voice to the pressure of my feet. He answered with the coldest indifference that it was the corpse of a galley-slave, who had succumbed to the fever, and had been flung there till he could be buried on the sea-shore sands in Istria. The hair on my head bristled with horror. But my happy disposition for seeing the ludicrous side of things soon came to my assistance.

After twelve days of much discomfort, and twelve noisome nights, passed in broken slumbers under the decks of that galley, which only too well deserved its name, our little fleet entered the port of Zara, principal city of Dalmatia. We went on shore at first privately and quietly; and after a few days the public ceremonies of official disembarkation were gone

[1] It seems from the names of these larger galleys that they were the official ships of the Provveditore, his own flag-ship and her attendant convoy. Romanin, op. cit., viii. 372 says that at this epoch Venice kept fifteen heavy galleys, ten lighters, nine sailing ships of the frigate build, and twenty-four armed craft of other descriptions. The galleys and sailing ships were commanded only by patricians. This was her peace establishment. (S)

through. The Provveditore Generale Jacopo Cavalli handed his baton of command over to the Provveditore Generale Girolamo Querini with all the formalities proper to the occasion. This solemnity, which is performed upon the open sea, to the sound of military music, the thunder of artillery, and the crackling of musket-shots, deserves to be witnessed by all who take an interest in imposing spectacles. An old man, fat and short of stature, with a pair of moustachios bristling up beneath his nostrils, a merry and most honest fellow to boot, who bore the name of Captain Girolamo Visinoni, was appointed master of these ceremonies, on account of his intimate acquaintance with their details. I had no other duty that day but to wear my best clothes, which did not cost much trouble.

Shortly after his arrival in Zara, Gozzi became seriously ill. Thinking he was on his death-bed, he sent for a confessor and received the last sacraments from a Dominican monk. He comments:

Our modern sages may laugh at this plebeian wish of mine to make my peace with Heaven; but I have never been able to dissociate philosophy from religion. Satisfied to remain a little child before the mysteries of faith, I do not envy wise men in their disengagement from spiritual terrors.

A heavy nasal hæmorrhage brought the fever to an end, causing Gozzi to make some caustic comments about the treatment of his ailment by the chief physician Danieli:

My ignorance could not reconcile this salutary crisis with Danieli's absolute prohibition of blood-letting in my malady. But I suppose that a score of learned physicians, each of them upon a different system of hypotheses, conjectures, well-based calculations, and trains of lucid argument, would be able to demonstrate the phenomenon to their own satisfaction and to the illumination or confusion of my stupid brain. Stupendous indeed are the mental powers which Almighty God has bestowed on men!

The expenses incurred during this illness left Gozzi short of money, but he was helped out of his difficulties by a man who was to become a lifelong friend: Innocenzo Massimo. He writes:

Under these painful circumstances I found a cordial and openhearted friend in Signor Innocenzo Massimo, nobleman of Padua and captain of halberdiers at the Dalmatian Court. This excellent gentleman, of rare distinction for his mental parts, the quickness of his spirit, his courage, energy, and honour, was the only intimate friend whom I possessed during my three years' absence from home. When they were over, our friendship continued undiminished by lapse of time, distance, and the various vicissitudes of life. I have enjoyed it through thirty-five years, and am sure that it will never fail me.

5

Short studies in the science of fortification and military exercises

On the restoration of my health, his Excellency placed me under Cavaliere Marchiori, Lieutenant-Colonel of Engineers, to learn mathematics as applied to fortification. This gentleman sent for me, and said that he had heard from my uncle of my aptitude for study, adding that the subject he proposed to teach me was of the greatest consequence to a soldier. I perceived at once that I was being treated on a different footing from the other volunteers, and that the studied forgetfulness of the Provveditore had been, as I suspected, a politic device to humble ambitious schemers. I thanked Signor Marchiori, and followed his instructions with pleasure, without however abandoning my own interest in literature.

He questioned me regarding my knowledge of arithmetic, which was only elementary; and when I saw that I must master it, in order to pursue the higher branch of study, I gave my whole head to the business. In the space of a month, I could cipher like a money-lender, and was ready to receive my master's teaching. My friend Massimo possessed a good collection of instruments for engineering draughtsmanship, and a library of French works on geometry, mathematics, and fortification, both of which he placed at my disposal, Signor Marchiori's lectures, long discussions with Signor Massimo, perusal of Euclid, Archimedes, and the French books, soon plunged me in the lore of points and lines and calculations. I burned with the enthusiasm, droll enough to my way of looking at the world, which inspires all students of this science. Yet I did not, like them, regard moral philosophy and humane literature as insignificant frivolities. I bore in mind for what good reasons the Emperor Vespasian dismissed the mathematicians who offered their assistance in the building of his Roman edifices. I knew that innumerable vessels, fabricated on the principles of science, have perished miserably in the tempests; that hundreds of fortresses, built by science, have been destroyed and captured by the same science; that inundations are continually sweeping away the dykes erected by science, to the ruin of thousands of families, and that the inundations of themselves are attributable to the admired masterpieces of science bequeathed to us by former generations; that, in spite of science and her creative energy, the buildings she erects are not secured from earthquakes, conflagrations, and the thunderbolt. It remains to be seen whether Professor Toaldo's lightning-conductors will prove effectual against the last of these disasters. Then I reckoned up the blessings and curses which this vaunted science has conferred on humanity, arriving at the conclusion that the harm which she has done infinitely exceeds the good. I shuddered at the hundreds of thousands of human beings ingeniously massacred in war or drowned at sea by her devices; and took more pleasure in consulting my watch, her wise invention, for the dinner-hour than at the hour of keeping an appointment with my lawyer. Without denying the utility of sciences, I stuck resolutely to the opinion that moral philosophy is of more importance to the human race than mechanical inventions, and deplored the pernicious influence of modern Lyceums and Polytechnic schools upon the mind of Europe.[1]

Signor Massimo and I kept house together in a little dwelling on the city walls, facing the sea. The sun, in his daily revolutions, struck this habitation on every side; and there was not an open space of wall or window-sill without its dial, fabricated by my skill, and adorned with appropriate but useless mottoes on the flight of time. A lieutenant named Giovanni Apergi, upright and pious, especially when the gout he had acquired in the world's pleasures made him turn his thoughts to Heaven, gave me friendly lessons in military drill. I soon learned to handle my musket, pike, and ensign; and sweated a shirt daily, fencing with Massimo, who was ferociously expert in that fiendish but gentlemanly art. We also spent some hours together over a great chess-board of his, covered with wooden soldiers, which we moved from square to square, forming squadrons, and studying the combinations which enable armies to kill with prodigality and to be killed with parsimony—fitting ourselves, in short, for manuring cemeteries in the most approved style.

I was already half a soldier, and meant to make myself perfect in my profession; not, however, without a firm resolve to quit the army[2] at the expiration of my three years' service.[3]

---

[1] With this last sentence Symonds summarizes a whole page of reflections, at the end of which Gozzi concludes that Rousseau's call for a return to nature was not wholly ill-conceived: 'The philosophy of Jean-Jacques Rousseau contains many errors, but not as many as are laid at his door' (*Memorie*, i. 59).

[2] This word is in the Italian *armata*. The *armata*, to which Gozzi belonged, was properly an armament of mixed naval and military forces, and *armata* would naturally be translated 'navy'. He was attached to it, however, in the quality of soldier, and was eligible for transfer into the land forces of the State in Lombardy. Thus he belonged to the Venetian army. (S)

[3] The remaining paragraphs of this chapter have been omitted as they are of little interest. Gozzi states that he found the society of his comrades in the main uncongenial, and records the death of Marchiori.

6

---

*This chapter proves that poetry is not as useless as people
commonly imagine*

I am bound to confess that my weakness for poetry and
Italian literature was great. In the Venetian service, and particularly in Dalmatia, there were very few indeed who shared
these tastes. I wrote and read my compositions to myself,
without seeking the applause of an audience or boring my
neighbours with things they do not care for, as is the wont of
most scribblers.

The secretary of the Generalate, Signor Giovanni Colombo,
took some interest in literature. I may mention, by the way,
that he afterwards rose to high dignity, which involved a
calamity for him, sweetened, however, by a splendid funeral;
in other words, he died Grand Chancellor of our most serene
Republic.[1] This man, of gentle spirit and jovial temper, knowing the epidemic of poetry which possessed the Gozzi family,
encouraged me to read him some of my trifles, and seemed to
take pleasure in listening to them. He owned a small but well-
chosen library which he courteously allowed me to use. My
verses, satirical for the most part and descriptive of characters
—without scurrility indeed, though based on accurate observation of both sexes—were communicated to him and
Massimo alone.

The town of Zara was bent on testifying its respect for our
Provveditore Generale Querini by a grand public display. A
large hall of wood was accordingly erected on the open space

[1] This was the highest office in the State to which a *cittadino* could
aspire. It conferred the rank of *cavaliere*. The Grand Chancellor
could open public despatches; he attended the sittings of the Grand
Council and the Senate, but without a vote, and was the official chief
of all the civil servants. (S)

before the fort, and hung with fine damask. Tickets of invitation were then distributed to various persons, who were to
compose an Academy upon the day of the solemnity. Every
academician had to recite two compositions in prose or verse,
as he thought fit. The subjects were set forth on the tickets,
and were as follows: first, is a prince who preserves, defends,
and improves his dominions in peace, more praiseworthy
than one who seeks to extend them by force of arms? The
second was to be a panegyric of the Provveditore Generale.
An old nobleman of Zara, named Giovanni Pellegrini, was
chosen to preside in the Academy and to dispense the invitations. He wore a black velvet suit and a huge blond wig, done
up into knotted curls, and possessed a fund of eloquence in
the style of Father Casimir Freschot[1] and Tesauro.[2]

I did not receive an invitation, which proves either that I
was an amateur of poetry unknown to fame, or that Signor
Pellegrini, in his gravity and wisdom, judged me a mere boy,
unworthy of consideration in an enterprise which he treated
with true Illyrico-Italian seriousness. Signor Colombo and my
friend Massimo urged me to prepare two compositions on the
published themes; but I reminded them that I had no right to
appear uninvited. Nevertheless, I amused myself by scribbling
a couple of sonnets, which I consigned to the bottom of my
pocket. As may be imagined, I defended peace in one, and did
my best to belaud his Excellency in the other.

The Provveditore Generale, attended by his officers and by
the magnates of the city, entered the temporary hall, and took
his seat upon a rich fauteuil raised many steps above the
ground. A covey of literary celebrities, collected Heaven
knows where, ranged their learned backs along a row of
chairs, which formed a semicircle round him.

Strolling outside the damasked tabernacle, I saw some

---

[1] C. Freschot (1640–1720), author of a *Nouvelle Relation de la ville et
république de Venise* (1709).
[2] Emanuele Tesauro (1591–1675), a Jesuit priest from Turin; historian,
tragedian, and exponent of baroque style, the theory of which he set
out in his *Cannocchiale aristotelico*, Venice, 1655.

servants who were preparing beverages and refreshments with a mighty bustle. I was thirsty, and thought I should not be committing a crime if I asked one of them for a lemonade. He replied that express orders had been given not to quench the thirst of anybody who was not a member of the Academy. This discourteous rebuff, repeated to the *sitio* of several officers, raised a spirit of silent revolt among us. I resolved to put a bold face on the matter, and to proclaim myself an academician, thinking that the title of poet might win for me the lemonade which was denied to the dignity and the weapons of an officer.

This little incident confirmed my opinion of the usefulness of poetry against the universal judgment which regards it as an inutility. Poetry stood me in good stead by procuring me a lemonade and saving me from dying of thirst. Having swallowed the beverage, I proceeded to one of the seats in the assembly, exciting some surprise among its members, who were, however, kind enough to tolerate my presence. For three whole hours the air resounded with long inflated erudite orations and poems not remarkable for sweetness. A yawn from the General now and then did honour to the Academy and the academicians. I must in justice say that some tolerable compositions, superior to what I had expected, struck my ears. A young abbé in holy orders gushed with poetic eloquence. I have heard that he is now become a bishop. Who knows whether poetry was not as serviceable to him in the matter of his mitre, as she was to me in the matter of my lemonade !

I declaimed my sonnets in their turn, the one which upheld the peaceable rather than the warring prince, somewhat in the manner of Boileau's epistle to Louis XIV, and the other one in praise of our Provveditore Generale Querini. The second of them, by Apollo's blessing, pleased his Excellency, and consequently was received with general approval. It established my reputation among the folk of Zara, and led to a comic scene two days later. The Provveditore Generale was in the habit of riding in the cool some four or five miles outside the city; a troop of officers galloped at his heels, and I galloped with them. While we were amusing ourselves in this way, his Excellency took a fancy to hear my sonnet over again; for it had now become famous, as often happens with trifles, which go the round of society upon the strength of adventitious circumstances. He called me loudly. I put spurs to my horse, while he, still galloping, ordered me to recite. I do not think a sonnet was ever declaimed in like manner since the creation of the world. Galloping after the great man, and almost bursting my lungs in the effort to make myself heard, with all the trills, gasps, cadences, semitones, clippings of words, and dissonances, which the movement of a horse at full speed could occasion, I recited the sonnet in a storm of sobs and sighs, and blessed my stars when I had pumped out the fourteenth line. Knowing the temper of the General, who was haughty and formidable in matters of importance, but sometimes whimsical in his diversions, I thought at the time that he must have been seeking a motive for laughter. And indeed, I believe this was the case. Anyhow, he can only have been deceived if he hoped to laugh more at the affair than I did. Yet I was rather afraid of becoming a laughing-stock to my riding-companions also. Foolish fear! These honest fellows, like true courtiers, vied with each other in congratulating me upon the partiality of his Excellency and the honour he had done me. They were even jealous of a bur-lesque scene in which I played the buffoon, and sorry that they had not enjoyed the luck of performing it themselves.

7

Little incidents, trifling observations, moral reflections of no value, gossip which is sure to make the reader yawn

Our forces had little to occupy them in those provinces, so that my sonnet in praise of peace exactly fitted. Some inter-esting incidents, and several journeys which I undertook, furnished me, however, with abundant matter for reflection. I shall here indulge myself by setting down a few observations which occur to my memory.

The regular troops which garrison the fortresses of Dalmatia had been recalled to Italy, in order to defend the neutrality of Venice during the wars which then prevailed among her neighbours. In these circumstances the Senate commissioned our Provveditore Generale to levy new forces from the subject tribes, not only for maintaining the military establishment of Dalmatia, but also for drafting a large number of Morlacchi[1] into Italy. It was a matter of no difficulty to enrol garrisons for the Illyrian fortresses; but the exportation of the Morlacchi cost his Excellency the greatest trouble. These ruffianly wild beasts, wholly destitute of education, are aware that they are subjects of Venice; yet their firm resolve is to indulge lawless instincts for robbery and murder as they list, refusing obedience in all things which do not suit their inclinations. To reason with them is the same as talking in a whisper to the deaf. They simply resisted the command to form themselves into a troop and leave their lairs for Italy.

Their chiefs, who were educated men, brave and loyal to their prince, strained every nerve to carry out these orders. It was found needful to recall the bandits, who swarm throughout those regions, outlawed for every sort of crime— robberies, homicides, arson, and such-like acts of heroism. Bribes too were offered of bounties and advanced pay, in order to induce the wild and stubborn peasants to cross the seas. I was present at the review of these Anthropophagi; for indeed they hardly merited a more civilized title. It took place on the beach at Zara under the eyes of the Provveditore, with ships under sail, ready for the embarkation of the conscripts. Pair by pair, they came up and received their stipend; upon which they expressed their joy by howling out some barbarous chant, and dancing off together with uncouth gambols

[1] The native Dalmatians of Slav origin, inhabiting the inland villages and country districts, were called by this name. (S)

to the transport ships. I revered God's handiwork in these savages while deploring their bad education, and felt a passing wish to explore the Eden of eternal beatitude in which the Morlacchi dwell.

It is certain that the Italian cities under our benign government were more disturbed than guarded by these brutal creatures. At Verona, in particular, they indulged their appetite for thieving, murdering, brawling, and defying discipline, without the least regard for others. At the close of a few months, they had to be sent back to their caves, in order to deliver the Veneto from an unbearable incubus. Even at the outset, their spirit of insubordination let itself be felt. Scarcely had the transports sailed, when the sight of the Illyrian mountains made them burn to leap on shore. The seamen did their best to restrain the unruly crew; but finding that they ran a risk of being cut in pieces, they finally unbarred the pens before this indomitable flock of rams.

What I am now writing may seem to have little to do with the narrative of my own life, and may look as though I wished to calumniate the natives of Dalmatia. The rulers of those territories will, however, bear me out in the following remarks. I have visited all the fortresses, many districts, and many villages of the two provinces. In some of the cities I found well-educated people, trustworthy, cordial, and liberal in sentiment. In places far removed from the Provveditore Generale's Court the manners of the population are incredibly rough. All the peasants may be described as cruel, superstitious, and irrational wild beasts. In their marriages, their funerals, their games, they preserve the customs of pagan antiquity. Reading Homer and Virgil gives a perfect conception of the Morlacchi. They hire a troop of women to lament over their dead. These professional mourners shriek by turns, relieving one another when voice and throat have been exhausted by dismal wailings tuned to a music which inspires terror. One of their pastimes is to balance a heavy piece of marble on the lifted palm of the right hand, and hurl it after taking a running jump. The fellow who projects this missile

in a straight line to the greatest distance, wins. One is reminded of the enormous boulders hurled by Diomede and
Turnus.

In their mountain homes the Morlacchi are fine fellows, useful to the State of Venice on occasions of war with the Turks,
their neighbours, whom they cordially detest. The inhabitants
of the coast make bold seamen, apt for fighting on the waters.
Toward Montenegro the tribes become even more like savages.
Families, who have been accustomed for some generations to
die peaceably in their beds or kennels, and cannot boast of a
fair number of murdered ancestors, are looked down upon
by the rest. On the beach outside the city walls of Budua, for
which these men leave their hills in summer-time to taste the
coolness of sea-breezes, I have witnessed their exploits with
the musket and have seen three corpses stretched upon the
sands. A member of one of the pacific families I have described, being taunted by some comrade, burned to wipe out
the shame of his kindred, and opened a glorious chapter in
their annals by slaughtering and being slaughtered. Fierce
battles and armed encounters between village and village are
frequent enough in those parts. The men of one village who
kill a man of the next village have no peace unless they pay
a hundred sequins or discharge their debt by the death of one
of their own folk. Such is the current tariff, fixed without
consulting their sovereign, among these people, who regard
brutality as justice. I learned much about these traits of
human nature from a village priest of Montenegro, who conversed with me nearly every day upon the beach at Budua.
He talked a strange Italian jargon, narrated the homicides of
his flock with complacency, and let it be understood that a
gun was better suited to his handling than the vessels of the
sanctuary.

The thirst for vengeance is never slaked there. It passes
from heir to heir like an entailed estate. Among the Morlacchi, who are less bloodthirsty than the Montenegrins, I
once saw a woman of some fifty years fling herself at the feet
of the Provveditore Generale, extract a mummied head from a

game-bag, and cast it on the ground before him, weeping as though her heart would burst, and calling aloud for pity and justice. For thirty years she had preserved this skull, the skull of her mother, who had been murdered. The assassins had long ago been brought to justice, but their punishment was insufficient to lay the demon of ferocity in this affectionate daughter. Accordingly, she presented herself indefatigably through a course of thirty years before each of the successive Provveditori Generali, with the same maternal skull in her game-bag, with the same shrieks and tears and cries for justice.

I liked seeing the Montenegrin women. They clothe themselves in black woollen stuffs after a fashion which was certainly not invented by coquetry. Their hair is parted, and falls over their cheeks on either shoulder, thickly plastered with butter, so as to form a kind of large shiny bonnet. They bear the burden of the hard work of the field and household. The wives are little better than slaves of the men. They kneel and kiss the men's hands whenever they meet; and yet they seem contented with their lot. Perhaps it would not be amiss if some Montenegrins came to Italy and changed our fashions with regard to women; for ours are somewhat too marked in the contrary direction.

Climate renders both the men and women of these provinces extremely prone to sensuality. Legislators, recognizing the impossibility of controlling lawless lust here, have fixed the fine for seduction of a girl with violence at a trifle above the sum which a libertine in Venice bestows on the purveyor of his venal pleasures. At the period of my residence in Dalmatia, the cities retained something of antique austerity. This did not, however, prevent the fair sex from conducting intrigues by stealth. It is possible that, since those days, enlightened and philosophical Italians, composing the courts of successive Provveditori Generali, may have removed the last obstacle of prejudice which gave a spice of danger to love-making.

In Dalmatia the women are handsome, inclining for the

E

most part toward a masculine robustness; among the Morlacchi of the villages, a Pygmalion who chose to expend some
bushels of sand in polishing the fair sex up, would obtain fine
breathing statues for his pains. These women of Illyria are
less constant in their love than those of Italy; but merit less
blame for their infidelity than the latter. The Illyrian is
blinded and constrained by her fervent temperament, by the
climate, by poverty and credulity; the Italian errs through
ambition, avarice, and caprice. I consider myself qualified for
speaking with decision on these points, as will appear from the
chapter I intend to write upon the love-adventures of my
youth.

The land of those provinces is in great measure mountain-
ous, stony, and barren. There are, however, large districts of
plain which might be extremely fertile. Neither the sterile nor
the fertile regions are under cultivation, but remain for the
most part fallow and unfruitful. Onions and garlic constitute
the favourite delicacies of the Morlacchi. The annual consumption of these vegetables is enormous; and it would not
be difficult to raise a large supply of both at home. They insist,
however, on importing them from Romagna; and when one
takes the peasants to task for their sluggish indifference to
their own interests, they reply that their ancestors never
planted onions, and that they have no mind to change their
customs. I often questioned educated inhabitants of those
regions upon the indolence and sloth which prevail in rural
Dalmatia. The answer I received was that nobody, without
exposing his life to peril, could make the Morlacchi do more
than they chose to do, or introduce the least reform into their
agriculture. I observed that the proprietors might always im-
port Italian labour and turn those fertile plains into a second
Apulia. This remark was met with bursts of laughter; and
when I asked the reason, my informants told me that many
Dalmatian gentlemen had brought Italian peasants over, but
that a few days after their arrival, they were found murdered
in the fields, without the assassins having ever been detected.
I perceived that my project was impracticable. Yet I won-

dered at my friends laughing rather than shedding tears, when they gave me these convincing answers.

I have too high a regard for the Arduini brothers[1] and our other agricultural experts to suggest that they should go and live among the Morlacchi and try to make Dalmatia and Illyria fertile and profitable to the State, but as it is, they cost our treasury more than they yield, through the expenses incidental to their forming our frontier against Turkey. However I never made it my business to meddle in affairs of public policy; and perhaps there are good reasons why these provinces should be left to their sterility. The opinion I have continually maintained and published, that we ought to begin by cultivating heads and hearts, has raised a swarm of hostile projectors against me. Such men take the truths of the gospel for biting satires, if they detect the least shadow of opposition to their views regarding personal interest, personal ambition, or particular prejudice. Yet the real miseries which I noticed in Dalmatia, the wretched pittance which proprietors draw from their estates, and the dishonesty of the peasants, suffice to demonstrate my principles of moral education beyond the possibility of contradiction.

During my three years in Dalmatia I used to eat superb game and magnificent fish for a mere nothing; often against my inclination, and only because the opportunity could not

---

[1] Giovanni (1714–95) and Pietro (1728–1805), from Caprino in the region of Verona. Giovanni Arduini was a pioneer in the fields of geology, mineralogy, and metallurgy. His most original contribution to science was his study of the chronology of rock-strata, which makes him the founder of stratigraphy. The Venetian Senate appointed him to the post of Soprintendente dell'Agricoltura, in the exercise of which he was called upon to make recommendations not only in the field of agriculture (land-drainage, the cultivation of hemp, mulberry-trees, etc.) but also about a wide range of other technical problems, such as those connected with the manufacture of salt and gunpowder. His brother, Pietro, studied botany under Pontedera at Padua, first as a student and later as *assistente* and keeper of the herb-garden, a position which enabled him to furnish Linnaeus with valuable data. In 1765 he was appointed to the recently founded Chair of Agriculture at Padua, the first of its kind in Italy.

be neglected. When you are in want of something, you rarely find it there. The fishermen, who live upon the rocky islands,[1] ply their trade when it pleases them. They take no thought for fasts, and sell fish for the most part on days when flesh is eaten. The fish too is brought to market stuffed into sacks. I could multiply these observations; but let what I have already said suffice. It is my firm opinion that the economists of our century are at fault when they propose material improvements and indulge in visions of opulence and gain, without considering moral education. Wealth is now regarded by the indigent with eyes of envy and the passion of a pirate; rich people act as though they knew not what it was to possess wealth, and make a shameless abuse of it in practice. The one class need to learn temperance, moderation, and obedience to duty; the other ought to be trained to reason and subordination. The sages of the present day entertain very different views from these. In their eyes nothing but material interest has any value; and instead of deploring bad morals and manners, they seem to glory in them.[2]

---

[1] *Scogli.* A long low island opposite the harbour of Zara is so called. (S)

[2] In these last five sentences Symonds summarizes the main points of a discussion in which Gozzi deplores the fact that scientists habitually overlook the importance of moral education. His remarks are aimed at the Paduan naturalist Alberto Fortis (1741–1803), whose *Viaggio in Dalmazia* contains a sympathetic description of the Morlacchi.

8

My theatrical talents; athletic exercise; imprudences of all kinds; dangers to which I exposed myself; with reflections which are always frivolous

All through the carnival, tragedies, dramas, and comedies used to be performed by amateurs in the Court-theatre, for the amusement of his Excellency, the patricians on the civil staff, officers of the garrison, and the good folk of Zara.[1]

Our troop was composed exclusively of male actors, as is the case in general with unprofessional theatres; and young men, dressed like women, played the female parts. I was selected to represent the *soubrette*.

On weighing the tastes of my audience, and taking into account the nation for whom I was to act, I invented a wholly new kind of character. I had myself dressed like a Dalmatian servant-girl, with hair divided at the temples, and done up with rose-coloured ribbands. My costume corresponded at all points to that of a coquettish housemaid of Sebenico. I discarded the Tuscan dialect, which is spoken by the *soubrettes* of our theatres in Italy, and having learned Illyrian pretty well by this time, I devised for my particular use a jargon of Venetian, altering the pronunciation and interspersing various Illyrian phrases. This produced a very humorous effect, and lent itself both in dialogue and improvised soliloquies to the expression of sentiments in keeping with my part. Courage and loquacity were always at my service; after studying the plot of a comedy, which had to be performed

[1] This chapter will be read with interest by students of the *Commedia dell'arte*. It throws light upon the way in which an actor of originality could adapt one of the fixed characters of that comedy, in this case the *servetta*, to his own talents and to local circumstances. (S)

extempore, I never found my readiness of wit at fault. Accordingly, the new and unexpected type of the *soubrette* which I invented was welcomed with enthusiasm alike by Italians and natives. It created a *furore* in my audience, and won for me universal sympathy.

My sketches of Dalmatian manners studied from the life, my satirical repartees to the mistresses I served, my piquant sallies upon incidents which formed the talk of the town and garrison, my ostentatious modesty, my snubs to impertinent admirers, my reflections and my lamentations, made the Provveditore Generale and the whole audience declare with tears of laughter running down their cheeks that I was the wittiest and most humorous *soubrette* who ever trod the boards of a theatre. They often bespoke improvised comedies, in order to enjoy the amusing chatter and Illyrico-Italian jargon of Luce; for I ought to add that I adopted this name, which is the same as our Lucia, instead of Smeraldina, Corallina, or Colombina.

Ladies in plenty were eager to know the young man who played Luce with such diablerie and ready wit upon the stage. But when they met him face to face in society, his reserve and taciturnity were so unlike the sprightliness of his assumed character, that they fairly lost their temper. Now that I am well stricken in years, I recognize that their disappointment was anything but a misfortune for me. The conduct of those few who concealed their feelings and pretended that my self-control and seriousness had charms to win their heart, justifies this moral reflection. Meanwhile my talent for comedy relieved me of all military duties so long as carnival lasted. Each year, at the commencement of this season, the Provveditore Generale sent for me, and affably requested me to devote my time and energy to his amusement in the Court-theatre.

During summer he set the fashion of pallone-playing, which had hitherto been unknown at Zara.[1] I had made myself an

---

[1] *Pallone* is a game played with a large leather ball, filled with air, and something like our football. In Italy it is struck with the hand, which is armed for the purpose with gloves or a flat short bat fixed on

adept in this game at our Friulian country-seat. Accordingly his Excellency urged me to display my accomplishments for the entertainment of the public. In a short time my seductive costume of fine white linen, with a waistband of black satin and fluttering ribands, cut a prominent figure among the competitors in this noble sport. My turn for study, literary talent, grave demeanour, and seriousness of character made far less impression on the fair sex than my success on the stage and the pallone-ground. It was these and these alone which put my chastity to the test and conquered it, as will appear in the chapter on my love-adventures. I might here indulge in a digression hardly flattering to women. But I prefer to congratulate them on their emancipation from the ideality of Petrarch's age. Now they are at liberty to float voluptuously on the tide of tender and electrical emotions, in company with youths congenial to their instincts, who have abandoned tedious studies for occupations hardly more exacting than a game at ball or the impersonation of a waiting-maid.

The truth of history compels me to touch upon some incidents which put my boyish courage to the proof; yet I must confess that my deeds of daring in Dalmatia were nothing better than mad and brainless acts of folly. While recording them, I dare hardly hope—although I should sincerely like to do so—that they will prove useful to parents by exposing the kind of life which young men lead on foreign service, or to sons by pointing out the errors of my ways.

We had no war on hand, and our valour was obliged to find a vent for itself. I should have passed for a poltroon if I had not joined the amusements and adventures of my comrades. These consisted for the most part in frantic gambling, serenading houses which returned our serenades with gunshots, entertaining women of the town at balls and supper-parties, brawling in the streets at night, disguising ourselves to frighten people, and breaking the slumbers of the good folk of the towns and fortresses where the Court happened to be

---

the palm. Sides are chosen, and the game roughly resembles tennis on a large scale. (S)

fixed. I remember that one summer night in the city of Spalato, eight or ten of us dressed up for the latter purpose. Each man put on a couple of shirts, thrusting his legs through the sleeves of one and his arms through the other, with a big white bonnet on his head and a pole in his hand. Thus attired, we scoured the town like spectres from the other world, knocking at doors, uttering horrid shrieks to rouse the population, and striking terror into the breasts of women and children. Now it is the custom there to leave the stable-doors open, because of the great heat at night. Accordingly we undid the halters of some fifty horses, and drove them before us, clattering our staves upon the pavement. The din was infernal. Folk leaped from their beds, thinking that the Turks had made a raid upon the town, and crying from their windows: 'Who the devil are you? Who goes there? Who goes there?' They screamed to the deaf, while we went clattering and driving on. In the morning the whole city was in an uproar, discussing last night's prodigy and scurrying about to catch the frightened animals.

My guitar-playing accomplishments made me indispensable in these dare-devil escapades of hare-brained boys, which by some miracle never seemed to reach the Provveditore Generale's ears. Had they done so, I suppose they would have been punished as they deserved; for he was a man who knew how to maintain discipline. The Italians and Illyrians do not dwell together without a certain half-concealed antipathy. This leads to frequent trials of strength and valour, in which the Italians are most to blame. They insult the natives and pick quarrels with a people famous for their daring and ferocity. The courage displayed in maintaining these quarrels and facing their attendant dangers deserves the name of folly rather than of bravery. After stating this truth, to which indeed I was never blind, I dare affirm that no one met musket-shots and menaces with a bolder front than I did. Physicians versed in the anatomy of the human frame may be able to explain my constitutional imperturbability under all circumstances of peril. I am content to account for it as sheer stupidity.

In the society of unemployed and lazy officers, a young man may be said to have worked miracles who preserves the good principles implanted in him at home. Unless he conforms to the tone and fashion of his comrades, he is sure to be derided and despised. If he does conform, he is likely to lose substance, health, and reputation at cards, with women, or by drinking. Besides this, he constantly risks life and limb in the so-called pastimes I have just described.

I am able to boast without exaggeration that I never played for high stakes, that I never surrendered myself to debauchery, that I preserved the sound principles of my home education, and yet that I was popular with all my comrades, owing to the clubbable and fraternal attitude which I assumed at some risk, it is true, yet always with the firm determination to leave a good character behind me when my term of service ended.

9

Shows how a young Cadet of Cavalry is capable of executing a military stratagem

Having described the dangers to which my system of conduct in the army exposed me, I ought in justice to myself to show that I was able on occasion to reconcile our absurd code of honour with prudence and diplomacy. With this object I will relate an incident, which is neither more nor less insignificant than the other events of my life.

The city of Zara is traversed by a main street of considerable length, extending from the piazza of S. Simeone to the gate called Porta Marina. Several lanes and alleys, leading downwards from the ramparts on the side towards the sea, debouch into this principal artery. It so happened that some of the officers, wishing to traverse one of these lanes on their

way to the promenade upon the ramparts, had been intercep-
ted by a man muffled in a mantle, who levelled an eloquent
enormous blunderbuss at their persons, and forced them to
change their route. This act of violence ought to have been
reported to the Provveditore Generale, and he would have
speedily restored order and freedom of passage. Our military
code of honour, however, forbade recourse of justice as an act
of cowardice; albeit some of my comrades found it not de-
rogatory to their courage to recoil before a blunderbuss.

My readers ought to be informed that a girl of the people,
called Tonina, one of the loveliest women whom eyes of man
have ever seen, lived in this lane. She had multitudes of admirers; and the cozening tricks she used to wheedle and entice
a pack of simpletons made her no better than any other cheap
venal beauty. Yet she contrived to sell her favours by the
sequin. A gentleman, whom I shall mention later on, was
madly in love with this little baggage. Wishing to keep the
treasure to himself, he adopted a truly Dalmatian mode of
testifying his devotion, and stood sentinel in her alley. On two
consecutive evenings the passage was barred; we talked of nothing else in the ante-chamber of the General, and laid plans
how to reassert our honour. A number of officers agreed to
face the blunderbuss; I received an invitation to join the
band; and acting on my system of good-fellowship, I readily
consented.

Our discussion took place in the ante-chamber; silence was
enjoined; we settled that each of the conspirators should wear
a white ribband on his hat, and that three hours after nightfall we should assemble under arms at our accustomed muster-
ing place. This was a billiard-saloon, whence we were to sally
forth to the assault of Buda.

An Illyrian nobleman, Signor Simeone C——, of handsome
person, honourable carriage, and a resolute temper, which inspired even soldiers with respect, although he held no military
grade, was sitting in a corner of the ante-chamber, half-asleep,
and apparently inattentive to our project. I knew him to be
frank and genial, and he had often professed sentiments of

sincere friendship for myself. After our scheme had been con-
certed, I passed into the reception-room of the palace. He
followed, and opened a conversation on indifferent topics, in
the course of which he drew me aside, changed his tone, and
began to speak as follows :

'The moment has arrived for me to testify the cordial
friendship which I entertain for you. I regret that you have
promised to join those fire-eaters this evening. On your
honour and secrecy I know that I can count. I am sure that
you will not reveal what I am about to disclose; else the higher
powers, whom we are bound to regard, might be involved,
and cowardice might be suspected in those whose courage is
indisputable. This preamble will enable you to judge what I
think of you, and to measure the extent of my friendship. I
am the man in the mask. Tonight there will be four blunderbusses in the alley. I shall lose my life; but several will lose
theirs before the lane is forced. I am sorry that you are in the
affair. Contrive to get out of your engagement. Let the rest
come, and enjoy their fill of pastime at the cost of life or
limb.'

This blunderbuss of an oration took me by surprise. But I
did not lose my senses or my tongue, and answered to the
following effect :

'I am amazed that you should have begun by professing
friendship and preaching caution. You do not seem to understand the first elements of the one or the simple meaning of
the other. I am obliged to you for one thing only, your belief
that I am incapable of divulging what you have just told me.
Upon this point alone your discernment is not at fault. I
would rather die than expose you. Yet you want me, under
threats, to break my word, and to render myself contemptible
in the eyes of all my comrades. This you call a proof of friendship. It is as clear as day, too, that you have yielded to a
hussy's importunities, risking your own life and the lives of
your friends upon a silly point of honour in a shameful
quarrel. This is the proof of your prudence. If you withdraw
from the engagement, no harm will be done, and cowardice

will only be imputed to a nameless mask. But if I break my word, you cannot free me from the imputation of having proved myself a renegade and a dastard. I shall become an object of scorn and abhorrence to the whole army. If I act as you desire, my oath of secrecy to you will violate the laws of friendship, prudence, everything which men hold sacred. Your promise of secrecy again puts my honour in peril. How can you be sure that one of your accomplices will not privily inform his Excellency of your name and your mad enterprise? Where shall I then be? No : it is clearly your duty to obey the counsels dictated by my loyal friendship and my sound prudence. Leave the alley open; and then you will in truth oblige me. Make love to your Tonina with something more to the purpose than a blunderbuss. Her physical shape excuses your weakness for her; her mind deserves your scorn; but I am not going to preach sermons on objects worthy or unworthy of love; I feel compassion for human frailty.'

It was obvious that Signor Simeone C—— felt the force of these arguments. But he writhed with rage under them, and showed no sign of consenting. In his fierce Dalmatian way he burst into bare protestation, swore that he would never quit the field, and wound up with a vow to sell his life as dearly as man ever did.

At this point I judged it needful to administer a dose of histrionic artifice. After gazing at him for some seconds with eyes which spoke volumes, I assumed the declamatory tone of a tragedian, and exclaimed : 'Well then, I promise to be the first to enter the lane this evening, and, without attacking you, I shall offer my breast to your fire. I have only this way left of proving to you that you are in no real sense of the word my friend.' Then I turned my back with a show of passion, taking care, however, to retire at a slow pace. Except for the ferocity instilled by education, he was at bottom an excellent goodhearted fellow. Seizing me by the arm, he begged me wait a moment. I saw that he was touched, and maintaining the tragic tone, persuaded him to leave the access to the alley free, without resigning his exclusive right to Tonina. For my part, I undertook never to reveal our secret. This promise I have kept for thirty-five years. Lapse of time and the probability of his decease—for he was much older than I—excuse me for now breaking it.

On three following nights I joined the allied forces at the billiard-room, armed to the teeth, and with a white ribbon flying from my hat-band. I was always the first to brave the blunderbusses, being sure that no resistance would be offered. Indeed, the victory, on which we piqued ourselves, had been won beforehand in my battle of words. The culpable conduct of Tonina, a girl of the people, who had exposed so many gentlemen to serious danger, remained fixed in my mind. I shall relate the sequel to this incident, which took a comic turn, in the next chapter. For the present, it is enough to add that Signor Simeone C——'s infatuation for this corsair of Venus rapidly declined, as is the wont of passion begotten by masculine appetite and feminine avarice. Tonina, however, did not lack lovers, and the badness of her nature continued to spread discord and foment disorder in our circle.

IO

The fair Tonina is rudely rebuked by me upon an accidental occasion in the theatre—Reflections on my life in Dalmatia

One evening during the last carnival of my three years' service, the Provveditore Generale bespoke an improvised comedy at the Court-theatre. The officers arranged a supper-party and a ball in private rooms, intending to pass the night gaily when the farce was over. I had to play the part of Luce, married to Pantalone, a vicious old man, broken in health and fortune. I was reduced to extreme poverty, with a daughter in the cradle, the fruit of my unhappy marriage.

There was a night-scene, in which I had to soliloquize, while rocking my child and singing it to sleep with some old ditty.

This lullaby I interrupted from time to time with the narrative of my misfortunes and with sallies which made the audience die of laughter. Bursts of applause brought the house down as I told my story, enlarged upon my reasons for marrying an old man, related the incidents of my life, alluded in modest monosyllables to what I had to bear, described what a fine figure of a woman I had been, and what a scarecrow matrimony had made me. I complained of cold, hunger, evil treatment. I did not make milk enough to suckle my baby; and what I made was sour, nay, venomous from fits of rage and all the sufferings I had to go through. This bad milk gave my darling, the fruit of my womb, the stomach-ache. It kept bleating all night like a lamb, and would not let me close an eye. The night was far advanced. I was waiting for my old fool of a husband. What could be keeping him abroad? He must surely be in the Calle del Pozzetto, notorious at Zara for its evil fame. I had a presentiment of coming troubles, moralized upon the woes of life, and burst into a flood of tears, which made everybody laugh. The truth was that one of our officers, Signor Antonio Zeno, who played the part of Pantalone excellently, had not turned up at the proper time to enter into dialogue with me. Until he arrived, I was forced to continue my soliloquy, which had already occupied the attention of the audience full fifteen minutes. A good extempore actor ought never to lose presence of mind, or to be at a loss for material. In order to prolong the scene, I pretended that my baby was crying, and that it would not go to sleep for all my lullabies and cradle-rocking. In a fit of impatience I took it up, unlaced my dress, and laid it with endearing caresses to my breasts to quiet it. This fresh absurdity, together with my lamentations over the non-existent teats I said the greedy little thing was biting, kept my audience in good humour. From time to time I turned my eyes to the sides, being really disturbed at Signor Zeno-Pantalone's non-appearance, and racking my brains in vain for some new matter to sustain the soliloquy.

Just then I happened to catch sight of Tonina seated in one of the front boxes of the theatre, resplendent with beauty, and attired in a gala dress which cast a glaring light upon her dubious career. She was laughing with more assurance and sense of fun than anybody at my jokes. The catastrophe which she had nearly caused flashed suddenly across my mind. I felt that I had discovered a treasure; and plunged like lightning into a new subject. What I proceeded to do was bold, I admit, yet quite within the limits of good taste upon our amateur stage, where personal allusions were allowed perhaps a little too liberally. I called my doll-baby by the name of Tonina, and addressed my speech to it. I caressed it, admired its features, flattered my maternal heart with the hope that Tonina would grow up a lovely girl. So far as I was concerned, I vowed to give her a good education, by example, precepts, chastisement, and watchful care. Then, taking a tone of gravity, I warned her that if, in spite of all my troubles, she fell into such and such faults, such and such acts of imprudence, such and such immoral ways, and caused such and such disturbances, she would be the worst Tonina in the world, and I prayed to God to cut her days short rather in the cradle. All the evil things I mentioned were faithfully copied from anecdotes about Tonina in the front box, with which my audience were only too well acquainted.

Never in my whole life have I known an improvised soliloquy to be so tumultuously applauded as this of mine was. The spectators at one point of the speech turned their faces with a simultaneous movement towards Tonina in her gala dress, clapping their hands and laughing till the theatre rang again. His Excellency, who had some inkling of the siren's ways, honoured my unexpected satire with explosions of unconcealed merriment. Tonina backed out of her box in a fit of fury, and escaped from the theatre, cursing my soliloquy and the man who made it. Pantalone finally arrived, and the comedy ended without any episode more mirthful than the scene between me and my baby.

Do not imagine that I have related this incident to brag about it. Although the young woman in question was a girl of the people, whose dissolute behaviour and ill-nature had been

the cause of many misadventures, and though the Provveditore Generale applauded my performance, I blamed myself,
when it was over, for yielding to a mere impulse of vanity,
and exhibiting my power as a comedian at the cost of committing an act of imprudence and indiscretion. Much has to
be condoned to youth which is never conceded to maturity.

I have now given some general notion of my ways of thinking and acting, my character and conduct, up to the age of
nineteen on to twenty. Nothing but the truth has dictated
these reminiscences, from which I have undoubtedly omitted
many things of similar importance. I am sure that if I had
been guilty of anything really wrong during this period, it
would not have escaped either my memory or my pen. I have
never hardened my heart against the stings of remorse, and I
would far rather frankly record facts to my discredit than
bear the stings of conscience by suppressing what is true. Re-
viewing the veracious picture of myself which I have painted,
friends will see in me a somewhat eccentric young man, but of
harmless disposition; enemies will take me for a worthless
scapegrace; the indifferent, who know me superficially by
sight, will discover someone very different from their conception based on my external qualities. At the proper place
and time I shall account for this not unreasonable and yet
fallacious conception formed of me by strangers. The reasons
will appear clearly in the detailed portrait I intend to execute
of myself, and which will surpass the best work of any
painter.

II

*The end of my three years' service—I cast up my accounts,
and reckon debts—My arrival in my home at Venice*

The three years of my military service were nearly at an end,
when I contracted a slow fever, not dangerous to life, but

tedious. The time had come for settling accounts, and seeing how I stood. My family, since I left home, had furnished me with only two bills of exchange, one for fourteen, the other for six sequins. My useless duties to the State had brought me thirty-eight lire per month. Against these receipts I balanced my expenses: so much for my daily food; so much for my lodging, clothing, and washing; so much for a servant, indispensable in my position; so much for two illnesses, together with the small sums spent on unavoidable pleasures of society. The result was that I found myself in debt to my friend Massimo for exactly the sum of fifty-six sequins and sixteen lire, or 200 ducats.[1]

If the necessities of life are not to be considered vices, this debt was certainly a modest one. Still it weighed upon my mind. I consoled myself by recalling my friend's nobleness of nature, and felt sure that I should be able to repay him on reaching home. I computed that the gross sum I had received during those three years amounted to 480 ducats; and I did not think I had been a spendthrift in consuming about 150 ducats a year on my total expenditure. I could indeed have saved something by attending the table which the Provveditore Generale kept daily for the officers of his Court and guard, but which his sublime Excellency never honoured with his presence. Little did he know what a gang of ruffians, with the exception of a few patient souls constrained by urgent need, defiled his table, or what low tricks were perpetrated at it. Since the day of my arrival I had heard the infamous and compromising talk which went on there, and watched the squabbles between guest and guest, and guests and serving-men, had seen the cups and platters flying through the air—and, like a naughty boy perhaps, I preferred to contract a debt of 200 ducats

[1] The sequin at this time was worth twenty-two *lire Venete*. The worth of the *lira* was about half a franc, says Romanin (op. cit., viii. 302). Romanin in the same place fixes the ducat at eight *lire*. Gozzi's debt amounted to 1,248 *lire*. This would make only 156 ducats at the above rate. But the relation of the ducat to the sequin and the *lira* is very obscure, and seems to have varied according to the kind of ducat. (S)

F

rather than accept a hospitality so prostituted to vile uses. I attended this table of Thyestes, as it seemed to me, only when I could not help it, on the days when I had to mount guard.

The financial statement I have just made will appear to many of my readers a mere trifle, unworthy of recording here. They are mistaken. When they have learned in what a state of desolation I found my father's house, and how I strove to stem the tide of prodigality and waste which was bringing our family to ruin, they will understand my reasons for insisting on these trifles. Heads heated by anger and resentment are only too ready to invent false accusations; and I shall soon be made to appear a prodigal, a reckless gambler, a consumer of the substance of my family during the three years I spent abroad. This is why I am so scrupulous in telling the plain truth about my cost of living in Dalmatia.

It was in the month of October when at last I embarked for Venice on the galley of his Excellency. Wind and weather were against us. After a painful voyage of twenty-two days, we came in sight of home, and I drew breath again. After paying my respects and returning thanks to the Cavaliere who had brought me back, I set off for our ancestral mansion at S. Cassiano, accompanied by Signor Massimo, whom I had invited to stay with me upon his way to Padua. There I hoped to be able to pay my friend some attention by giving him good quarters during his sojourn in Venice.

12

Disagreeable discoveries relating to our family affairs, which dissipate all illusions I may have formed

Leaving the horrors of the galley for the ancient home of my ancestors, I palpitated between pleasure at escaping into freedom, hope of being able to make my friend comfortable, and uneasiness lest this hope might prove ill-founded.

We reached the entrance, and my companion gazed with wonder at the stately structure of the mansion, which has really all the appearance of a palace. As a connoisseur of architecture, he complimented me upon its fine design. I answered, what indeed he was about to discover by experience, that attractive exteriors sometimes mask discomfort and annoyance. He had plenty of time to admire the façade, while I kept knocking loudly at the house-door. I might as well have knocked at the portal of a sepulchre. At last a woman, named Eugenia, the guardian-angel of this wilderness, ran to open. To my inquiries she answered, yawning, that the family were in Friuli, but that my brother Gasparo was momently expected. Our luggage had now been brought from the boat, and we began to ascend a handsome marble staircase. No one could have expected that this fine flight of steps would lead to squalor and the haunts of indigence. Yet on surmounting the last stair this was what revealed itself. The stone floors were worn into holes and fissures, which spread in all directions like a cancer. The broken window panes let blasts from every point of the compass play freely to and fro within the draughty chambers. The hangings on the walls were ragged, smirched with smoke and dust, fluttering in tatters. Not a piece remained of that fine gallery of pictures which my grandfather had bequeathed as heirlooms to the family. I only saw some portraits of my ancestors by Titian and Tintoretto still staring from their ancient frames. I gazed at them; they gazed at me; they wore a look of sadness and amazement, as though inquiring how the wealth which they had gathered for their offspring had been dissipated.

I have hitherto omitted to mention that our family archives contain an old worm-eaten manuscript, in which are registered the tithes[1] paid to the public treasury. From this document it appears that the father of my great-grandfather was taxed on upwards of ten thousand ducats of income. It is perhaps a folly to moralize on such things; yet the recollection

[1] *Decime.* Taxes annually raised upon the whole property of a Venetian. (S)

of those mournful portraits gazing down upon me in the squalor of our ancient habitation prompts me to tell an idle truth. Nobody will be the wiser for it; certainly none of our posterity in this prodigal age. My grandfather left an only son and a good estate settled in tail on heirs-male in perpetuity. Four excellent residences, all of them well-furnished, one in Venice, another in Padua, another in Pordenone, another in the Friulian country-town of Vicinale, were included in this entail, as appears from his last will and testament. Little did he think that the solemn appointments of the dead would be so lightly binding on the living.

I had informed my friend Massimo of the exact state of our affairs at home, so far as these were known to me. I could not acquaint him with the grave disasters which had happened in my three years' absence, being myself in blessed ignorance as yet. The news that my two elder sisters had been married inclined me to expect that our domestic circumstances were improving. Cruel deception wrapped me round, and a hundred speechless but eloquent mouths were now proclaiming, from the walls and chambers of my home, how utterly deceived I had been.

Before long I broke, as usual, into laughter, and gaily begged my comrade's pardon for bringing him to such a wretched hostelry. I assured him that my heart, at any rate, was not so ruined as my dwelling, and engaged him in conversation, while we roamed around its chambers, every nook of which increased my mirth by some new aspect of dilapidation. Then I bade him refresh his spirits with a survey of the noble façade; till at last we settled down as well as circumstances permitted. Two days afterwards, my brother Gasparo arrived. I presented the stranger I had brought to share our hospitality, frankly expressing my sense of his worth and my obligations to him as a friend. Upon this we established ourselves in a little society of three, enlivened by the conversation of my brother who, even with a fever on him, never failed to be witty.

Gasparo and I were anxiously awaiting an opportunity to

talk alone like brothers after my long absence. When the moment came, I inquired after my poor father, our mother, and the circumstances of the family. What I had already seen on my arrival prepared me for the disagreeable news I had to hear. With his usual philosophy, but not without an occasional sign of painful emotion, he gave me the following details. The family was reduced to really tragic straits. Our father lived on, but speechless and paralytic, in the same state as when I left him. My two elder sisters, Marina and Emilia, were married respectively to the Conte Michele di Prata and the Conte Giovan Daniele di Montereale. About ten thousand ducats had been promised for their dowries. To raise this sum, such and such portions of the estate had been sold, and a debt of more than two thousand ducats had been contracted. A lawsuit was pending between the family and the Conte Montereale concerning part of the dowry still due to him. Our other three sisters, Laura, Girolama, and Chiara, were growing into womanhood, and gave much to think of for their future.

I saw, to my great annoyance, that it would be impossible to liquidate my debt upon the spot. But all these terrifying details did not make me regret my resignation of the post of cadet noble in the cavalry. A few days later, Signor Massimo left for Padua with the assurance that his two hundred ducats would be paid in course of time by me. Upon this matter he only expressed the sentiments of cordial friendship.

It was not too late in the season for a visit to the country. I felt a strong desire to reach Friuli, and to kiss the hands of my unhappy father. Thither then I went, together with my brother, armed with a giant's fortitude, which was not long in being put to proof.

13

*Fresh discoveries regarding the condition of our family
—Vain hopes and wasted will to be of use—I abandon
myself to my old literary studies*

Our country-house had been originally constructed on an old-fashioned, roomy, and convenient scale, with numbers of out-buildings. It was now reduced to one of those dilapidated farms which I have described in my burlesque poem *Marfisa the Bizarre*, canto xii., stanza 126.[1] Two-thirds of the edifice had been demolished, and the materials sold. The remaining fragments were inhabited, but bore written on their front: 'Here once was Troy.'

Prepared as I was by the misery of our town-house for the desolation of this rural mansion, I hardly cared to cast a glance upon it. What I noticed on arriving was a certain air of jollity and gladness, breathing health, betokening content-ment, which all the faces of the village people wore. Amid the jubilations of relatives, guests, serving-folk and lads about the farm, not omitting a pack of barking dogs, I descended from the calèche with my brother. A whole crowd of people, whom I did not know and could not number, fell upon my neck to bid me welcome. Something of a military carriage, which I had picked up abroad, but which had no relation to my real self, made our farm-folk stare upon me like a comet.

Then I raised my eyes, and saw my poor father at a window in the upper storey, with trembling limbs, dragging himself forward on his stick to catch a glimpse of me. All the blood turned suddenly and galloped through my veins. I rushed up the stairs, burst into the room where he was standing, seized one of his hands, and kissed it in a transport of filial affection:

[1] *La Marfisa bizzarra.* See *Opere*, Venice, Colombani, 1772–92, vii. 393.

He fell upon my shoulder, more paralytic that he had been when I last embraced him, and, in his inability to speak, broke into a piteous fit of weeping. The effort I made to restrain my own tears, lest they should add to his unhappiness, made me feel as though my lungs would burst. Leaning on my arm, he slowly tottered after me, and little by little we reached another room which he frequented. October was nearly over, and the cold in that Friulian climate was very sensible. A good fire burned on the hearth, near which stood the arm-chair of my father, who for seven years had dragged his life out in this wretched state. All the resources of medical science had been tried in vain. Physicians sometimes agreed and sometimes differed about his treatment. But their concord and their discord were equally impotent to effect a cure; and he had not yet reached the age of fifty-five.

I found my mother in the same apartment. She uttered sentiments which were not inappropriate to her maternal character, but in a frigid tone and with an air of stately self-control. I always loved and respected her, not merely from a sense of duty, but with a true filial instinct. She, on her side, used frequently to protest when there was no need for protestation, that she loved all her nine children with exactly the same amount of affection. She often repeated the following words with gravity, raising her eyebrows as she spoke : 'Cut off one of my fingers and I suffer pain; cut off a second and I suffer'; and so on through nine fingers, amputated by the same figure of speech, with equal agony in each case. Notwithstanding this, I believe that the loss of eight fingers would not have given her the same pain as that of the first-born finger, in other words, of my brother Gasparo. He is still alive, a man of honour, and a sage if ever sage existed; and I feel sure that he would admit the truth of this statement, if called on to confirm it.

In my long and anxious study of human nature, I have seen so many mothers with the weakness of my own, that I never dreamed of blaming her. It seemed right to me that my brother's mental gifts and noble qualities should earn for him more of her love than she bestowed on all her other eight children. Mothers, however, who are so devoted to a son, generally spoil him, not only by extolling what is good in his character, but also by defending his natural frailties. Acting thus, my mother favoured Gasparo's marriage, which subjected her beloved son to a real martyrdom. Her lifelong devotion to him, and the prejudice displayed in his favour by her will, only served to increase the unhappiness of a man whom I always loved, love still, and shall love as friend and brother till the end of my days on earth. This digression was rendered necessary by what will follow in my Memoirs.

The room was soon full of relatives and intimate friends, all curious about me. My father strove to ply me with questions, but his tongue refused its office, and he relapsed into weeping. Sad at heart as I was for him, I contrived to relate the most amusing anecdotes I could remember concerning my life in Dalmatia and my travels. In this way I kept him laughing, together with the whole company, through the rest of that day.

The perfect country air; a table abundantly served with rural dainties, though somewhat deficient in elegance; the joviality, wit, and pleasant sallies which never failed in our domestic circle—all this prevented me from attending to the defects of our establishment. Next day I began to discover that the real cause of trouble was not in the building, but in the minds of its inhabitants. I could not have explained why, but I seemed to be a person of importance in the eyes of everybody. My three sisters confided to me in secret that my brother Gasparo's wife, in close alliance with my mother, who doted on her as the consort of her favoured first-born, ruled all the affairs of the family, which were rapidly going from bad to worse. My father's authority as head of the house had ceased to be more than a mere instrument for carrying out what my sister-in-law advised and my mother sanctioned. Unless I managed to stem the tide of extravagance, we should all be plunged into an abyss of ruin. One of my sisters, Girolama, a girl devoted to reading, writing, and translating from the

French—for she too was bitten with our family cacoethes—spoke like a sibyl, gravely and eloquently, on these painful topics. At the same time, my brother's wife contrived secret interviews, in which she explained to me that her husband was indolent, torpid, drowned in fruitless studies, devoted to the company of a certain clever person, and wholly averse from thoughts or cares about domestic matters. She had done everything in her power—God knew she had. She would go on doing her best—God should see she would. Then she described her plans and projects, which, to tell the truth, were pure poetical stupidities. She vowed that she was not in any sense the mistress of the establishment, the administrator of the estate, or the disposer of its revenues; she merely gave advice, made suggestions, and exerted herself for the common benefit and to supply the needs of the family in general. She exhorted me to speak seriously to her husband; I was to make him abandon his unprofitable studies, make him, above all things, give up those visits of taste and soul, which did so much harm; in fine, I was to force him to sustain his wife in her stupendous labours, and to concentrate his thoughts upon his children, who were five in number.

When I came to analyse the curious compound of truths, lies, and fancies which issued from the fevered brains of this poor lady—always hard at work, always embarrassed in a labyrinth of business—I seemed to perceive that what moved her most was the fear of being made responsible for our financial failure. It was also clear that her original ambition of acting the part of prime minister in a realm which only existed in her own imagination, kept her always on the stretch; while a certain little devil of feminine jealousy against her husband added to her disquietude. He, good fellow, had forgotten the long collection of Petrarchan poems written by him for her honour in the past, and which she had repaid with the gift of five children. Not the least little sonnet issued from his pen to celebrate her now. His lyrics were addressed to another idol of the moment.

Meanwhile she set great store upon her personal importance. Every member of our family, who wanted a ducat, a pair of shoes, or something of the sort, came to her with humble supplications, imploring her good offices at head-quarters—and Heaven knew where head-quarters were. This honour and glory made up to her for all her heroic labours in the little realm, which she administered with real authority, though her right to do so was contested, and her schemes were pindarically unpractical.

My younger brother, Almorò, was also at our villa, on a holiday from school—the non-existent school he never went to. His education seemed to have been of the slightest, and his wardrobe left even more to be desired. A boy of good heart and parts, however; gay-spirited and innocent; he was not old enough and had not time to reflect upon our troubles; setting snares for little birds was all his pastime, and when he talked to me, I heard only of the number and the kinds of birds he caught, and the important adventures he had met with in his fowling expeditions.

My father did not converse with me, because he could not; my mother, because she would not. Gasparo's five children with their quarrels and their games broke in upon the only solace which I had, that of reading and writing.

To all the complaints I heard, to all the exhortations which were daily heaped upon me, I gave one only answer: we will see and think it over.

One thing emerged with distinctness from this hurlyburly of our family. The government of affairs was in the hands of the women, under the shadow of my father's authority. If therefore I attempted any salutary innovation in the wasp's nest of my relatives, in opposition to the current regime, which I detested, I should be misrepresented to him, preju-diced as he was by education, susceptible and hot-blooded by temperament, enfeebled by chronic illness; and he was still the master, still my father, loved and respected by me. I doubted whether anything which I could do would not prove in-effectual or worse. I was afraid of becoming the object of everybody's hatred; for I observed that personal considerations, rather than wise reflection and moderate ambitions, were the motive principles of all the folk I had to deal with. Finally I dreaded giving such a shock to my father's declining frame as would cut short the few days of life which still remained to him. The sequel will show that these anticipations were not ill-founded.

In these circumstances I determined to exercise the strictest self-control, and to bear with everything during my father's lifetime. Literature and my favourite studies of the world meanwhile would suffice to entertain me. Knowing that my uncle Almorò Cesare Tiepolo was in the country on an estate of his not far from where we lived, I went to pay him my respects. He inquired how I had been treated in Dalmatia by his Excellency Querini. I answered that he had treated me very well indeed, but that he could not give me any permanent commission, because our troops had been drafted into Italy. He then proposed to recommend me to his Excellency the Provveditore Generale at Verona. I replied that I was grateful for his interest on my behalf, but that Mars had not inspired me with a vocation for military service. I foresaw that I should have to employ all my energies upon the affairs of my family, which were calling loudly for my assistance. Shaking his head and pursing up his lips, he answered that what I said was only too true.

14

Return from Friuli to Venice with my family—I pursue my chosen path in life, and open new veins of experience—Yet further painful discoveries as to our circumstances—The beginnings of domestic discord

The month of November was wearing away when our family began to think of Venice. It amused me to watch the preparations for our journey and our luggage, which in no wise resembled that of the General's suite I had been used to. My father, an invalid; my mother, serious and diplomatical; my sister-in-law, the woman of business; my brother Gasparo, wool-gathering; our little sisters, intent upon the custody of their old-fashioned bonnets; Almorò, plunged in grief at leaving his birds and cages, which he consigned by something like a last will and testament to the bailiff; I, giving myself military airs, quite out of season; some serving-maids and men in worn-out livery; a few cats and dogs; these composed our travelling party, which might have been compared to a troupe of comedians upon the march.

I shall perhaps be told that there was no reason to enumerate these humiliating circumstances. But I have never had to blush for unworthy actions in my family; and it seems to me a poor philosophy that feels ashamed where no shame is. Such as it was, our caravan arrived in Venice, joking and laughing all the way. There we installed ourselves with as much disorder and as little comfort as was proper to a fine large mansion with nothing to fill its empty spaces.

For my own use I chose out a little room at the top of the house, where I set up a rickety table, provided myself with a huge inkstand and plenty of pens and paper, and spent at least six hours a day in reading and scribbling poetic nonsense. This was my best amusement; but I ought to add that I devoted some of my time to the cafés, studying types of character and listening to conversation; nor did I neglect our theatres, where I saw the various tragedies and comedies which appeared. My brother Gasparo had already given several serious pieces to the stage. They pleased the public then; and though they may be out of fashion now, they would not fail to please me still. I know the instability of taste too well to change my old opinions.

I had mixed with all sorts of men and learned to know their characters—generals, admirals, noblemen, great lords, officers, soldiers, the people of Illyrian cities, the Morlacchi of the village, Mainotti, Pastrovicchi, convicts, galley-slaves. It was time, I thought, to become acquainted with my own Venetians. I began by cultivating a set of men who go in Venice by the name of *cortigiani*.[1] My companions of this kind were chiefly shopkeepers and handicraftsmen, with a priest or two among the number; clever fellows, respectable, and versed in all the ways of our Venetian world. Their courage and readiness to take part in quarrels won them the respect of the common people, and they carried the art of getting the maximum of pleasure at a minimum of outlay to perfection. On certain holidays I joined their boating-parties, and went to shoot birds on the marshes with them. Or else we lunched together on the Giudecca, at Campalto, Malcontenta, Murano, Burano, and other neighbouring islands. My share of the expenses on these occasions was not much above six-pence, and I gained the hearty good-will of my companions by contributing some slices of excellent Friulian ham to our common table. The characters and manners of these men

[1] Gozzi's description of the Venetian *cortesan* may serve as illustration to a popular play of Goldoni's, *Momolo cortesan*. This was the first comedy of character Goldoni composed. Its title-rôle was written for a celebrated Pantalone, Golinetti (see Goldoni's *Memoirs*, Part I, chap. 40). When he printed it, he translated the title into *L'uomo di mondo (The Man of the World)*, finding no exact equivalent for the Venetian term *cortesan*. Goldoni's account of the character tallies with Gozzi's. (S)

delighted me; I took pleasure in listening to the stories of their quarrels, reconciliations, love-adventures, misfortunes, accidents of all kinds, told in racy Venetian dialect, with the liveliness which is natural to our folk. What is more, I learned much from them. Alas! the race of *cortigiani* has degenerated, like everything else in this corrupt age. When I chance to meet a survivor of the honest jolly crew, he strikes his forehead, and confesses that the good days of his youth are irrecoverable, and that the *cortigiano* is an extinct species.

Meanwhile I took good care to interfere with nobody and nothing in the household. This I did for my poor father's sake. But I kept my eyes open to observe the intrigues, schemes, and movements of the government. Some Jews, some brokers, and a crowd of women were always coming and going on secret conferences with my sister-in-law. These attracted my attention, and formed the subject of my earnest cogitations. It grieved me to see my brother Gasparo immersed in his philosophy and poetry, never for one moment giving the least thought to domestic economy. It grieved me; but I grieved in silence. There was one circumstance, however, which fairly put me out of patience. We had three sisters in the house; and a swarm of drones, hulking young fellows of the freest manners, kept buzzing round them. When I came home and found these visitors at the accustomed chatter, I used to scowl at them, lift my hat and put it on again, turn my back, and climb the stairs to my own den, with the fixed intention of making the gentlemen perceive how little their company attracted me. This manœuvre had its effect. My sister-in-law took it upon her to read me a matronly lecture on the impropriety of insulting friends of the family by my rough ways. I replied that I knew very well what friendship was, but that I could distinguish the false from the true; I was not conscious of having been rude to anybody; my father was the master, and if he did not mind some things which seemed to my inexperience imprudent and irregular, a mere lad's opinions were not worthy of consideration. This hint of my displeasure made all the women of the house regard me like a serpent. Even my three sisters, who loved me sincerely, and were excellent creatures, imbued with the soundest religious principles, could not help harbouring a trifle of suspicion in their feminine brains. For the rest, I said what I thought when I was consulted upon affairs of no importance. My advice in such matters pleased nobody. I ran on little errands if these were intrusted to me; and above all, I devoted some hours of every evening to my father, who always received me with tenderness and tears.

From conversation with my sisters I learned that the five thousand ducats raised by sale of lands in Friuli, ostensibly to make up portions for my married sisters, had either not been paid by the purchasers or had only reached the hands of the husbands in part. The same had happened with the drapery, linen, and jewels, for which a large debt had been contracted with a company of merchants. These and similar confidences made it clear to my mind that the marriages of my two sisters had not been arranged for their settlement in life so much as with the view of raising money under colourable pretexts, and of alienating entailed property with some show of legality. In fact, I scented disastrous dealings of the sort which are known in Venice by the name of *stocchi*.[1] As natural consequences of this crooked policy, urgent needs for ready money and embarrassments of all sorts had ensued,

[1] In these and several passages which follow, Gozzi ascribes the pecuniary embarrassment of his family to the maladministration of his mother, aided by his sister-in-law. It is only fair to say that Gasparo Gozzi's correspondence confirms his veracity. That favourite and favoured eldest son complains bitterly that, even to the last days of her life, his mother insisted on managing the property, and that she made underhand contracts to the prejudice of himself and his children. It was, in fact, a misfortune for the Gozzi that their father, Jacopo Antonio, married into a patrician family of higher rank and pretensions than his own. Angela Tiepolo, knowing herself to be one of the last representatives of a very noble house, with considerable expectations from her childless brother, drove her easy-going husband into ruinous expenditure, and domineered over her kindred by right of a marriage which savoured of a mésalliance. See the article upon her in Litta's *Famiglie celebri*, sub tit. 'Tiepolo.' (S)

which led to fresh expedients and ever-growing financial distress.

Without attributing malice to any one, I merely blamed the bad luck of our family, owing to which my grandfather's fine estate had passed into the hands of women under two administrations, and had been wasted by a course of insane irregularities. I took care to send an accurate report of our domestic circumstances to my brother Francesco at Corfu. And now I must embark upon the sea of my worst troubles.

15

I become, without fault of my own, quite unjustly, the object of hatred to all members of my household— Resolve to return to Dalmatia—My father's death

It had not escaped my notice that my mother and sister-in-law were in the habit of going abroad together in the mornings. During the five winter months they wore masks, and their proceedings had all the appearance of some secret business.[1] Now Carnival was over. We had reached the month of March 1745, a date which will be always painful to my recollection. Every morning the two ladies left the house together, no longer masked, but wearing the *zendado*.[2] I asked my sisters if they knew the object of these daily expeditions. They answered to the following effect: all they knew for certain was that my father's invalid condition made a residence in Venice irksome to him; now that the spring was advancing, he wished to go into Friuli with my mother, leaving our sister-in-law at the head of affairs in Venice; meanwhile the

[1] The *bautta* and the mask were permitted at Venice from the first Sunday in October until Ash Wednesday. (S)

[2] This was a very long scarf of black silk, which, draped above the head, and falling over the shoulders, was tied in a knot, and allowed to hang on both sides of the wearer's skirts. The mask or *bautta* was only permitted during the prolonged Venetian Carnival. (S)

treasury was empty, the barns and cellars of our country-house had nothing left in them. I shrugged my shoulders, and kept silence.

A few days afterwards, while I was attempting to drive away care by study in my little upper chamber, my three sisters entered. They were weeping, and my first fear was lest my father should have died. Reassuring me upon this point, they passionately besought me to interpose between the family and shameful ruin. I alone was capable of doing this. The secret expeditions of my mother and sister-in-law had resulted in a contract with a certain Signor Francesco Zini, cloth merchant. He undertook to pay down six hundred ducats in exchange for our ancestral mansion, agreeing, moreover, to hand over a little dwelling of his own in the distant quarter of S. Jacopo dall' Orio. They added that my father was ready to give his assent to this bargain, and my brothers Gasparo and Almorò would offer no opposition. I felt deeply moved by the distress of these poor girls as well as by my own keen sense of humiliation. Between their sobs they urged me to prevent the shameful and disastrous contract; and when they concluded by enjoining the strictest secrecy upon myself in the transaction, a gulf of dissensions, disagreeableness, and misery of all kinds seemed to yawn before my feet. Our pressing want of money, the contract verbally completed by my mother and sister-in-law, my father's consent, the adhesion of my brothers to the scheme, the obligation to secrecy laid upon me by my sisters, my own bad reputation in the household as a disturber of domestic quiet, my lack of friends and supporters in Venice, all filled me with terror. Yet I resolved to try what I could do to gratify my father's desire for the country, and put a stop to this humiliating contract. With that object in view I also undertook a secret mission and went to visit Signor Francesco Zini.

I laid myself open to him in terms of flattering politeness, appealing to his excellent disposition, and pointing out that he was about to enter on a business which would expose him to risk and us to notable humiliation. I told him that my

G

father had been an invalid for many years, that our ancestral mansion was subject to a strict entail, that on my father's death he would lose his money and the house, that all the sons of the family were not prepared to sanction the contract, that one of them was in the Levant, that I had not the least intention of assenting, and that the utmost I could do would be to abandon the house at my father's express command. Then I passed to the pathetic. I described a numerous family departing with their scanty bundles from the loved paternal nest, bowed down with grief and shame before the eyes of all their neighbours, who would be exclaiming: 'See those gentlefolk upon the move, because their home has been sold over their heads!' I proved to him that if he gained a fine house to live in, he would also gain an odious and ugly reputation. Finally, I besought him, as a man of worth, to seize some plausible pretext for breaking a bargain which, happily for his advantage and our own, had not been ratified.

Over the fat, red, small-pox-pitted features of Signor Zini spread amazement and perplexity. He did not understand my rigmarole, he said; he was an honest man, pouring out his blood, not water, to obtain the house; my mother and sister-in-law, together with the broker of this honourable bargain, had assured him that my father wished to conclude it, and that all his sons were prepared to emancipate themselves from the paternal authority, in order to be able to sign the contract, thus giving it validity, and securing the rightful interest of the innocent purchaser. The affair had been settled, the necessary deeds were waiting on the bureau of Marchese Suarez, his advocate. Most assuredly, unless my father's male heirs procured their emancipation, in order to give validity to the contract in perpetuity, he would not unbutton his pockets to disburse a penny; he was not a fool, to be imposed upon with fibs and fables.

I commended the fat gentleman's perspicacity and caution; repeated that I had no intention of procuring my emancipation, and that nothing on earth would force me to consent; once more I begged him to find some excuse for breaking off the bargain; and wound up by imploring him to keep silence upon my interference in the matter. I made it clear that only a brute, devoid of Christian charity, would reject a son's entreaties, and render him odious to mother and father without any advantage to himself. He promised to respect my secrecy, wagging his huge scarlet jowl and lifting his night-cap, with so many protestations of being touched to the heart, that I ought to have been put upon my guard. I did not yet know human nature, and retired as happy as if I had taken Gibraltar by assault, feeling confident that my prudence and discretion had averted a lamentable catastrophe.

Nothing was said by me about the course which I had followed, even to my three sisters. I reflected that they were women, and awaited a quiet termination of the affair, trusting to Signor Zini's humanity. Meanwhile I ruminated how to procure my father's removal to the country, and how to help the family without waiting for the harvest, which would be finished in three months. I computed the value of my clothes, my watch, my snuff-box; prepared as I was then, to sell everything I possessed. But these calculations only reduced me to despair. My one real friend was Signor Massimo, then at Padua. I remembered that I already owed him two hundred ducats, and that he was living on an allowance from his father. Yet I knew that both father and son, as well as a brother of my comrade, were no less generous towards persons on whose character for loyalty and friendship they relied, than they were suspicious of intriguers and impostors. I was also aware that they were in a position to render me substantial services. How often, during the tempestuous vicissitudes of my existence, have I not had the opportunity to verify this fact!

While thus engaged in studying ways and means, Signor Zini broke rudely in upon my meditations. Possessed with the desire to obtain our dwelling for his own, he divulged the secret of my visit, and exposed what I had said to him in terms of his own choosing. My belief is that his communication amounted to this—unless the hot-headed impetuous young fellow, who had come to treat with him, were brought to reason, and compelled to sign the contract, he refused to disburse two shillings.

I was in my upper chamber, studying as usual, and talking with my brother Almorò about his wretched schooling, when my mother appeared one day. Something of philosophical severity in her toilette, something imposing in her manner, which concealed, however, an internal irritation, proclaimed the gravity of her mission. She addressed herself pointedly to me, with the features of a judge rather than a mother, and began a long narration of the straits to which we were reduced. She said that, God be blessed, she had been inspired and assisted to discover six hundred ducats in the hands of a benevolent merchant, which would be placed immediately at her disposal upon such and such conditions. The notary was ready to engross the necessary deeds; and she begged me to declare what I thought about this special providence.

At the bottom of her heart I read Signor Zini's act of treason, and saw that I was lost. However, I answered respectfully that a contract of this kind struck me as anything but providential; still my father had full power to do what he thought fit, without rendering an account of his actions to his sons. She flamed up, and cried with a threatening air that my consent was also needed; she could not believe that I should be so rash and headstrong as to prevent a plan which would relieve my father and the family in our present painful circumstances. I could have uttered several truths without a wish to wound; but certain truths, once spoken, wound incurably. Therefore, I contented myself with observing that I was ready to shed my blood for my father, but that I could not assent to a contract so humiliating and ruinous, the last of a whole series dictated by suicidal policy. People who understood economy were in the habit of calculating and making provisions for the future, not of selling or mortgaging their property to meet embarrassments created by their own extravagance. The latter course was rapidly bringing our whole family to the workhouse. Under a disastrous financial system our income had been reduced to three thousand ducats; yet I could not comprehend how we were in such straits as she had described. When people were unable to maintain a decent state in the capital, they could live at ease in the country at one-third of the same cost. Houses ought to be let, and not sold. Still my father had the power to make any contract he thought right; only I did not believe him capable of forcing me to give consent against my will and judgment.

The gestures of submission, respect, and supplication with which I accompanied this speech had no power to mollify the pungency of its significance. My mother rose, with her arms akimbo, and inquired who it was I meant to blame for our misfortuncs. Instead of telling the bitter and irrefutable truth, I said that I only blamed fate and the misfortunes themselves. 'I reckon,' she replied with a smile of fury, 'that you will give in your adhesion.' 'Indeed I shall not,' was my answer; and the profound bow with which I spoke these words had the appearance of impertinent irony, although God knows I did not mean it. This was enough to fan the smothered flames into a Vesuvius in eruption. My mother bent her stormy brows upon me—upon the sixth finger of her maternal hands —and broke into the following declamation. From the moment of my return she had prophesied, like Cassandra, that I should turn the household upside down. She did not know me for one of her own children. The intimacy of a certain friend to whom I had attached myself was ruining the family, as it had ruined me. (Poor innocent generous Signor Massimo!) If I had behaved well during my three years' service, his Excellency Querini would certainly have rewarded me with some good military situation. As it was, my excursion into Dalmatia had been a source of burdensome expense. I had led a vicious life there . . . she knew . . . she did not mean to speak . . . but . . . enough . . . and my debt of two hundred ducats to Massimo was merely a sum lost by me at basset.

Now this debt had not yet been paid, and had therefore been of no inconvenience to my family. Such extravagant accusation took me by surprise; and the reader will now perceive the reason of the accounts which I rendered in a former passage of these Memoirs. I should perhaps have flown into a fury alien to my real nature, if these reproofs had been based on truth. The wounding allusion to Signor Massimo nearly roused me, but I preserved my self-control. It was clear that my mother had been deeply prejudiced and cruelly instigated against me. The consciousness of my innocence and a sense of duty made me stand before her rigid and mute as a statue. With an impulse of affection, maternal as it seemed, my mother took my brother Almorò by the arm, and gazing at me with contempt, which strove to be compassionate, she addressed these words to him: 'Come away, my dear boy; let us leave that madman to the error of his ways!' Then she turned her back and led him from the room, as though she were saving an innocent creature from some fearful danger.

Convinced by this tragi-comedy that I was the victim of a family cabal, I saw no other course open but to resume my commission as a cadet of cavalry. I left my room, went downstairs, and found all the family (except my father) assembled in commotion, listening to the commiserations of their usual friends enraged against me. It had been proclaimed aloud that I had called them all thieves, retorted against my mother with scandalous and impious audacity, and betrayed my determination to make myself the tyrant of the household. Even my three sisters, who had urged me into opposition, showed themselves sulkily scornful; and though I might have exposed them before the whole company, I did not deign to do so. Confirmed in my resolve to leave Venice for Dalmatia, I buckled on my sword, wasted no words about my intention, and repaired to the Riva degli Schiavoni, to see if I could find a ship for Zara. There I discovered that a *trabaccolo* would set sail in four or five days. The captain was a certain Bernetich. I took down his name, and, wrapped up in my own dark thoughts, spent all that day in exile, wandering far from home.

On my return, I noticed that, though everybody wore a crabbed face against me, something had happened to their satisfaction. Signor Zini, it appeared, was willing to execute the contract without requiring my consent. I did not know that my brother Francesco had left a power of attorney to act for him in Gasparo's hands. With voices of triumph they all exclaimed together that the great sacrifice was to be solemnly and legally performed next day. I did not care to inquire how things had been brought to this conclusion; but putting on as cheerful a face as possible, I went to keep my poor father company as usual for a few hours in the evening.

It will be as well at this point to describe the topography of our house. It was originally built for two separate residences, with double entrances upon the street and water-side, two staircases and two cisterns. At the time when it was planned, the Gozzis formed two families, which were afterwards reduced to one. We occupied the lower floor and some apartments in the highest storey. The second floor was let for 150 ducats a year to an honest ironmonger called Uccelli; but this portion of the mansion had also been sold upon my father's life, by one of those contracts which were only too frequent in our family, for the sum of 1,200 ducats to his Excellency the Procuratore Sagredo.

I did all in my power to avoid the least allusion to the painful scenes of the preceding day; but my dear father kept gazing earnestly at me, and shedding tears from time to time. In vain I tried to inspire him with happier thoughts. Would that I could banish all recollection of that night, which was one of the most sombre, the most painful, in the whole course of my existence. Paralysed and dumb for seven long years, he yet retained his mental faculties in their full vigour. Summoning all his force, by signs and stammerings and tears, he made it only too clear how much he suffered from the miserable straits to which the family had been reduced. He also continued to express his sympathy with me for my dislike to sign the projected contract. To my surprise and grief, he intimated that I had only a brief time to wait; his swift approaching death would restore to us the upper dwelling, which had been sold upon his life, and which was much better than the one we occupied. This inarticulate but eloquent discourse ended in a flood of tears. Deeply moved to the bottom of my heart, I strove to tranquillize his mind, and direct his thoughts from such afflicting topics. I perceived that no pains had been spared to make me odious in my father's eyes, and that this had been done without the least regard for his infirmity. Yet I did not attempt to justify my conduct, and said nothing about my firm resolve to leave home. His departure for Friuli had been fixed for the third day after this fatal evening, and I mentally decided to set out for Dalmatia two days later on. My assumed cheerfulness, and the merry turn I gave to all those dismal subjects of reflection, seemed to tranquillize him. Then he tried to lift himself from his arm-chair, as though to get to bed. I helped to raise him, but he tottered more than usual, and sank with his knees towards the ground. I took him in my arms to keep him from falling. Agonizing moment! It was clear that a last stroke of apoplexy was carrying away my father from my arms. In a loud voice and with perfect articulation he pronounced the words: 'I am dying!' They fell like lead upon my heart, with such cruel force that I nearly dropped. My mother, who was present, fled from the room. I called aloud for aid. Servants hurried in; one of these I dispatched for medical assistance, while the others helped me to place my poor dear father, now quite incapable of any movement, on his bed. A physician, Doctor Bonariva by name, had him bled at once. But nothing could be done to save his life. Assisted by Don Pietro Pighetti, now Canon of S. Marco, in the last religious duties of our creed, he displayed all the signs of Christian resignation and intelligence; and after eight hours of oppression, toilsome suffering, and the pangs of death, my unhappy parent closed his eyes upon the vast obscurity in which his family was plunged.

The affairs of the family were in such a precarious state that Gozzi was compelled to borrow a further sum of money from his friend Massimo in order to give his father a decent burial. The nominal head of the family was now the eldest of the sons, Gasparo, but he showed no inclination to assume

his responsibilities and continued to let his wife dictate to the
family. On Francesco Gozzi's return from the Levant, Gasparo's wife was persuaded to hand over the administration of
the family's affairs to her three brothers, but insisted that they
put their signatures to her account-book as an acknowledge-
ment of the correctness of her accounting. This they did in
order to pacify her, but according to Carlo they did not really
understand her book-keeping. It was a mistake which was to
have awkward consequences later. Francesco went off to look
after the estates in Friuli, but his indulgent nature made him a
poor administrator, and his blunders dissipated still further
the family's revenues. Carlo decided that the time had come
when he must assert himself more forcefully if the family was
not to be completely ruined. Assuming sole responsibility for
the direction of affairs, he took steps to initiate a programme
of economy.

16

*The dogs of the law are let loose on me by my family—It is
impossible to avoid a separation*

As time went on, my steady intention to remove our family
into the country, and my other plans of reform, roused my
domestic antagonists to various pettifogging stratagems. The
black-robed seedy myrmidons of the courts began to haunt
our dwelling, taking inventories of every nail on the pretext
of my mother's dowry, delivering demands in form from my
three sisters for maintenance and marriage portions, presenting bills for drapery and jewels furnished by a company of
merchants to the tune of 1,500 ducats, and suing on the part of
my two brothers-in-law for some 4,000 ducats owed to them.
Little creditors of all descriptions rose in swarms around us;
and what was still more astounding, my sister-in-law advanced
a claim of 900 ducats, due to her, she said, upon the statement

of accounts which we had signed so negligently. One would have thought the myrmidons and ban-dogs of the law had been unleashed by hunters bent on driving a wild beast from his lair; while the satisfaction and triumph depicted on the faces of my relatives showed too clearly who were the real authors of this legal persecution.

I bore the brunt of these attacks with my habitual philosophy of laughter, drew closer to my brother Almorò, and informed Francesco by letter of what was being conspired against us. Count Francesco Santonini helped me at this pinch with excellent advice. Under his direction I took the following measures. Francesco received instructions to hold fast by every rood of our Friulian property, and to send me copies of any writs which might be served upon him there. I recognized my mother's dowry, and offered annual payments to the merchants and my brothers-in-law. To my sisters I replied in writing that their maintenance should be duly attended to, but that it was impossible to create marriage portions for them under the conditions of entail to which the estate was subjected. With regard to the monstrous claims advanced by my sister-in-law, I flatly denied their validity until they had been submitted to a court of justice. Then I proceeded to meet the current expenditure of our establishment as well as I was able, while waiting for the time of harvest; and all this I did without mooting the question of Gasparo's separation from our brotherhood, in the hope that little by little things would settle down in peace and quietness. Vain and idle expectation ! My reforms, by cutting at the root of vested interests, and checking the arbitrary sway of Heaven knows whom, merely fanned the flames of rage which burned against me. In a private memorial, addressed to my mother, brother, sister-in-law, and sisters, I finally explained the impossibility of supporting the family any longer at Venice, exposed as I was to annoying and expensive litigation with the very persons who ate and drank at the same table. I might just as well have talked to images. Writs issued by my mother, my sister-in-law, my sisters, fell in showers. Slights and insults thickened daily. Our common table had become a pit of hell, worthy to be sung by Dante. To such a state of misery had irrational dissensions brought a set of relatives who really loved each other.

In order to shelter Almorò and myself from the wordy missiles which fell like hail all dinner-time, I had a little table laid for us two in a separate apartment. The covers were removed with rudeness, on the pretext that the linen, plates, dishes, &c., belonged to my mother's dowry, and that if I wanted such furniture I must buy it. Pushed in this way to extremities, I decided to leave a house which had become for me a hell on earth. Perhaps it was impolitic to take this step. But I could not stand these petty persecutions longer. Before quitting the infernal regions, I begged permission from my mother to take away the beds in which my brother Almorò and I enjoyed our troubled slumbers, offering to pay their price to the credit of her dowry. She replied with a sardonic smile of discontent that she could not grant my request, since the beds were needed by the family. I accepted this refusal with hilarity.

> *E quindi uscimmo a riveder le stelle.*
> And thence we issued to review the stars.

17

Calumnious reports, negotiations, a legal partition of our family estate, tranquillity sought in vain

I had hardly settled down with my brother Almorò in the remote quarter of S. Caterina, where lodgings are cheap in proportion to their inconvenience and discomfort, before the whole town began to talk about our doings. Three of the brothers Gozzi, it was rumoured, had laid violent hands upon the family estate; their eldest brother with his wife and five children; their three unmarried sisters, and their mother, a

Venetian noblewoman worthy of all respect, had been plunged in tears and indigence by the barbarous inhumanity of these unnatural monsters. The hovel I had hired, and where I suffocated with Almorò in the smoke of a miserable kitchen, ill-furnished and waited on by an old beldame called Jacopa, was besieged by the myrmidons of the law. Everything was done to dislodge me from the city, and to make me abandon the line of action on which I had resolved. Democritus and my innocence came to my aid; and I determined to stand firm with silent and passive resistance.

In these painful circumstances I heard to my great sorrow that my brother's wife had persuaded him to become the lessee of the theatre of S. Angelo at Venice.[1] Her romantic turn of fancy, together with her love of domination, made her conceive wild hopes of profit from this scheme. A company of actors were engaged at fixed salaries; and she was to play the part of controller, purse-holder, and stage-manager for the troupe at Venice and on the mainland. Moved by pity for my brother and his innocent children, I did everything I could, without appearing personally in the matter, to dissuade this hot-headed woman from so perilous an enterprise. She repelled all such attempts with scorn, being firmly convinced that she would gain a fortune and make her brothers-in-law bite their nails with envy.

I saw that the division of our patrimony could no longer be postponed, and civilly intimated to Gasparo that the time was come for taking this supreme step. Articles were accordingly drawn up, whereby the several parcels of our estate in Friuli, Venice, Bergamo, and Vicenza were partitioned into four lots. Provision was made for the repayment of my mother's dowry and for the proper maintenance of my three sisters, all of whom elected to reside with Gasparo. A fund was formed for the liquidation of debts, the charge of which devolved on me. I undertook to render an annual report of this operation,

---

[1] The theatres of Venice were called by the names of the parishes in which they stood, or of non-parochial churches to which they were contiguous. S. Angelo was one of the smaller. (S)

showing how I had bestowed the monies in my hands as trustee for the family. Nothing was fixed about my sister-in-law's claims for reimbursement; but it will be seen that when her theatrical speculation proved a ruinous failure, I had to take these also into account. Gasparo expressed a wish to obtain the upper dwelling in our mansion as part of his share. The lower dwelling was conceded to Francesco, Almorò and myself. To my mother and sisters we offered the hospitality of sons and brothers, in case at any time they should repent of their decision to abide with Gasparo.

It might be imagined that, while these negotiations were in progress, I had no time to spend on literary occupations. Nothing could be further from the fact. I found in them my solace and distraction, pouring forth multitudes of compositions, for the most part humorous and alien to the cares which weighed upon my mind. The course of my Memoirs will bring to light many curious incidents which these literary pastimes occasioned, and the narration of which will prove, I hope, far from saddening to my readers.

18

I enter on a period of toilsome litigation, and become acquainted with Venetian lawyers

I should have been an arrant fool had I flattered myself with the hope that this partition would introduce the olive-branch of peace into our midst. On the contrary, I looked forward, and with justice, to all kinds of coming troubles. Three-quarters of the estate were saved from extravagant administration by the process: but the minds of Gasparo's family had been almost incurably embittered by the same cause. When I wanted to lay my hands upon our documents, in order to study the nature of various entails and trusts under which the estates were settled, I found that all these papers had been sold out of spite. Who had done this I did not learn, but I was informed in great secrecy by a servant-maid that they had been sold to a certain pork-butcher. I repaired immediately to his shop, and was only just in time to repurchase some abstracts and wills, which had not yet been used to wrap up sausages. Then I set to work in the offices of notaries and advocates and in the public archives, following the scent afforded by my recovered papers. More than eighty bulky suits in my own handwriting remain to show how patiently I studied the rights and claims of our estate, and now I prepared myself for the task of laying these before the courts.

At this epoch I made acquaintance with the celebrated pleader, Antonio Testa, under whose direction and advice I embarked upon a series of litigations which kept me fully occupied for eighteen years, and in the course of which I became acquainted with the men who haunt our palace of justice, and learned the chicaneries of legal warfare. Inveterate abuses, introduced in the remote past, and complicated by the ingenuity of lawyers through successive generations (most of them men of subtle brains, some of them devoid of moral rectitude), have been built up into a system of pleading as false as it is firmly grounded and imbued with ineradicable insincerity. This system consists, for the most part, of quibbling upon side-issues, throwing dust in the eyes of judges, cavilling, misrepresenting, taking advantage of technical errors, doing everything in short to gain a cause by indirect means. And from this false system neither honourable nor dishonest advocates are able to depart.

In justice to the legal profession, I must, however, say that I found many practicians who combined the gifts of eloquence and intellectual fervour with urbanity, cordiality, prudence, and disinterested zeal. Outside the vicious circle of their system they were men of loyalty and honour. Among these I ought to pay a particular tribute to my friendly counsel and defender, Signor Testa. Knowing my circumstances and my upright motives, he refused to take the fees which were his due, and not unfrequently opened his purse to me at a pinch in my necessities. I have never met a lawyer more quick at seizing the strong and weak points of a case, more rapid in his analysis of piles of documents, more sagacious in divining the probable issue of a suit, or more acute in calculating the mental powers, the bias, and the equity of judges. Time and the circumstances of our several lives have drawn us somewhat apart. But nothing can diminish the feeling of deep gratitude which I shall always cherish for one who helped to heal the distractions and to improve the fallen fortunes of my family.[1]

Over a period of eighteen years, with the assistance of the lawyer Testa, Gozzi successfully fought a number of actions for the recovery of estates and property in Friuli, Vicenza, Venice, and Bergamo, which had been alienated from the family by fraudulent evasions of entail. The most considerable of his lawsuits was against the Marchese Antonio Terzi, a nobleman of Bergamo. Financial difficulties compelled Gozzi to drop this action for some years, but he reinstituted proceedings in 1766 and, after a three-year struggle, managed to win his case.[2]

In addition to this litigation with outsiders, Gozzi had trouble on his hands within the family itself. Quite soon after the settlement described in Chapter 17, he was forced to bring an action against Gasparo's family to evict them from the ground-floor of the house at Venice, which had been allocated to him under the terms of the partition. Gozzi does not wish to be thought guilty of acting inhumanely, and so he is careful to recount the circumstances which brought about this domestic litigation. His explanation is that, after the partition of the family property, he had decided for reasons of economy to move into cheaper accommodation and to put a tenant into his half of the house at Venice. In fact, without waiting for Gasparo to move out, he had let the ground-floor to the Countess Elisabetta Ghellini, widow of the patrician Barbarigo Balbi,

---

[1] In this chapter Symonds has considerably abridged the original text.

[2] See below, pp. 203 f.

who had already given up her former place of residence and was anxious to move at once into her new home. He had had no choice, therefore, but to evict Gasparo's family by force.

Gozzi's friendship with the Countess Ghellini Balbi, his frequent visits to her house in the course of these negotiations, naturally gave rise to gossip, and there were rumours of a secret marriage. Whether Gozzi really entertained the idea of matrimony is open to question. He himself ridicules the idea and accuses his relatives of deliberately spreading the rumour in order to discredit him.

Be this as it may, the successful eviction of Gasparo's family was not the end of Carlo's litigation with his sister-in-law, for she caused fresh trouble by reviving her claim for reimbursement of monies expended by her in the management of the family's affairs during the lifetime of Gozzi's father. She won her action and Gozzi paid her 700 ducats. He complains that there was a miscarriage of justice and that his sister-in-law won her case only because her legal adviser (a pettifogging lawyer named Giovannantonio Guseo, who is more than once the object of Gozzi's diatribes) was prepared to commit perjury on her behalf.

19

I should not have believed what is narrated in this chapter, if I had not seen it with my own eyes

I was excessively pained to observe that the bitterness created in my brother Gasparo's family by the events I have narrated remained unconquerable. It is true that they concealed, as far as possible, their grudge against me, whenever I paid them visits and treated them with brotherly good-will. This grudge, however, could not help showing itself in public; and it did so in a monstrous fashion, which I should not have credited unless I had been an eye-witness of the scandal.

My brothers and I were in the habit, during carnival-time, of frequently attending the theatre of S. Angelo, which was under the direction of my sister-in-law far rather than her husband. Amusement was less our object than the wish to support, so far as in us lay, a speculation to which we feared our brother had been sacrificed. We persuaded Signora Ghellini Balbi to accompany us; and she entered into our designs by applauding as heartily as any of the audience.

They had given at this theatre a translation of the French comedy called *Aesop at the Court*, which succeeded partly by the elegance of my brother's Italian version, and partly by its novelty. Rumour told us that the sequel, by the same French author, entitled, *Aesop in the Town*, was being translated and would soon appear. We were eager to be present at the first night, to back the piece with our approval, and to witness its triumph.

A worthy fellow, who aired his eloquence at Gasparo's house and also in our own, took me apart one day, and spoke with an air of secrecy and consternation to the following effect: 'You must know that the forthcoming play of *Aesop in the Town* will contain a scene, interpolated, not translated from the original, in which you, your brothers Francesco and Almorò, and Signora Ghellini Balbi, are held up in a cruel satire to the public scorn. Do not let my name transpire; but take means to prevent this scandal; the comedy will be re-presented in five days from now.' I was far from disbelieving that what my friend said was the truth; yet I took care to let no sign of my belief escape me. I thanked him for the friendly interest which had prompted him to warn me, but laughed the matter off as something beyond the range of possibility. He strained every nerve to convince me, but got nothing for his pains beyond smiles and ironical protestations of gratitude. I left him there fuming with anger at my obstinate hilarity.

I kept guard over my tongue in the presence of my brothers and the lady, and made a show of great anxiety to see the new play produced upon the boards. At last the first night came, and we all provided ourselves with a convenient box

H

for the occasion. We were disappointed to find the theatre ill-attended, and to notice the comedy dragged. *Aesop at the Court* had caught the public by something piquant in its chief character, by his grotesque, crook-backed figure, and by the appropriate fables which had been written with real dramatic skill for the part. *Aesop in the Town* was no less worthy of attention, but the novelty had evaporated; it seemed a plagiarism of the former piece, and wearied the audience like a composition which has lost its salt. At length the interpolated scene, of which my friend had warned me, came on.[1]

An ancient dame, attired in black, made her entrance, and unfolded the tale of her self-styled calamities to Aesop. Pouring forth an interminable catalogue of woes, she enumerated all the lies which had been circulated against myself and Signora Balbi at the period of our family dissensions. The ancient dame summed up by saying that she had been turned out of house and home, together with a loving son, three daughters, a daughter-in-law, and five grandchildren, by three of her own male children, the barbarous perverted offspring of her womb. Then she appealed with tears for counsel and advice to Aesop, who expressed his sympathy in a frigidly elaborated fable. The ancient dame, attired in black, was an exact image of our poor mother, who had been blinded by a touch of spite against me and by the darling object of her favouritism into allowing herself to be exposed in this way on a public stage for the mirth of the populace.

The scene was very long; it had nothing to do with the action of the piece, having been foisted in to gratify a private animosity. The audience, ignorant of what it meant, began to yawn; and it contributed in no small measure to the failure of the play.

---

[1] This scene has actually been preserved and printed in Gasparo Gozzi's works: *Opere*, Padova, Minerva, 1818–20, vol. vii. It forms the 6th scene of the 3rd act of *Esopo in città*, and is very much as Carlo Gozzi describes it. The ancient lady throws the principal blame for her domestic sufferings upon a certain 'Sicofante, Dottor legista di questa città', whom I take to be Carlo's lawyer, Testa. (S)

While this indecent and malignant episode was dragging its slow length along, I saw Signora Ghellini Balbi becoming momently more taciturn and out of humour, my two brothers flaming into anger and preparing for some act of violence. The shouts of laughter with which I greeted this abortion of a satire added fuel to their fire, and Francesco, spurred by martial ardour, was on the point of defying the players. He only made me laugh the louder; but I had some difficulty in persuading my companions to quench their indignation in a cup of water, and to wrap themselves around with imperturbable indifference. They obeyed me. If we had made a disturbance, we should have put the cap on our own heads. As it was, our cold behaviour snuffed out the whole episode, without awaking anybody's interest. And such will, peradventure, be the fate of these Memoirs I am writing of my life.

In concluding this episode, which I leave my readers to characterize with stronger epithets than I shall use, I wish to affirm that I never believed, or can believe, that my brother Gasparo lent his pen or his assent to the production of the scene in question.

2O

A long and serious illness—My recovery—The doctors differ—One of my sisters takes the veil— Beginnings of literary squabbles, and other trifles

In the midst of these annoyances, I found the time and strength to pursue my literary studies, especially in the now neglected art of poetry, and enjoyed excellent health; when suddenly, one night, a violent hæmorrhage from the lungs warned me that the life of mortals hangs upon the frailest thread.

Bleeding, vegetable diet, and a frugality in food, which few, I think, are capable of continuing for as long a space of time as I can, together with my philosophical indifference to death, restored me to something like a tolerable state of health.

It seemed to me at this period that my two brothers[1] and I, who always kept together, were in a position to settle down again in our paternal home. Signora Ghellini Balbi, who had rented the house for more than five years, politely retired at my request, and found another habitation at S. Agostino. I furnished our ancestral nest as decently as I was able; and we were soon installed there. It was then that I invited my youngest sister to leave her convent[2] and join us, travelling myself to Pordenone for this purpose.

Whether through weakness, or human influence, or Divine inspiration, I know not; but I found the good girl obstinate against my prayers, my anger, and my threats. She entreated with a holy stubbornness to be left in prison, to be indulged in her desire to pass her lifetime in that blessed aviary of virgins. I commanded her to come home for at least three or four months. At the end of that time, if she still persisted in her pious fanaticism, I promised to play the part of executioner at her request. She replied with a serious enthusiasm, which made me laugh, that she knew enough of the world to be experienced in its wickedness; and when I insisted, she met me with rather less than heavenly doggedness by remarking that nothing short of cutting her in pieces would make her quit the convent-gratings. Though I did not believe that this ultimatum was dictated by the angels, I bent my head in order to avoid a scandal. On taking the veil, she received those appointments and allowances which are usually bestowed upon the brides of Christ.

Were I to fix my thoughts upon the troubles which my four married sisters have had to suffer and still suffer—and I am only too well informed about them—I should be obliged

[1] Francesco and Almorò.

[2] When Gozzi moved out of the family residence at Venice, his youngest sister Chiara expressed a wish to go and live with him, but agreed to go temporarily into the convent of S. Maria degli Angeli at Pordenone until such time as her brother could offer proper accommodation.

to admit that the youngest chose the better part in life. They were always in straits, always weeping, with their gentle natures and their illimitable powers of endurance. One of them died before my eyes, to my deep sorrow, only because she was a wife. Meanwhile, the nun, beloved by her sisters, placidly smiled at things which we, refined in pleasures, finding nowhere solid pleasure for our satisfaction, would call barbarous tortures, and took delight in little treats, which we philosophers, past-masters in the arts of greed, are wont to scorn and turn our backs upon. In due course she attained the highest rank of Abbess in her convent; and I believe she was more gratified with this honour than Louis XVI with his titles of King of France and of Navarre.[1]

Time had at length allayed the discords of our family. My two remaining sisters found husbands. My brother Gasparo obtained a post at the University of Padua, which brought him 600 ducats a year, besides pecuniary gratifications for extraordinary services.[2] This proves that literature is not wholly unremunerated in Venice. In addition to these emoluments, he found another way, legitimate indeed, but one which seems incredible, for accumulating the sequins so much needed after his theatrical disaster. There was not a marriage, a taking of the veil among our noble families, an election of a Doge, or Procurator, or Grand Chancellor, without my brother being engaged to produce the panegyrics or poems which are usual on such occasions—more sought perhaps by fashion than by studious readers. The patricians made it their custom to reward him with 100 sequins, which contributed to the splendour of their families, but did him little good, for in his hands money found wings and flew away.

These details have little to do with my Memoirs; yet they are honourable to my nation, and are not without a certain

[1] This was written in 1780, but when it was printed in 1797, Louis XVI had little reason to be proud of his titles. (S)

[2] In 1762 he was appointed *Vicesoprintendente alle stampe e alle materie letterarie*. He was promoted to the position of *Soprintendente* two years later. He drew up several reports embodying proposals for the reform of the university at Padua and of schools at Padua and Venice.

bearing on my subject. Poetical trifles, published by me in collections, found favour by some aspect of novelty and by genial satire on contemporary fashions. Unluckily, they got me the reputation of a good poet and good writer. Accordingly, many of our lords tried to press me into the ranks of the *Raccoglitori*—collectors and compilers of occasional verse-books. They did not know that I had adopted for my motto that line of Berni :

> *Voleva far da sè, non comandato.*
> His master he would be, and no man's man.

Whenever they did me the honour to force this function on me, I civilly declined, and sent their messengers on to my brother, without, however, refusing compositions of my own, which swelled the collections, to their gain or loss as chance might have it.

I never abandoned the scheme I had formed of moving at law against the Marchese Terzi of Bergamo in a suit for the recovery of lands and rights belonging to us. But while I was engaged on the preliminary business, a fresh attack of pulmonary hæmorrhage cooled my ardour. Many learned physicians whom I consulted, looked upon me as a victim of consumption, at the point of death. Beggars in the street, when they saw me pass, promised to pray for my life if I would fling them a copper. The cleverest professors of medicine at Padua prescribed ass's milk, which was tantamount to saying : 'Phthisical creature, go and make your peace with Heaven!' My own doctor in ordinary, Arcadio Cappello by name, now dead—an old man, experienced, well acquainted with my constitution, and a philosopher to boot—forbade me milk as though it had been poison. 'You,' he said, 'are suffering from a nasty malady. Yet it has not the origin, nor has it made the progress, which these eminent physicians fancy. If you let your illness prey upon your mind, you will die. If you have the strength and heart to throw aside all thoughts about it, you will recover. It has in you no other basis than a hypochondriacal habit, which you have contracted by a sedentary life of worry, business, and excessive study. Raw milk of any kind is a pure poison in your case. Live regularly, cast aside reflections on your symptoms, take horse-exercise two or three hours a day. These are your best medicines.'

Marchese Terzi owes no thanks to my malady. Bloodless as I was, through what I lost by hæmorrhage and venesection, my intellect enjoyed the highest qualities of penetration and acumen. Stretched out upon my bed, I had the necessary papers for my lawsuit brought to me—abstracts and wills re-covered from the pork-butcher; a whole paraphernalia of documents forbidden by my doctors—and set up a scheme of proofs and arguments, so clear and so convincing that they subsequently drove my enemy to desperate measures.

These annoying relapses of my malady continued for two years and a half to fall upon me when I least expected them. They were enough to dishearten any man less stupid than my-self, and make him despair of living. Contrary to the advice of several physicians, who protested with wide-open horror-stricken eyes that riding would inflame my blood, burst the arteries of my lungs, and drown me in my own blood, I followed the prescription of Doctor Arcadio Cappello. He proved to be right. Regular diet, contempt for my symptoms, and horse-exercise completed my cure. It is now twenty years and more since I have been reminded that I was ever sub-ject to this indisposition.

As I have often had occasion to remark, no business, no quarrels, no lawsuits, and no illnesses prevented me from de-voting some hours every day to poetry. This being the case, when controversies arose in Venice on philology and the higher Italian literature—controversies of which I mean to render some account in the following chapters—I went on vomiting blood from my veins, and scribbling sonnets, satires, essays in defence of our great writers, treatises on style, pole-mics against Chiari and Goldoni and their followers. All these trifles, when I read them aloud, made my friends laugh, as well as my doctor and the surgeons who attended on me.

21

Concerning my physical and mental qualities

In the course of these Memoirs I have promised more than once to give an exact description of my external appearance and internal qualities, and also to narrate the story of my love-affairs.

In stature I am tall. Of this I am made conscious by the large amount of cloth needed for my cloaks, and by the frequent knocks I give my forehead on entering rooms with low doors. I have the good luck to be neither crook-backed, lame, blind, nor squint-eyed. I call this good luck; and yet if I were afflicted with one or other of these deformities, I should bear it with the same lightness of heart at Venice as Scarron put up with his deformities in Paris.

This is all I know or have to say about my physical frame. From early youth I have left to women the trouble of telling me that I was handsome with a view to flatter me, or that I was ugly with a view to irritate, in neither of which attempts have they succeeded. Dirt and squalor I always loathed. Otherwise, if I ever chanced to wear clothes of a new cut, this was due to my tailor, and not to my orders. Ask Giuseppe Fornace, my rogue of a snip for over forty years, if I ever pestered him about such matters, as so many do. From the year 1735 to 1780, at which date I am writing, I stuck to the same mode of dressing my hair with heroic constancy. Fashion has changed perhaps a hundred times during this period, yet I have never deviated from my adopted style of coiffure. In like manner I have worn the same type of buckles; except when I happened to break a pair, and was forced to change them from square to oval; and then I did so at the instance of the goldsmith, who made me take the lightest in his shop, because they would break sooner and give him more to do in mending them.

Men who talk little and think much, to which class, per-

adventure, I belong, being immersed in their own meditations, catch the habit of knitting their brows in the travail of
reflection. This gives them an air of incivility, sternness,
almost ferocity. Though I am gay by nature, as appears from
my published writings, yet the innumerable thoughts which
kept my brains in a turmoil, through anxieties about our
family, lawsuits, schemes of economy, literary plans, and so
forth, bred in me a trick of contracting my forehead and
frowning, which, combined with my slow gait, taciturnity,
and preference for solitary places, won me the reputation
among those who were not my familiar friends of being a
surly, sullen, unapproachable fellow, perhaps even an enemy
of mankind. Many who have come upon me, pondering, with
knitted brows and gloomy downcast eyes, will have suspected
that I was planning how to kill an enemy, while really I was
constructing the plot of my *Green Bird*.

In the society of people new to me, I always appeared
drowsy, stupid, silent, and lethargic, until I had studied their
characters and ways of thinking. Afterwards I turned out
quite the opposite; not, however, that I may not have remained a fool; but I was one of those fools who utter lacon-
isms, less tiresome to the company than interminable flowery
speeches.

I was not miserly, because I always loathed that vice, nor
prodigal, for the sole reason that I was not rich. I cannot form
any conception of the influence which wealth might have
exercised over my imagination and my moral nature, both
being doubtless not more free from foibles than in the case of
other men and women.

I might have earned considerably by my numerous published works, but I made a present of them all to comedians
and booksellers, or to persons who sought to profit by
giving them to the press. Perhaps I shall not be believed when I
say that I invariably refused such profit for myself. Yet this
is the fact. Some who are aware that I was far from rich, will
take me to task for my indifference to gain; they will attribute
my generosity to vainglory or to stupidity. I had, however,

my own reasons, which were as follows. My writings were always marked by freedom, boldness, pungency, and satire upon public manners; at the same time, moral and playful in expression. Being unpaid, they gained the advantage of a certain decent independence, which secured for them toleration, appreciation, and applause on their own merits. Had I been paid for them, they would have lost their prestige; my antagonists might have stigmatized them as a parcel of insufferable mercenary calumnies, and I should have been exposed to universal odium.

In addition to this : there is no degradation for men of letters in Italy worse than that of writing for hire in the employ of publishers or of our wretched comedians. The publishers begin by caressing authors, with a view to getting hold of their works; then they turn round and cast their pretended losses in the author's teeth. To hear them, you would imagine that books for which they had begged on their knees before they sent them to press, were now a load of useless stones encumbering their shelves. The wretched pence they fling at a writer for some masterpiece on which he has distilled the best part of his brains, are doled out with the air of bestowing alms. More fuss is made about it, and it costs more effort, than if the money were being paid for masses for the dead, who have no need to clothe and feed themselves. All this is bad enough. But Apollo protect a poet from being reduced to serve a troop of our comedians at wages! There is not a galley-slave more abjectly condemned to servitude than he. There is not a stevedore who carries half the weight that he does; not an ass who gets more blows and fouler language, if his drama fails to draw the whole world in a fever of excitement to the theatre.

For these reasons, I have always shrunk from letting out my pen to hire. On the frequent occasions when family affairs and litigation have emptied my purse, I always chose rather to borrow from friends than to plunge into the mire and rake up a few filthy stinking sequins. In the one case I incurred the pleasing burden of gratitude to my obligers; in the second I should have bent beneath the weight of shameful self-abasement.

Not even the brotherly terms on which I lived with comedians, nor my free gift to them through five-and-twenty years of all my writings for the stage, preserved me from the acts of ingratitude, and the annoyances which are described in the ensuing chapters of my Memoirs. Think then what would have become of me if I had been their salaried poet!

Italy lacks noblemen to play the part of Maecenas, and to protect men of letters and the theatre. Had there been such, and had they thought me worthy of their munificence, I should not have blushed to receive it. Knowing my country, however, and Venice in particular, I never allowed myself to indulge flattering dreams of any such honourable patronage.

Sustained by my natural, keen sense of the ludicrous, I have never even felt saddened by seeing the morality, which I held for sound and sought to diffuse through my writings, turned upside down by the insidious subtleties and sophisms of our century. On the contrary, it amused me vastly to notice how all the men and all the women of this age believed in good faith that they had become philosophers. It has afforded me a constant source of indescribable recreation to study the fantastic jargons which have sprung up like mushrooms, the obscure and forced ways of expressing thoughts, spawned by misty self-styled science, invested with bombastic terms and phrases alien to the genius of our language. Not less have I diverted myself with the spectacle of all the various passions to which humanity is subject, suddenly unleashed, playing their parts with the freedom of emancipated imps, let loose from their hiding-place by famous discoverers—just like those devils in the tale of Bonaventura Despériers, whom Solomon sealed up in a cauldron and buried beneath the ground until a pack of wiseacres dug them up and sent them scampering across the world again.[1]

---

[1] Despériers (b. 1500–10, d. 1544) was servant to Marguerite de Navarre, and a writer of Rabelaisian humour. His two principal works are *Cybalum mundi* and *Nouvelles Récréations et joyeux devis*. (S; Ed.)

The spectacle of women turned into men, men turned into women, and both men and women turned into monkeys; all of them immersed in discoveries and inventions and the kaleidoscopic whirligigs of fashion; corrupting and seducing one another with the eagerness of hounds upon the scent; vying in their lusts and ruinous extravagances; destroying the fortunes of their families by turns; laughing at Plato and Petrarch; leaving real sensibility to languish in disuse, and giving its respectable name to the thinly veiled brutality of the senses; turning indecency into decency; calling all who differ from them hypocrites, and burning incense with philosophical solemnity to Priapus—these things ought perhaps to have presented themselves to my eyes in the form of a lamentable tragedy; yet I could never see in them more than a farce, which delighted while it stupefied me.

I have made but few intimate friendships, being of opinion that a man of many friends is the real friend of none. Neither time, nor distance, nor even occasional rudeness, interrupted the rare friendships which I contracted for life, and which are still as firm as ever.

Now and then, I have given way to angry impulses on sustaining affronts or injuries; and at such times men of phlegmatic temper are more decided in their action than the irascible. Reflection, however, always calmed me down; nor was I ever disposed to endure the wretchedness which comes from fostering rancour or meditating revenge.

I am inclined to laugh both at *esprits faibles*, who believe in everything, and at *esprits forts*, who pretend that they believe in nothing. Yet I hold that the latter are really weaker, and I am sure that they do more harm, than the former.

Notwithstanding my invincible habit of laughing, I am firmly persuaded that man is a sublimely noble animal, raised infinitely far above the brutes. Consequently I could not condescend to regard myself as a bit of dung or mud, a dog or a pig, in the humble manner of freethinkers. In spite of all the pernicious systems generated by men of ambitious and seductive intellect, we are forced to believe ourselves higher in the scale of beings, and more perfect, than they are willing to admit. Although we may not be able to define with certainty what we are, we know at any rate beyond all contradiction what we are not. Let the freethinking pigs and hens rout in their mud and scratch in their midden; let us laugh and quiz them, or weep and pity them; but let us hold fast to the beliefs transmitted to us by an august line of philosophers, far wiser, far more worthy of attention, than these sages of the muck and dungheap. The modern caprice of turning all things topsy-turvy, which makes Epicurus an honest man, Seneca an impostor; which holds up Voltaire, Rousseau, Helvétius, Mirabeau, &c., to our veneration, while it pours contempt upon the fathers of the Church; this and all the other impious doctrines scattered broadcast in our century by sensual fanatics, more fit for the mad-house than the university, have no fascination for my mind. I contemplate the disastrous influence exercised by atheism over whole nations. This confirms me still more in the faith of my forefathers. When I think of those fanatics, the sages of the muck and midden, when I think of mankind deceived by them, I repeat in their behoof the sacred words of Christ upon the cross: 'Father, forgive them, for they know not what they do.' Finally, I assert that I have always kept alive in me the flame of our august religion, and that this has been for me my greatest stay and solace during every affliction. The philosophers of the moment may laugh at me; I am quite contented for them to regard me as a dullard, besotted by what they choose to stigmatize as prejudice.

22

Story of my first love, with an unexpected termination

In order to relate the trifling stories of my love-adventures, I must return to the period of my early manhood. I ought indeed to blush while telling them, at the age which I have reached; but I promised the tales, and I shall give them with all candour, even though I have to blush the while.

Being a man, I felt the sympathy for women which all men feel. As soon as I could comprehend the difference between the sexes—and one arrives betimes at such discretion—women appeared to me a kind of earthly goddesses. I far preferred the society of a woman to that of a man. It happened, however, that education and religious principles were so deeply rooted in my nature, and acted on me so powerfully as checks to inclination, that they made me in those salad days extremely modest and reserved. I hardly know whether this modesty and this reserve of mine were quite agreeable to all the girls of my acquaintance during the years of my first manhood.

I can take my oath that I left my father's house, at the age of sixteen, on military service in Dalmatia, innocent—I will not say in thoughts—but most innocent as to the acts of love. The town of Zara was the rock on which this frail bark of my innocency foundered; and since I hope to make my readers laugh at my peculiar bent in love-making, and also by the tales of my amours, I will first describe my character in this respect, and then proceed to the narratives.

I always preserved a tincture of romantic metaphysics with regard to love. The brutality of the senses had less to do with my peccadilloes than a delicate inclination and tenderness of heart. I cherished so lofty and respectful a conception of feminine honour and virtue that any women who abandoned themselves to facile pleasures were abhorrent to my taste. A *fille de joie*, as the voluptuaries say, appeared to me more frightful, more disgusting, than the Orc described by Boiardo.[1] Never have I employed the iniquitous art of seduction by suggestive language, nor have I ever allowed myself the slightest freedom which might stimulate desire. Languishing in soft and thrilling sentiments, I demanded from a woman sympathy and inclination of like nature with my own. If she fell, I thought that this should only happen through one of those blind and sudden transports which suppress our reason on both sides, the mutual violence of which admits of no control. Nothing could have been more charming to my fancy than the contemplation of a woman, blushing, terrified, with eyes cast down to earth, after yielding to the blind force of affection in self-abandonment to impulse. I should have remembered how she made for me the greatest of all sacrifices— that of honour and of virtue, on which I set so high a value. I should have worshipped her like a deity. I could have spent my life's blood in consoling her; and without swearing eternal constancy, I should have been most stable on my side in loving such a mistress. On the other hand, I could have safely defied all men alive upon the earth to take a more sudden, more resolute, and more irreversible step of separation than myself, however much it cost me, if only I discovered in that woman a character different from what I had imagined and conceived of her, while all the same I should have maintained her honour and good repute at the cost of my own life.

This delicate or eccentric way of mine in thinking about love exposed me to facile deceptions in my youthful years, when the blood boils, and self-love has some right to illusion, and the great acquirement of experience is yet to be made.

The narratives of my first loves will confer but little honour on the fair sex; but before I enter on them I must protest that I have always made allowance for the misfortune under which, perhaps, I suffered, of having had bad luck in love;

[1] The Orc was a huge sea-monster, shaped like a gigantic crab. It first appeared in Boiardo's *Orlando innamorato* (Bk. iii. Canto 3), and was afterwards developed by Ariosto, *Orlando furioso* (Canto 17). (S)

which does not shake my conviction that many phœnixes may be alive with whom I was unworthy to consort.

After living through the mortal illness which I suffered during the first days of my residence at Zara, I moved into one of the so-called *Quartieroni* situated on the beautiful walls of Zara, and built for the use of officers. A very good room, which I furnished suitably to my moderate means, together with a kitchen, formed the whole of my apartment. I engaged a soldier for my service at a small remuneration. He had orders to retire in the evening to his quarters, leaving me a light burning. I remained alone; went to bed, with a book and a candle at my side; read, yawned, and fell asleep.

Now to attack the tale of my first love-adventure! Its details will perhaps prove tiresome, but they may yet be profitable to the inexperience of youngsters.

Opposite my windows, at a certain distance, rose the dwelling of three sisters, noble by birth, but sunk in poverty which had nothing to do with noble blood. An officer, their brother, sent them trifling monies from his foreign station, and they earned a little for their livelihood by various woman's work, with which I saw them occupied. The eldest of these three Graces would not have been ugly, if her bloodshot eyes, rimmed round with scarlet, had not obscured the lustre of her countenance. The second was one of those bewitching rogues who are bound to please. Not tall, but well-made, and a brunette; her hair black and long; eyes very black and sparkling. Under her demure aspect there transpired a force of physique and a vivacity which were certainly seductive. The third was still a girl, lively, spirited, with possibilities of good or evil in her make.

I never saw these three nymphs except by accident, when I opened the window at which I used to wash my hands, and when their windows were also open, which happened seldom. They saluted me with a becoming bow. I answered with equal decorum and sobriety. Meanwhile, I did not fail, as time went on, to notice that whenever I opened my window to wash my hands, that little devil, the second sister, lost no time in opening her window too, and washed her hands precisely while I was washing mine; also, when she bent her lovely head to greet me, she kept those fine black eyes of hers fixed on my face in a sort of dream, and with a kind of languor well fitted to captivate a lad. I felt, indeed, a certain tickling at my heartstrings; but the austere thoughts to which I was accustomed, cured me of that weakness; and without failing in civility, I kept myself within the bounds of grave indifference.

A Genoese woman, to whom I paid a trifle for ironing my scanty linen, came one morning with some of my shirts in a basket. Upon the washing lay a very fine carnation. 'Whose is that flower?' I asked. 'It is sent to you,' she answered, 'and from the hands of a lovely girl, your neighbour, for whom you have the cruelty to take no heed.' The carnation and the diplomatic message—and well knew I from whence both came—increased the itching at my heart-strings. Nevertheless, I answered the ambassadress in terms like these : 'Thank that lovely damsel on my part; but do not fail to tell her that she is wasting her flowers to little purpose.'

My head began to spin round and my heart to soften. At the same time, when I reflected that I had no wish to enter into matrimonial engagements, which were wholly excluded from my plan of life, nor yet to prejudice the reputation of a girl by traffic with her—furthermore, when I considered how little money I possessed, to be bestowed on one in whom I recognized so much of beauty—I stamped out all the sparks of sympathy which drew me towards her. I began by never washing my hands at the window, in order to escape the arrows of those thievish eyes. This act of retirement was ineffectual; indeed, it led to worse consequences.

One day I was called to attend upon my old friend, the officer Giovanni Apergi, who had been my master in military exercises, and who was now in bed, racked and afflicted with aches acquired in youthful dissipation. He had his lodgings on the walls, not far from mine, in the house of a woman well advanced in years, the wife of a notary. Thither then I went.

The elderly housekeeper began to twit me with my rustic

I

manners. Gradually she passed to sharp but motherly reproof; in a youngster of from sixteen to seventeen, like myself, the sobriety of a man of fifty had all the effect of caricature; in particular, my treatment of well-bred handsome girls, devotedly in love with me, my driving them to desperation and tears by indifference and what appeared like scorn, did not deserve the name of prudence; it was nothing short of clownishness and tyranny. My friend, the officer, pulling wry faces and shrieking at the twinges of pain he was suffering as a consequence of his amours, chimed in with similar reproaches: I was a little simpleton, a fool who did not know his own good fortune. 'Oh, if I only had your youth, your health, your opportunities!' These exclamations were interrupted by groans occasioned by the spasms of pain that were his legacy from Cupid.

Just when I was preparing to defend myself, someone knocked, and the dangerous beauty came into the room, under the pretext of inquiring after the health of the officer. Her entrance checked my speech and made my heart beat faster. The conversation turned on general and decorous topics. The girl discovered qualities of wit and understanding; she was not very talkative, but sensible and modest. Her eyes, which might in poetry have been called stars, told me clearly that I was an ingrate. Her visit to the sick man was really intended for the sound. At its close, she remarked that she had sent her servant back, because her elder sister was confined to bed by fever; might she beg for some one to conduct her home? 'This gentleman,' replied the elderly woman, pointing at once to me, 'will be able to oblige you.' 'Oh, I do not wish to put him to trouble; I am not worthy of the honour.' The cunning creature said this with ironical seriousness. I made the usual polite offer of my services, and rose to accompany her. We had not far to go, and during the brief journey both were silent. As she leant upon my arm, which was steadier than marble, I felt her tremble sensibly, and we were in the month of July. This tremor ran through my vitals, and made me tremble more than she did.

When we reached her dwelling, she begged me to step in and to give her the pleasure of a few minutes' conversation. We went upstairs, and I beheld a home breathing of indigence in all its details. In the room which I was asked to enter, her elder sister (the one with the red eyes) lay sound asleep upon a decent bed, notably different from the rest of the furniture. She was really ill, and we did not wish to wake her; so our conversation proceeded in a low voice. My beauty began to knit a stocking, and made me sit upon a little wretched sofa at her side. She whispered, with downcast eyes, that some weeks ago she had conceived the greatest esteem for me, but that she feared she had not earned gratitude for her lively sentiments of regard. I answered in a whisper, but with raised eyes, that I believed in her sincerity; I did not suppose that she was flattering me; yet I was inquisitive to learn how she had come to entertain such partiality for a young man un- known to her, who was not worthy to excite the sentiments she had described. She replied, still whispering, but lifting her eyes a little, that she had told the simple truth. Her heart had first been touched when she saw me play the part of Luce, the *soubrette*, in the theatre. Afterwards, while watching me on the pallone-ground, this impression had been deepened. I listened with some repulsion to the motives of her passion, nor could I refrain from answering, with a laugh: 'Surely modest girls are taken by the mental gifts and sterling quali- ties of a young man, not by such follies as you deign to mention.' She dropped her fine eyes, mortified by this home- thrust. Then she replied with a finesse I hardly expected from a Dalmatian: 'You cannot deny that public exploits, univer- sally applauded, in a young man, have some right to impress a girl's imagination. I could indeed have defended my heart against these promptings, if your person had not pleased me; if you had not shown yourself in private to be governed by principles of modesty, sobriety, and prudence; if the whole city were not edified by your behaviour, and ringing with per- petual eulogies of conduct rare indeed among those madcap fellows of the garrison. These reports confirmed my passion;

and if now I find it scorned by you, I know not to what extremities despair will drive me.' The speech flattered my *amour propre*. Tears, which she attempted to conceal, fell from her fine eyes, and stirred my sensibility. The beauty of the little devil bewitched me. However, I summoned reason to my aid, and replied with gentle calmness: 'Dear lady, I should be a monster if I were not grateful to you for your kind and precious sentiments. Still I am only a lad, dependent on my family, without the resources of fortune. Unable as I am to think of marriage, I should injure you and should commit a dishonourable action were I to frequent your society. The tenderness, which I feel only too deeply for you, might lead me also on my own side into some disaster. Precisely because I love you, it is my duty to shrink from anything which could be hurtful to you; and because you love me, it is your duty to shun what might prove disastrous to myself. Do not be hurt by what I have to say. I shall not cease to cherish in my breast an ardent affection for yourself; but from this hour forward I must avoid all opportunities of being in your company, not less for my own than for your advantage.'

The stocking she was knitting fell to the floor. She took one of my hands and clasped it to her bosom. Leaning her lovely cheek against my shoulder and shedding tears, she whispered: 'Dear friend, how little you know me! Your prudent and ingenuous speech has only added to the ardour of my soul. Could you suspect that my poverty was laying a trap for your thrift? Could you imagine that I was a dissolute girl, or that I was angling for a husband? You are mistaken. I make allowances for your mistake. But, for pity's sake, learn to know me better. Grant me from time to time some moments of your charming conversation. We will watch for these precious moments with discretion. Unless you are a tiger of cruelty, do not abandon me to the unbearable torments of a burning heart.' Her tears began to fall in showers. For my part, I remained deeply moved, confused, and, I confess, madly in love with this charming girl, who had so cleverly expressed a passion quite in harmony with my own idealistic tendencies. I promised to renew our meetings; and indeed this promise was made at least as much to my own heart as to hers. She showed the liveliest signs of satisfaction; but at this moment her sister woke. I explained the accident which brought me to their house; and then my innamorata led me to the staircase. There we shook and kissed hands. I departed, over head and ears in love, a captivated blockhead.

We continued to find occasions for our meetings, and with less of caution than we had agreed upon. During several days our conversations were playful, witty, piquant. It was an exchange of deep sentiments, of sighs, of little terms of endearment, of tender, restrained embraces, of caresses, of ecstasies, of languors, pallors, trembling glances—of all those sweets, in short, which constitute the greatest charm, the most delicate, the most enduring delights of love. On my side, the restraint of modesty was not yet broken. On the girl's side, it did not seem to be so. One day, after playing pallone, I changed my shirt, and went to walk alone upon the ramparts. It was very hot, and I looked forward to the refreshment of the sea-breeze. Passing the house of the notary's wife, with whom my friend, the pain-racked officer, lodged, I heard my name called. Looking up, I saw the woman with my idol at the window. They asked me in, and I entered gladly. A walk upon the ramparts was proposed; and the officer, who happened to be a little better, wished to join our party. He gave his arm to the elderly dame; I offered mine to the blooming girl. He walked slowly, limping on his gouty toes. I walked slowly for a different reason; my heart, and not my toe, was smitten; besides, my sweetheart and I were more at liberty together, if we kept the other couple well in front. Meanwhile night began to fall. After taking a short turn, the officer complained of pain in his feet, and begged leave to go back with his elderly companion, adding that I could see my lady home when we had enjoyed enough of the evening cool together. The pair departed, while I remained with my innamorata, lost in the ecstasies of love.

The hours passed like minutes. We walked in a dream, each fanning the other's passion with all the spoken and silent expressions of ardent love. At length, as it was now quite dark, we decided to turn our backs on the cool night air, which was by now for us more hot than cold. The road back to my beloved's house led us down a narrow alley close to my own quarters. The little hussy asked me to please her by showing her my lodgings. I took out my key and opened the door. We went in.

My valet had as usual left the lamp on a pedestal table by the side of the bed. 'This then is the bed in which you sleep all by yourself,' said the girl, seating herself upon it. I sat beside her, and we began to exchange caresses, sighs, and delicious embraces, not wholly chaste. Our hearts were all but leaping from our breasts. The solitude, the darkness, the faint glimmer of the lamp, made us somewhat bolder than usual; and yet common sense, together with my doubts and fears, kept me still within the bounds of propriety and virtuous restraint.

'What a simpleton, to be sure!' the libertines will say. 'You have kept us listening long enough to the tale of your scruples and cold feet. Get a move on. Do like Dido and Aeneas, and start the nymphs howling in their caves.' Savages, be patient. You do not know the true delights of love, if you think that they consist only in quenching one's desires like an animal.

'You are wiser and crueller than I,' said the girl, resting her beautiful, flushed face on my breast. 'I know the reason of your cautious concern,' she went on, 'and I love you all the more for it. Would that I still possessed that precious flower of my virginity, that I might sacrifice it, freely and with all my heart, to you and to you alone. But I am afraid to offend you by concealing a secret over which I have wept many tears. Two years ago I was seduced by a colonel, who took me by force and then cruelly abandoned me within three days of my terrible misfortune. Why are not all men like you? I cannot tell you how great an effort it costs me to disclose an act of shame which no other girl would reveal. But I would think it more shameful not to be frank with a friend whom I adore. Do not hate me; or else kill me.'

So saying, she burst out weeping, and I could feel my breast wet with her tears. Her story filled me with uncertainty and bitter reflections. The colonel she had mentioned was in truth a notorious seducer, who was rather like Sinadab in my allegorical drama *Zobeide*. This character, when he had had his pleasure with a girl for a few days, used to change her into a heifer and turn her out to pasture. The colonel's position of authority in the province of Dalmatia protected him from the rigours of the law.

The girl lifted her lovely, tearstained eyes towards me, and seeing that I was hesitant and upset, she heaved a deep sigh and exclaimed : 'Alas, you hate me. Kill me; kill me, for pity's sake.' Then she returned to her weeping and to my chest. I bent down to console and caress her, not knowing what I was saying or doing. She threw herself impetuously upon my neck, panting, and kissing me for the first time on the lips. Her breath was like ambrosia. It made my senses reel and penetrated my vitals. Whether it was to hide her blushes or to hearten me up, I know not, but she blew out the lamp, and . . . the nymphs began to howl.

I will draw a heavy curtain over that night of rapture which two young lovers spent under the spell of an ardent passion. Towards dawn I accompanied my priceless jewel to her house. Our affection for one another was twice as strong as before. We planned fresh moments of bliss for the future, convinced that our arrangements were discreet. She could hardly tear herself away from my side, but eventually we parted, and I went home to bed. However, with a brain teeming with novel impressions and a conscience pricked by occasional feelings of remorse, I could not close my eyes all night.

The intrigue continued for two months, with equal ardour on both sides. Blinded as we were by passion, we thought that it was hidden from all eyes; and yet perchance we were but playing the comedy of *The Open Secret*.[1] At any rate, I

[1] *Il pubblico secreto*, one of Gozzi's own comedies. (S)

must admit that I found in this girl a mistress exactly suited to my metaphysical ineptitude. She showed herself always tender, always in ecstasy, always afraid to lose me, always candid. Knowing how poor she was, I often wanted to divide my poverty with her. I used prayers, almost violence, to win her consent to this partition of my substance. But she took it as an unbearable insult, and broke into rage in her refusals, exclaiming with kisses which drew my soul forth to her crimson lips: 'Your heart is my true riches.'

Certainly, a young man in his first love-passage sees awry, and makes mistakes through mere stupidity. The end of this amour, which seemed interminable, was brought about by an incident sufficiently absurd, and far removed from my delicate idealism. It happened that the Provveditore Generale was summoned to Bocche di Cataro, in order to settle some disputes between the tribe called Pastrovicchi and the Turks. I had to take sail with the Court. Good God! what agonies there were, what rendings of the heart, what tears, what vows of fidelity, at this cruel parting between two young creatures drowned in love! My absence lasted about forty days, which seemed to me as many years. Scarcely had I returned, and was rushing to my goddess, when a certain Count Vilio of Desenzano, master of the horse to the General, who had stayed behind at Zara (a man sufficiently dissolute in his amours, but a good and sincere friend), came up to me and spoke as follows: 'Gozzi, I know that you are on the best of terms with such and such a girl. I should be acting wrongly if I did not inform you of what has happened in your absence, the truth of which I hold on sure foundations. You have a rival, in the general's steward, who has pursued the girl for a long time without success. He remained in Zara during your absence and made good use of his opportunity. I cannot tell you what stratagem he employed, but I know for certain that he had intercourse with her. The scoundrel suffers from the pox, which naturally he will have passed on to the unfortunate girl, so I am concerned for your health. You have received my warning; rule yourself accordingly.' These words were

scorpions to my heart. Nevertheless, I chose to assume indifference, and put a bold face on the matter. So I forced myself to laugh, and answered, stammering perhaps a trifle, that
it was quite true I knew the girl, but that my intercourse with
her had always been blameless, and that I had no cause to
fear. I had invariably found her so modest and reserved that I
suspected he must have been taken in by a bragging impostor,
to the infinite injury of the poor girl's character. 'I am not
mistaken, by gad,' cried Vilio in his Brescian way. 'You are of
years to know the world. I have done my duty as a friend,
and that is enough for me.'

He left me with my head stunned, my spirit in confusion,
staggering upon my feet. From my earliest boyhood, I have
always made a point of exercising self-control. Accordingly,
I now stifled the imperious impulse which urged me to embrace my mistress. I did not merely postpone my visit, but I
kept my windows shut, avoiding every opportunity of setting
eyes on her. The Genoese laundress brought me diplomatic
messages; to these I returned laconic and meaningless answers,
without betraying the reason of my sudden coldness. Some
notes were refused with heroic, or shall I call it asinine endurance. At the same time, I nourished in my breast a lively
desire that my mistress might be innocent, and that the accusation of so base a fault might be proved a vile mendacious
calumny. I hoped to arrive at the truth somehow, by adhering
to severe and barbarous measures.

In course of time I obtained only too positive confirmation
of my fears. Walking one day upon the ramparts, the elderly
dame, of whom I have already spoken, called me from her
window, and begged me to come up. She had a word or two to
say to me. I assented, and entered the house. Divining that she
wished to speak about my mistress, I armed myself with
caution. My plan was to allege decent excuses for my conduct, without touching the repulsive wound. However, I had
not divined the whole. She led me into a room, where, to my
surprise, I beheld the idol of my first affections, seated and
shedding tears. 'What I wanted to say to you,' exclaimed the

dame, 'you will hear from the lips of this afflicted damsel.' On this, she left the room, while I remained like a statue before the beauty I had adored, and who was still supremely charming in my sight. She lifted her forehead, and began to load me with the bitterest reproaches. I did not allow her to run on, but told her with resolute plainness that a young woman who, during my absence, had played so false was no longer worthy of my love. She turned pale, crying aloud: 'What scoundrelly scandal-monger has dared . . .' Again I cut her speech short, adding: 'Do not tire yourself by attempting the justification of your conduct. I know the whole truth from an infallible source. I am neither inconstant, nor a dreamer, nor ungrateful, nor unjust.' The assurance with which I uttered these words made the poor girl lower her face, as though she was ashamed that I should look at her. Then bursting into a passion of tears, broken with sobs, she brought these incoherent phrases forth: 'You are right . . . I am no longer worthy of you . . . The devil has been pursuing me for a long time in vain. He went to my eldest sister to get her to coax me into compliance. He promised her two bushels of flour if she succeeded. The constant entreaties, exhortations, and threats to which the bitch subjected me . . . It was loathsome . . . Cursed sister! Cursed flour! Cursed poverty!' She was unable to continue, and I thought her tears would suffocate her. I was fit to drop to earth with the vertigo caused by this confession, which left no flattering hopes of innocence. My senses still painted a Venus in that desolated beauty. My romantic head and heart painted her a horrid Fury from the pit of hell. I kept silence. In my purse were some ducats, few indeed, but yet I had them. I took these coins out, and, speechless still, I let them gently drop into the loveliest bosom I have ever seen. Then I turned my back and fled. Half mad with grief, I bounded down the staircase like a greyhound, screaming with the ecstasy of one possessed by devils: 'Cursed steward! Cursed sister! Cursed flour! Cursed poverty!'

Since then I never saw the object of my first love. I thought

I must have died under the pressure of a passion which gnawed my entrails, but which, although I was but a boy, I had the cruel strength to subjugate. Soon afterwards I learned with satisfaction that the unhappy girl had married an officer, but I never sought to trace her out or to hear more about her history.

23

The story of my second love-affair, with fewer platonisms and a more comic ending than the last

About that time the Provveditore Generale found that he had need of my quarters for storing the appurtenances of his stables and of the coach-house, which were situated beneath the *Quartieroni*. Accordingly, I removed into a little pavilion, which my friend Signor Innocenzo Massimo and I had taken. It stood upon the ramparts. We could not occupy this dwelling long; for it was distant from the Court and from our place of duty. Moreover, when the winter season arrived, heavy rains, a terrible north wind, and snowfalls made our nest uninhabitable. Massimo had some acquaintance with a shopkeeper and tradesman, who lived inside the town, and owned a house with rooms to spare and many conveniences. This man was married to a fine woman, plump and blooming; and God forgive me if I think it probable that Massimo was more intimate with the wife than the husband! Anyhow, he made arrangements with this excellent couple to rent two rooms, one for me, the other for himself, in close communication. We agreed for these rooms by the month, taking our meals with the masters; their table was homely but abundant, and the food excellent.

The couple were not blessed with children, but the man had adopted a poor girl, in order to perform an act of Christian charity. This child, who had scarcely reached her thirteenth year, dined and supped with us, as the adopted daughter of the house. Her behaviour betrayed nothing but the innocence belonging to her age. She had blond hair, large blue eyes, an expression at once soft and languid, a pale complexion tinged with rose. She was rather thin than fleshy, but her figure was straight, lithe, and beautifully formed; in stature she promised to be tall, with something of the majestic in her build. This girl came to dress me and arrange my hair for the part of Luce, whenever I played at the Court theatre. She joked and laughed, and turned me round to look at me. I made some harmless witticisms in reply. At this she laughed the louder. Such was our custom; but one evening, after she had done my hair for Luce, she suddenly gave me three or four kisses on my cheeks and lips. I was astonished. Yet I thought the girl so guileless, that I supposed she must have imagined she was kissing someone of her own sex, seeing me dressed like a female. This scene was repeated every evening with additions; and I began to perceive that her kisses, which were accompanied by laboured breathing, were not as innocent as I supposed. Respect for my host's roof induced me to reprove her kindly but seriously, and so as not to rouse resentment in the girl. I warned her that such kisses between man and woman were forbidden by our confessors.

She laughed and told me in an undertone to be quiet and not to cause a commotion. She begged me to leave my bedroom door ajar that night, because when everyone had gone to bed and was asleep, she would come and visit me. She had something to tell me in the strictest confidence.

'What on earth can the little hussy wish to tell me?' I asked myself.

I was curious, however, and even felt a certain affection for the elf-like creature, whose behaviour at table and about the house would have done credit to Santa Rosa herself. So I was persuaded to leave my door open.

A little after midnight, as I was beginning to doze, she appeared at my bedside, half undressed. She began by pinching me until I was wide awake, and then she put her arms around my neck and showered provocative kisses upon me, saying: 'My poor young idiot, what sort of a man do you take him for, this so-called father of mine, who tells me off so roundly and treats me so sternly when we are in company? I will tell you. He is a real swine. He took me into his house, with a show of charity, as his adopted daughter; but in secret the brute has always had his way with me, and still does now, though his good wife suspects nothing. He is a jealous beast and torments me like a devil when we are alone together. You, on the other hand, are a young man after my own heart. I am madly in love with you, and with your help I intend to find some relief from the tyranny of this middle-aged swine. Now I have told you everything. I hope you feel kindly towards me.'

She gave me no time to reflect, but laid siege to my virtue by resuming the music of her ardent kisses. My powers of reasoning evaporated before this sprite of thirteen years, as beautiful in her dishabille as an angel from heaven. Under the compulsion of a bold, impetuous passion, she sucked up my soul between her parted lips and breathed her own soul into my mouth in return. And here I shall draw the customary curtain over the second of my amorous transgressions.

Romantic idealism played no part in this secret liaison, which was sheer, reckless folly, entirely physical in character. When I discovered that this butterfly was a truly terrible adversary in our nocturnal duels of love; when I saw her on the following day, going about the house and serving at table, all serious, with downcast eyes and an edifying air of modesty, I was captivated. I . faithfully imitated her caution and serious demeanour, though not without occasional twinges of remorse and apprehension lest the illicit traffic be discovered. The secret command to leave my door open was issued, not every day, but frequently. She took pains to appear at my bedside on each occasion with increased ardour, finding fresh transports of passion with which to send my senses reeling and throw me into those ecstasies which oblige me to draw my curtain.

About a month remained before our Provveditore Generale Querini took sail for Venice. His successor was already at Zara; and I had arranged my own departure to suit with that of my superior. I must admit, however, that I was so captivated by that little hussy's ways, that all my strength of mind could not prevent me from looking forward with real sadness to our parting.

A comic accident, which happened three days before I quitted Zara, cured me on the instant, and made me bless the hour of my embarkation for home. In order to make my narrative intelligible, I shall be obliged to describe the plan and the construction of the house we occupied. After ascending the first stone staircase, one entered a large hall. At the end of this hall, on the right hand, were two chambers, in one of which the married couple slept, while Massimo occupied the other. At the head of the staircase, on the left, lay my bedroom, near the door of which another opening led to the foot of a long ladder of thirty or more wooden steps. By this one mounted to a floor above. Just at the top of the ladder was a dormer window, looking out upon the roof, for the convenience of work-people, when tiles had to be replaced and other repairs made. At one side of the window you found a little chamber, the chaste cell in which my mistress slept.

The putative father of the girl, that charitable man, had conceived no suspicion with regard to me; her behaviour and mine in public was marked with indifference, so well sustained that it suggested nothing to arouse a doubt about us. He was furiously jealous, however, and had some inklings that a certain young man, who inhabited the next house, might crawl along the roof at night like a cat, and get in by the window, if his adopted daughter left it open. His working jealousy suggested the following device. How it was executed, I do not know. But he secretly attached a thick log to the dormer window by a slender cord, in such a way that it was impossible to open the window without snapping the twine, and letting the log fall headlong down the ladder with a fearful crash. This trap was meant to act as an alarm to the paternal guardian. One night, while I was sweetly sleeping, an infernal uproar, as of something tumbling down the wooden stairs which ran along the hoarding at my pillow's head, woke me up with an awful fright. I thought my sweetheart must have fallen, but it was only the log which went heavily lumbering down.

I jumped out of bed in my shirt, caught up a light, and sallied forth to give assistance to the wretched girl. While I was opening my door, I spied the putative father in his shirt with a light in one hand and a long naked scimitar clenched in the other, running like mad and rushing up the stairs to execute summary vengeance. His wife in her shirt hurried after, shrieking to make him stop. Massimo in his shirt, with a light, and with his brandished sword, issued at the same time from his bedroom, judging by the din that thieves were in the house. The husband ran upstairs, swearing. The wife followed, howling. I followed the wife, in dumb bewilderment. Massimo followed me, shouting: 'Who is it? What is it? Make room for me! Leave me to do the business!' The scene was quite dramatic. The dormer window stood wide open. The girl in her smock had fallen, huddled together, terrified, and trembling, just beneath it. Her crime was manifest. We had much ado, all three of us, to curb the rage of the so-called putative father, who had now become an Orlando Furioso, and was bent on cutting the throat of his adopted daughter. The row was terrible. During the long examinations which ensued, and in which, thanks to Heaven, no mention was made of me, it came out that, not content with receiving nocturnal visits from the young roof-climber, our paragon of modesty often went softly down the staircase in the night, opened the front door, and entertained any number of fellows in a pantry on the ground-floor.

All these matters were finally made up with sermons, threats, entreaties for forgiveness, promises, vows to never do the like again, and a change of dormitory for the vestal. I left Zara, light of heart, three days after this event, horrified at the memory of my second love-affair with a thirteen-year-old Messalina.

24

*Story of my third love-affair, which, though it is true
history, women may, if they please, regard as fiction*

After my return to Venice occurred the events which I shall
now proceed to narrate. This third amour was also the last of
any essential importance in my life. During its development
the romance and idealism of my nature, the delicacy of my
emotions, seemed to meet with perfect correspondence in a
mistress whose sublime sentiments matched my own. Why I
say *seemed*, will appear in the sequel of this story, out of
which Boccaccio might have formed a first-rate *novella*. The
recital must be lengthy; but I crave indulgence from my
readers, feeling that the numerous episodes which it contains
and the abundance of curious material deserve a careful
handling.

I occupied some little rooms at the top of our house in
Venice. Here I used to sleep, and pass whole days in study.
From time to time, while I was working, an angel's voice
arrested my attention, singing melancholy airs attuned to
sad and plaintive melodies. This lovely voice came from a
house which was only divided by a very narrow alley from
my apartment. My window opened on the house in question;
and so it happened, as a matter of course, that one fine day
I caught sight of its possessor sitting at her window sewing.
Leaning at one of my windows, I found myself so close to the
lady that civility obliged me to salute her. She returned my
bow with courteous gravity. It was a young woman of about
seventeen, married, and endowed with all the charms which
nature can confer. Her demeanour was stately; complexion,
very white; stature, middle-sized; the look of her eyes gentle
and modest. She was neither plump nor lean. Her bust presented an agreeable firmness; her arms were rounded, and she

had the most beautiful hands. A scarlet riband bound her forehead, and was tied in a bow behind her thick and flowing tresses. On her countenance dwelt a fixed expression of profound sadness, which compelled attention. In spite of these distinguished qualities, I was far from engaging my romantic heart upon the spot. My adventures at Zara were too fresh in my memory, and taught me some experience.

When one has a beautiful young woman for one's next-door neighbour, it is easy to pass by degrees from daily compliments and salutations to a certain sort of intimacy. One begins to ask: 'How are you?' or 'Did you sleep well last night?' One exchanges complaints upon the subject of the weather, the sirocco, the rain. At length, after some days passed in such inquiries on topics common to all stupid people, one is anxious to show that one is not as stupid as the rest of the world.

I asked her one morning why she invariably exercised her charming voice in mournful songs and plaintive music. She replied that her temperament inclined to melancholy; that she sang to distract her thoughts, and that she only found relief in sadness. 'But you are young,' I said. 'I see that you are well provided; I recognize that you have wit and understanding; you ought to overcome your temperament by wise reflections; and yet, I cannot deny it, there is always something in your eyes and in your face which betrays a chagrin unsuited to your years. I cannot comprehend it.' She answered with much grace, and with a captivating half-smile, that since she was not a man, she could not know what impression the affairs of the world made upon the minds of men, and since I was not a woman, I could not know what impression they make upon the minds of women. This reply, which had a flavour of philosophy, sent a little arrow to my heart. The modest demeanour, the seriousness, and the cultivation of this Venetian lady pictured her to me immeasurably different from the Dalmatian women I had known. I began to flatter myself that here perhaps I had discovered the virtuous mistress for whom my romantic, metaphysical, delicate heart was sighing. A crowd of reflections came to break the dream, and

K

I contented myself with complimenting her upon her answer. Afterwards, I rather avoided occasions for seeing and talking with her.

Certainly she must have had plenty of work to finish; for I observed her every day seated at the same window sewing with melancholy seriousness. While shunning, so far as this was possible, the danger of conversing with her, my poor heart felt it would be less than civil not to speak a word from time to time. Accordingly we now and then engaged in short dialogues. They turned upon philosophical and moral topics —absurdities in life, human nature, fashion. I tried to take a lively tone, and entered upon some innocent witticisms, in order to dispel her gloom. But I rarely succeeded in waking a smile on her fair lips. Her replies were always sensible, decorous, ingenious, and acute. While debating some knotty point which admitted controversy, she forgot to work, left her needle sticking in the stuff, looked me earnestly in the face and listened to my remarks as though she were reading a book which compelled her to concentrate her mind. Flattering suggestions filled my head. I sought to extinguish them, and grew still more abstemious in the indulgence of our colloquies.

More than a month had passed in this way, when I noticed, on opening a conversation of the usual kind, that the young woman gazed hard at me and blushed a little, without my being able to assign any cause for her blushes. A few indifferent sentences were exchanged. Still I perceived her to be restless and impatient, as though she were annoyed by my keeping to generalities and not saying something she was waiting for. I did not, and really could not, make it out. I might have imagined she was expecting a declaration. But she did not look like a woman of that sort, and I was neither bold nor eager enough to risk it. At length I thought it best to remark that I saw she had things to think over, and that I would not infringe upon her leisure further. I bowed, and was about to take my leave. 'Please, do not go!' she exclaimed in some distress, and rising at the same time from her chair: 'Did you not receive, two days ago, a note from me in answer to one of yours, together with a miniature?' 'What note? What answer? What miniature?' cried I in astonishment: 'I know nothing about the matter.' 'Are you telling the truth?' she asked, turning pale as she spoke. I assured her on my honour that I did not know what she referred to. 'Good God!' she said with a sigh, and sinking back half-fainting on her chair: 'Unhappy me! I am betrayed.' 'But what is it all about?' continued I, in a low voice, from my window, truly grieved to be unable to assist her. Ultimately, after a pause of profound discouragement, she rose and said that in her position she had extreme need of advice. She had obtained her husband's permission to go that day after dinner to visit an aunt of hers, a nun, on the Giudecca. Therefore she begged me to repair at twenty-one o'clock to the *sotto portico* by the *ponte storto* at S. Apollinare.[1] There I should see, waiting or arriving, a gondola with a white handkerchief hung out of one of its windows. I was to get boldly into this gondola, and I should find her inside. 'Then you will hear all about the circumstances in which my want of caution has involved me.' This she spoke with continued agitation. 'I have no one but you to go to for advice. If I deserve compassion, do not fail me. I believe enough in your discretion to confide in you.' With these words she bowed and rapidly retired.

I remained fixed to the spot, like a man of plaster; my brains working, without detecting the least clue to the conundrum; firmly resolved, however, to seek out the *sotto portico*, the *ponte storto*, and the gondola. I took my dinner in haste, nearly choked myself, and alleging business of the last importance, flew off to the *ponte storto*. The gondola was in

[1] These words have so much local colouring that they must be left in the text and explained in a note. A *sotto portico* at Venice is formed by the projection of houses over the narrow path which skirts a small canal or *rio;* the first floor of the houses rests on pillars at the waterside. A *ponte storto* is a bridge built askew across a *rio*, not at right angles to the water, but slanting. A *riva* is the quay of stone which runs along the canals of Venice, here and there broken by steps descending into the water and serving as landing-places. (S)

position at a *riva*, with the flag of the white handkerchief hung out. I entered it in haste, impelled perhaps by the desire to join the lovely woman, perhaps by curiosity to hear the explanation of the letters and the miniature. When I entered, there she was, resplendent with gems of price at her ears, her throat, her fingers, underneath the *zendado*.[1] She made room for me beside her, and gave orders to the gondolier that he should draw the curtain, and row towards the Giudecca to a monastery which she named.

She opened our conversation by apologizing for having given me so much trouble, and by begging me not to form a sinister conception of her character. The invitation, it was true, exposed her to the risk of being taken for a light woman, considering her obligations as a wife. To this she added that she had already formed a flattering opinion of my discretion, prudence, honourable conduct, and upright ways of thinking. She proceeded to tell me that she found herself much embarrassed by circumstances. She asked me if I knew a woman and a man, a poor married couple, whom her husband lodged under his roof, renting them a room and a kitchen on the ground-floor. I replied with the frankness of veracity that I was perfectly ignorant regarding the persons whom she indicated; far from being aware that they dwelt in her house, I did not know of their existence in the universe. At this answer, she closed her eyes and lips, as though in pain; then she resumed: 'And yet the man assured me that he knew you perfectly, and possessed your thorough confidence; furthermore, he brought me this note from you, in the greatest secrecy; you can read it, and discover whether I am speaking true.' Upon this she drew the *billet* from her bosom, and handed it to me.

I opened it with amazement, and saw at once that I had never written it. I read it through, and found in it the divagations of a most consummate lady-killer, full of panegyrics on the fair one's charms, oceans of nauseous adulation, stuffed out with verses filched from Metastasio. I was on the point of

[1] See above, p. 72, n. 2.

giving way to laughter. The concluding moral of the letter was
that I (who was not I), being desperately in love with her, and
forecasting the impossibility of keeping company with her,
saw my only hope in the possession of her portrait; if I could
obtain but this, and keep it close to a heart wounded by
Cupid's dart, this would have been an immense relief to my
intense passion.

'Is it conceivable, madam,' said I, after reading this precious
effusion, 'that you have conceived a gracious inclination towards me, grounded on my discretion, on my prudence, on
my good principles, on my ways of thinking, and that after
all this you have accepted such ridiculous and stupid stuff as
a composition addressed by me to you?' 'So it is,' she
answered: 'we women cannot wholly divest us of a certain
vanity, which makes us foolish and blind. Added to the letter,
the man who brought it uttered words, as though they came
from you, which betrayed me into an imprudence that will
cost me many tears, I fear. I answered the letter with some
civil sentiments, cordially expressed; and as I happened to
have by me a miniature, set in jewels, and ordered by my
husband, I consigned this to the man in question, together
with my note, feeling sure that if I were obliged to show the
picture to my husband, you would have returned it to me. It
seems then that you have received neither the portrait nor my
letter in reply?' 'Is it possible,' I answered, 'that you are still
in doubt about my having done this thing? Do you still
believe me capable of such an action?' 'No, no!' she said:
'I see only too well that you have nothing to do with the
affair. Poor wretched me! to what am I exposed then? A
letter written by my hand . . . that portrait . . . in the keeping
of that man . . . my husband! . . . For heaven's sake, give me
some good counsel!' She abandoned herself to tears.

I could do nothing but express my astonishment at the
cleverness of the thief. I tried to tranquillize her; then I said
that, if I had to give advice, it was necessary that I should be
informed about the man and wife who occupied her house,
and about the intimacy she maintained with them. She

replied that the husband seemed to be a good sort of fellow, who gained something by a transport-boat he kept. 'The wife is a most excellent poor creature, and a devoted daughter of the church. She is attached to me, and I to her. I often keep her in my company, have often helped her in her need, and she has shown herself amply grateful. You know that, between women, we exchange confidences which we do not communicate to men. She is aware of certain troubles which beset me, and which I need not speak to you about; and she feels sorry for me. She has heard me talking at the window with you, and has joked me on the subject. I made no secret to her of my inclination, adding however that I knew my duties as a wife, and that I had overcome the weakness. She laughed at me, and encouraged me to be a little less regardful on this point. That is really all I have to tell you, and I think I shall have said perhaps too much.' So she spoke, and dropped her eyes. 'You have not said enough,' I put in : 'that excellent Christian woman, your confidante—tell me, did she ever see your portrait set in jewels?' 'Oh, yes! I often showed it to her.' 'Well, the excellent and so forth woman has told everything to her excellent husband. They have laid their heads together, and devised the roguery of the forged letter to abstract your jewelled miniature. The worst is that the excellent pair had some secretary to help them in their infernal conciliabulum.' 'Is it possible?' exclaimed she, like one bewitched. 'You may be more than sure that it is so; and shortly you will obtain proof of this infallible certainty.' 'But what can I do?' 'Give me some hints about your husband's character, and how he treats you.' 'My husband adores me. I live upon the most loyal terms with him. He is austere, and does not wish to be visited at home. But whenever I ask leave to go and pay my compliments to relatives or female friends, he grants me permission without asking further questions.' 'I do not deny that your want of caution has placed you in a position of delicacy and danger. Nevertheless, I will give you the advice, which I think the only one under these uncomfortable circumstances. That excellent Christian woman, your confidante, does she know perhaps that I was going to meet you in the gondola today?' 'No, sir! certainly not, because she was not at home.' 'I am glad to hear it. This, then, is my advice. Forget everything about the miniature, just as though you had never possessed it; bear the loss with patience, because there is no help for it. If you attempted to reclaim it, the villain of a thief and his devout wife and the secretary, finding their roguery exposed, might bring you into the most serious trouble. If your husband has a whim to see the miniature, you can always pretend to look for it and not to find it, affect despair, and insinuate a theft. Do not let yourself be seen henceforward at the window talking with me. Go even to the length of informing your confidante that you intend to subjugate an unbecoming inclination. Treat the pair of scoundrels with your customary friendliness, and be very cautious not to betray the least suspicion or the slightest sign of coolness. Should the impostor bring you another forged letter under the same cloak of secrecy, as I think he is pretty sure to do, take and keep it, but tell him quietly that you do not mean to return an answer; nay, send a message through the knave to me, to this effect—that you beg me to cease troubling you with letters; that you have made wholesome reflections, remembering the duty which an honest woman owes her husband. You may add that you have discovered me to be a wild young fellow of the worst character, and that you are very sorry to have entrusted me with your miniature. Paint me as black as you can to the rascal; if he takes up the cudgels in my defence, as he is sure to do in order to seduce you, abide by your determination, without displaying any anger, but only asking him to break the thread of these communications which annoy you. You may, if matters take a turn in that direction, waste a ducat or two upon the ruffian, provided he swears that he will accept no further messages or notes from me. This is the best advice which I can give you in a matter of considerable peril to your reputation. Pray carry my directions out with caution and ability. Remember that your good name is in the hands of people who are diabolically capable of blackening it before your husband to defend themselves. I flatter myself that before many days are past you will find that my counsel was a sound one.'

The young woman declared herself convinced by my reasoning. She promised to execute the plan which I had traced, and vowed that her esteem for me had been increased. At this point we reached the Giudecca, where she had to disembark. With a modest pressure of one of her soft hands on mine, she thanked me for the trouble I had taken on her behalf, begging me to maintain my cordial feelings towards her, and assuring me that she prized our friendship among the great good fortunes of her life. I left her gondola, and reached Venice by another boat, considerably further gone in love, but with my brain confused and labouring. Love and the curious story I had heard kept me on the stretch.

A week or more passed before I saw her again. Yet I was always anxious to meet her, and to hear how she had managed with those sharpers. At last she showed herself one morning in her workroom; and while I was passing along by my open window, she threw a paper tied to a pebble into the room; then disappeared. I picked the missive up, and read the scroll, of which the purport was to this effect: She had to pay a visit to a friend after dinner; her husband had given his permission; could I meet her at the former hour, and at the former *ponte storto?* There I should see a gondola waiting with the former ensign of the handkerchief. She begged me to jump into the boat; for she was sorely pressed to tell me something. I went accordingly, and found my lady at the rendezvous. She seemed more beautiful than I had ever seen her, because her face wore a certain look of cheerfulness which was not usual to it. She ordered the gondolier, who was not the same as on the previous occasion, to take a circuit by the Grand Canal, and afterwards to land her in a certain *rio* at Santa Margherita. Then she turned to me and said that I was a famous prophet of events to come. From her bosom she drew forth another note and handed it to me. It was written in the same hand as the first. The caricature of passion was the same. I, who was not I, thanked her for the portrait; vowed that I kept it continually before my eyes or next to my heart. I, who was not I, complained loudly that she had deserted the window; I was miserable, yet I comforted myself by thinking that she kept apart from prudent motives. I, who was not I, had no doubts of her kindness; as a proof of this, being obliged to wait for a draft, in order to meet certain payments, and the draft not having yet arrived, I, who was not I, begged for the loan of twenty sequins, to discharge my obligations. I promised to repay them religiously within the month. She might give the money to the bearer, a person known to me, a man of the most perfect confidence, &c., &c.

I confess that I was angry after reading this. The lady laughed at my indignant outburst. 'How did you deal with the impostor?' I cried. 'Exactly as you counselled me,' she answered: 'excuse me if I painted you as black as possible to the fellow. He stood confused and wanted to explain; but on seeing that my mind was made up, he held his tongue, completely mortified. I ordered him to talk no more to me about you, and to accept no further messages or letters. Then I gave him a sequin, on the clear understanding that he should never utter a word again to me concerning you. I told him that I was resolved to break off all relations with you. To what extent our relations have been broken off, you can see for yourself now in this gondola; and they will only come to an end when you reject my friendship, which event I should reckon as my great disaster. I swear this on my honour.

'I must report another favourable circumstance,' she continued: 'my husband surprised the rogue in the act of stealing some ducats from a secret drawer in his bureau. He told the man to pack out with his wife, threatening to send him to prison if they did not quit our premises at once.' 'Were you clever enough,' I said, 'to affect a great sorrow for those unfortunate robbers, sent about their business?' 'I did indeed try to exhibit the signs of unaffected sorrow,' she replied; 'I even made them believe that I had sought to melt my husband's heart with prayers and tears, but that I found him firm as marble. I gave them some alms, and three days ago they dislodged.'

'Well done!' I exclaimed : 'the affair could not have gone better than it does. Now, even if your husband asks to see the portrait, it will be easy to persuade him that they stole it. You will incur no sin of falsehood; for steal it they did, in good sooth, the arrant pair of sharpers.' 'Ah!' cried she, 'why cannot I enjoy the privilege of your society at home? What relief would my oppressed soul find in the company of such a friend! My sadness would assuredly be dissipated. Alas! it is impossible. My husband is too strict upon the point of visitors. I must abandon this desire. Yet do not cease to love me; and believe that my sentiment for you exceeds the limits of mere esteem. Be sure that I shall find occasions for our meeting, if indeed these be not irksome to yourself. Your modesty and reserve embolden me. I know my duties as a married woman, and would die sooner than prove myself disloyal to them.' We had now arrived at Santa Margherita. She clasped my hand with one of the loveliest hands a woman ever had. I wished to lift it to my lips. She drew it back, and even deigned to bend as though to kiss my own. That I could not permit, but leapt from the gondola, a simpleton besotted and befooled by passion. Then she proceeded on her way to the house she meant to visit.

This heroine of seventeen summers, beautiful as an angel, had inflamed my Quixotic heart. It would be a crime, I reflected, not to give myself up to a Lucretia like her, so thoroughly in harmony with my own sentiments regarding love. 'Yes, surely, surely I have found the phœnix I was yearning for!'

A few days afterwards the pebble was once more flung into my chamber. The paper wrapped around it spoke of *ponte storto*, gondola, a visit to a cousin in childbed. I flew to the assignation. Nor can I describe the exultation, the vivacity, the grace, with which I was welcomed. Our conversation was both lively and tender; an interchange of

sentiments diversified by sallies of wit. Our caresses were confined to clasped hands and gentle pressure of the fingers at
some *mot* which caught our fancy. She never let fall an equivocal word, or gave the slightest hint of impropriety. We were
a pair of sweethearts madly in love with one another, yet respectful, and apparently contented with the ecstasies of
mutual affection. The pebble and the scroll, the *ponte storto*,
and the gondola were often put in requisition. I cannot say
what pretexts she discovered to explain her conduct to her
husband. The truth was that her visits for the most part consisted in our rowing together to the Giudecca or to Murano,
where we entered a garden of some lonely cottage, and ate a
dish of salad with a slice of ham, always laughing, always
swearing that we loved each other dearly, always well-
behaved, and always melting into sighs at parting. I noticed
that in all this innocent but stolen traffic she changed her
gondola and gondolier each time. This did credit to her
caution. We had reached the perfection of a guiltless friendship—to all appearances, I mean—the inner workings of
imagination and desires are uncontrollable. *You* had become
thou, and yet our love delights consisted merely in each
other's company, exchanging thoughts, clasping hands, and
listening now and then to hearts which beat like hammers.

One day I begged her to tell me the story of her marriage.
She replied in a playful tone: 'You will laugh; but you must
know I am a countess. My father, Count so-and-so, had only
two daughters. He is a spendthrift, and has wasted all his
patrimony. Having no means to portion off us girls, he gave
my sister in marriage to a corn-factor. A substantial merchant
of about fifty years fell in love with me, and my father
married me to him without a farthing of dowry. At that time
I was only fifteen. Two years have passed since I became the
wife of a man who, barring the austerity of his old-fashioned
manners, is excellent, who maintains me in opulence, and who
worships me.' (I knew all about the Count her father, his
prodigality and vicious living.) 'But during the two years of
your marriage,' said I, 'have you had no children?' The young

lady showed some displeasure at this question. She blushed deeply, and replied with a grave haughtiness : 'Your curiosity leads you rather too far.' I was stung by this rebuke, and begged her pardon for the question I had asked, although I could not perceive anything offensive in it. My mortification touched her sympathy, and pressing my hand, she continued as follows : 'A friend like you has the right to be acquainted with the misfortune which I willingly endure, but which saddens and embitters my existence. Know then that my poor husband is far gone in lung-disease; consumed with fever, powerless; in fact, he is no husband. Nearly all night long he sheds bitter tears, entreating forgiveness for the sacrifice imposed upon me of my youth. His words are so ingenuous, so cordial, that they make me weep in my turn, less for my own than for his misfortune. I try to comfort him, to flatter him with the hope that he may yet recover. I assure you that if my blood could be of help, I would give it all to save his life. He has executed a legal instrument, recognizing my marriage dowry at a sum of 8,000 ducats, and is constantly trying to secure my toleration by generous gifts. One day he pours ducats into my lap, then sequins, then great golden medals; at another time it is a ring or a sprig of brilliants; now he brings stuffs for dresses or bales of the finest linen, always repeating : "Put them by, dear girl. Before long you will be a widow. It is the desire of my soul that in the future you may enjoy happier days than those which now enchain you to a fatal union." There then is the story of my marriage. You now know what you wished to know about my circumstances.' Soon after she resumed, changing her tone to one of pride and dignity : 'I am afraid that this confession, which you have extorted from me, may occasion you to form a wrong conception of my character. Do not indulge the suspicion that I have sought your friendship in order to obtain vile compensations. If I discovered the least sign in you of such dishonouring dirty thoughts, I should lose at once the feeling which drew me towards you, and our friendship would be irrevocably broken.'

I need hardly say that this discovery of a Penelope in my mistress was exactly what thrilled my metaphysical heart with the most delicious ecstasy. Six months meanwhile had flown, and we were still at boiling-point. I used to write her tender and platonic sonnets, which she prized like gems, fully appreciating their sense and literary qualities. She would snatch them from my hand and drop them into her lovely bosom—a rarer gem than any of my sonnets. I also wrote songs for the tunes she knew; and these she used to sing at home, unseen by me, surpassing the most famous sirens of the stage by the truth and depth of her feeling. I am afraid that my readers will be fatigued by the long history of this semi-platonic amour. Yet the time has now arrived when I must confess that it degenerated at last into a mere vulgar *liaison*. It pains me; but truth demands that I should do so. Indeed, it was hardly to be expected that a young man of twenty and a girl of seventeen should carry on so romantic and ethereal a friendship for ever.

One day, having received the usual invitation, I entered the gondola. It was the month of April, a month that remained etched upon my memory for ever. My idol was attired in a loose-fitting mantle. Had there been an artist there to paint her, he would have executed a superb picture of Venus, I am sure.

At Murano we entered a garden, at one end of which was a comfortably-furnished pavilion, where meals were served. We ate and drank, toasting one another with lively affection. Luncheon over, we sat down on a settee of inviting softness, and held hands. We were silent for a moment. I saw her beautiful cheeks first turn pale and then blush red. As for myself, I cannot say whether I was pale or flushed, but certainly my blood was in a turmoil. She made as if to rise and draw away from me. I restrained her with but a small effort. She sighed deeply and fell back again upon the sofa at my side. Perhaps it was the ardour of youth, or the virtue of the April day, or the now irresistible force of attraction; whatever the reason, we suddenly found ourselves locked in each other's arms, our lips pressed passionately together, each drinking in the vital spirit of the other, reason and virtue thrown to the winds. An outburst of avid sensuality; a faintly whispered 'no', which was the sweetest assent that a man ever heard; a mixture of bashfulness, of ecstasy, of sighing, of inexpressible rapture; then a mutual sense of delicious languor . . . and the virtuous platonism of the previous six months was at an end.

The young woman sat up again, regaining her composure. Then, with downcast eyes, she said timidly : 'Dear friend, forgive me for leading you astray. Let it not diminish your regard for me.'

'No, my beloved,' I replied, 'I am the offender. It is I who have led you astray. Do not hate me for it.'

Like Sofronia and Olindo in Tasso's *Jerusalem Delivered*, when they each confess to stealing the picture of Our Lady, we both wished to affirm our guilt. But the only effect of this heroic contest was that we fell more deliriously in love than before and repeated our transgression, to which the delight of contemplation now lent a fresh piquancy. The six months of platonic love were followed by another six months of blind, unbridled sensual passion. We frequently resorted to the consolations of the gondola, Murano, the garden, the pavilion, luncheon, and the soft settee, the accomplice in our crime.

I should perhaps have drawn my curtain, instead of painting such a vivid picture of my guilty relations with the young woman, but the details were so firmly fixed in my mind that I was unable to restrain my pen when I recalled them. Moreover I have since been punished for my misdeeds by the pain they subsequently caused me, and so my narrative may serve as a lesson to those young people who are prepared to read about the unexpected conclusion of this love-affair, which I had imagined could go on for ever.

One day I saw my mistress seated with a very sad expression at her window. I inquired what had happened. She answered in a low voice that she had things of importance to communicate, and begged me to be punctual at the gondola, the *ponte storto*. Nothing more. I trembled to think that she might wish to inform me that she was pregnant. Seeing that her husband was consumptive and impotent, and highly principled into the bargain, the situation was gravely embarrassing. However, my fears were unfounded. She told me that she was much distressed about her husband. He was very ill. The doctors had recommended him to seek the temperate air of Padua and the advice of its physicians.

He had departed in tears, leaving her alone with a somnolent old serving-woman. I was genuinely sorry for the cause of her distress; but the news relieved me of my worst fears. After expatiating on the sad occurrence and over-acting her grief, I thought, even to the extent of shedding tears, she entered into a discourse which presented a singular mixture of good sense, tenderness, and artifice. 'My friend,' she said, 'it is certain that I must be left a widow after a few days. How can a widow in my youthful years exist alone, without protection? I shall only have my father's house to seek as an asylum. He is a man of broken fortunes, burdened with debts, enslaved to the vices of extravagance. My natural submission to him as a daughter will be the ruin of my fortune. After a short space of time I shall be left young, widowed, and in indigence. I have no one to confide in except yourself, to whom I have yielded up my heart, my virtue, and my reputation. In my closet I have stored a considerable sum of money, jewels, gold and silver objects of value. Will you oblige me by taking care of these things, so that my father may not lay his talons on them, under the pretext of guarding my interests in the expected event of my poor husband's death? Should he succeed in doing so, I am certain that before two months are over the whole will be dissipated. You will not refuse me this favour? Little by little I will convey to your keeping all that I possess. I shall also place in your hands the deed by which my husband recognized the dowry of which I spoke to you upon another occasion. My father knows nothing of this document; and in the sad event of my husband's death it may well be possible that I shall need the assistance of some lawyer to prove my rights and the maintenance which they secure me. For the direction of these affairs I trust in you. You love me, and I doubt not that you will give me your assistance in these painful circumstances.'

I saw clearly that the object of this speech was to bring me to a marriage without mentioning the subject. Now I was extremely averse to matrimony for two reasons. First, because I abhorred indissoluble ties of any sort. Secondly, because my brothers were married, with large families, and I could not stomach the prospect of charging our estate with jointures, and of procreating a brood of little Gozzis, all paupers. Nevertheless, I loved the young woman, felt sincerely grateful towards her, and in spite of what had happened between us, believed her to be virtuous and capable of making me a faithful wife. My heart adapted itself in quiet to the coming change, and conquered its aversion to a matrimonial bond.

A very surprising event, which I am about to describe, released me from all obligations to my mistress, dispelled my dreams of marriage, and nearly broke my heart.

Well, I did my best to comfort the fair lady. I told her that perhaps her husband's case was not so desperate as she imagined. Next I firmly refused to become the depository of her property. My reasons were as follows. In the first place, I had no receptacle to which the goods could be transferred with secrecy and safety. In the next place, her husband might survive and make inquiries. This would compromise the reputation of both her and me. I thanked her for the confidence she reposed in me, and vowed that she should always, at the hour of need, find me ready to support her as the guardian of her rights, her friend, and a man devoted to her person. She expressed herself satisfied with my decision; and once again we abandoned ourselves to the transports of a love which only grew in strength with its indulgence. She was an extraordinary woman; perfectly beautiful, always grateful, always new. Even in her hours of passion she preserved a modesty which overwhelmed my reason. Would that the six months of our platonic love had been prolonged into a lifetime, instead of yielding place to sensuality! In that case, the un-expected accident, which cut short our intercourse in a single moment, would not have inflicted the wound it did upon my feelings.

A friend of mine came about this time to Venice on busi-ness, and took up his quarters with me. He observed me ex-changing some words with this young lady, and began to banter me, loudly praising my good taste. I played the part of a prudish youngster, exaggerated the virtues of my neighbour, and protested that I had never so much as set foot in her house —which was indeed the truth. It was not easy to deceive my friend in anything regarding the fair sex. He positively refused to believe me, swearing he was sure I was the favoured lover of the beauty, and that he had read our secret in the eyes of both. 'You are a loyal friend to me,' he added; 'but in the matter of your love-affairs, I have always found you too re-served. Between comrades there ought to be perfect confi-dence; and you insult me by making a mystery of such trifles.' 'I can boast of no intimacy whatever with that respectable lady,' I replied; 'but in order to prove my sincerity towards my friend, I will inform you that even if I enjoyed such an intimacy as you suspect, I would rather cut my tongue out than reveal it to any man alive. For me the honour of women is like a sanctuary. Nothing can convince me that men are bound by friendship to expose the frailty and the shame of a mistress who has sacrificed her virtue, trusting that the man she loves will keep the secret of her fault; nor do I believe that such honourable reticence can be wounding to a friend.' We argued a little on this point, I maintaining my position, he treating it with ridicule, and twitting me with holding the opinions of a musty Spanish romance.

Meanwhile he was always on the watch to catch sight of my goddess, and to exchange conversation with her at the window. He drenched her with fulsome compliments upon her beauty, her elegance, and her discretion, artfully inter-weaving his flatteries with reference to the close friendship which had united himself and me for many years. To hear

L

him, one would have thought that we were more than brothers. She soon began to listen with pleasure, entering deeper and deeper into the spirit of these dialogues. Though ready to die of irritation, I forced myself to appear indifferent. I knew the man to be an honourable and a cordial friend; but with regard to women, I knew that he was one of the most redoubtable pirates, the most energetic, the most fertile in resources, who ever ploughed the seas of Venus. He was older than I; a fine man, however, eloquent, sharp-witted, lively, resolute, and expeditious.

Some days went by in these preliminaries, and the date of his departure was approaching. In other circumstances I should have been sorry at the prospect of parting from him. Now I looked forward to it with impatience. One morning I heard him telling her that he had taken a box at the theatre of S. Luca, and that he was going there that evening with his beloved friend. He added that it would cheer her up to join our party, breathe the air, and divert her spirits at the play. She declined the invitation with civility. He insisted, and called on me to back him up. She looked me in the face, as though to say: 'What do you think of this project?' My friend kept his eyes firmly fixed on mine, waiting to detect any sign which might suggest a *No*. I did not like to betray my uneasiness, and felt embarrassed. I thought it sufficient to remark that the lady knew her own mind best; she had refused; therefore she must have good reason for refusing; I could only approve her decision. 'How!' cried my friend, 'are you so barbarous as not to give this lady courage to escape for once from her sad solitude? Do you mean to say that we are not persons of honour, to whose protection she can safely confide herself? Answer me that question.' 'I cannot deny that we are,' said I. 'Well, then,' interposed the coquette upon the moment, much to my surprise, 'I am expecting a young woman of my acquaintance, who comes every evening to keep me company, and to sleep with me, during the absence of my husband. We will join you together, masked. Wait for us about two hours after nightfall at the opening of this *calle.*[1] 'Excellent!' exclaimed my friend with exultation; 'we will pass a merry evening. After the comedy we will go to sup at a restaurant. It will not be my fault if we do not shine tonight.' I was more dead than alive at this discovery. Yet I tried to keep up the appearance of indifference. Can it be possible, I said in my own heart, that these few hours have sufficed to pervert a young lady whom I have so long known as virtuous? Can these few hours have robbed me of a mistress whom I esteem so highly, who loves me, and who is seeking to win my hand in marriage?

The bargain was concluded, and at the hour appointed we found the two women in masks at the opening of the *calle*. My friend swooped like a falcon on my mistress. I remained to man the other girl. She was a blonde, well in flesh, and far from ugly; but at that moment I did not take thought whether she was male or female. My friend in front kept pouring out a deluge of fine sentiments in whispers, without stopping to draw breath, except when he drew a long sigh. I sighed deeper than he did, and with better reason. Can it be possible, I thought, that yonder heroine will fall into his snare so lightly?

We reached the theatre and entered the box. The blonde gave her whole attention to the play. My friend did not suffer the idol of my heart to listen to a syllable. He kept on breathing into her ear a torrent of seductive poisonous trash. What it was all about I knew not, though I saw her turning red and losing self-control. I chafed with rage internally, but pretended to follow the comedy, of which I remember nothing but that it seemed to be interminable. When it was over, we repaired to the Luna—as before, in couples—my friend with my mistress, I with the blonde. I never caught a syllable of the stuff which he dribbled incessantly into his companion's ears. Supper was ordered; a room was placed at our disposal, and candles lighted. My friend, meanwhile, never interrupted

[1] The narrow foot-paths between lines of houses at Venice are so called. They frequently have scarcely space enough for two men to walk abreast. (S)

his flood of eloquence, and without paying the slightest attention either to me or to the blonde, stuck tight to the arm of
my beloved and walked her up and down the room. I could
see her face burning like live coals; but in my heart an even
hotter fire was raging.

After passing to and fro like a pair of infatuated lovers, they
entered an adjoining room, which was in darkness and which,
as I had previously observed, contained a makeshift bed. From
this they did not return. Stormy thoughts occupied my confused mind. I dropped down beside my blonde companion
without knowing where I was, as silent with anguish as she
was silent by inclination. Nearly a quarter of an hour later
the couple emerged in a state of disarray which revealed
plainly the terrible incident which had occurred.

The ruthless woman came up to me with friendly demonstrations. One of those blind impulses, which it is impossible
to control, made me send her reeling three steps backwards.
She hung her head, confused with chagrin. My friend looked
on in astonishment. The blonde opened her eyes and mouth
as wide as she was able. I pulled myself together, ashamed
perhaps at having shown my anger; then, as though nothing
had happened, I began to complain of the host : Why did he
not bring our supper? It was getting late, and the ladies ought
to be going home. I noticed that my mistress shed some furtive
tears. Just then the supper was served, and we sat down to
table. For me it was nothing better than the banquet of Thyestes. Still I set myself to abusing the comedy, which I had not
heard, and the host, and the viands, swallowing a morsel now
and then, which tasted in my mouth like arsenic. My friend
betrayed a certain perplexity of mind; yet he consumed the
food without aversion. My mistress was gloomy, and scarcely
raised a mouthful to her lips with trembling fingers. The
blonde fell to with a good appetite, and partook of every
dish. When the bill was paid, we conducted the ladies back to
their house, and wished them good-night.

No sooner were we alone together, than my friend turned
to me and said : 'It is all your fault. You denied that you

were intimate with that young woman. Had you confessed the truth to your friend, he would have respected your amour. It is your fault, and the loss is yours.' 'What I told you was the truth,' I answered: 'but permit me now to tell you another truth. I am sure that she consented to join our company, relying upon me, and on my guarantee—which I gave at your request—that we were honourable men, to whom she could commit herself with safety. I cannot regard it as honourable in a friend to wheedle his comrade into playing the ignoble part which you have thrust upon me.' 'What twaddle!' exclaimed he. 'Between friends such things are not weighed in your romantic scales. True friendship has nothing to do with passing pleasures of this nature. You have far too sublime a conception of feminine virtue. My opinion is quite different. The most skilful arithmetician could not calculate the number of my conquests. Women may be frigid, emotional, prudent, or chaste, but I have found them all alike when it comes to making love, and very little skill on my part sufficed to disarm them all. I take my pastime, and let others take theirs.' 'If a ram could talk,' I answered, 'and if I were to question him about his love-affairs with the ewes of his flock, he would express precisely the same sentiments as yours.' 'Well, well!' he retorted: 'you are young yet. A few years will teach you that, as regards the sex you reverence, I am a better philosopher than you are. That little blonde, by the way, has taken my fancy. The other woman told me where she lives. To-morrow I mean to attack the fortress, and I will duly report my victory to you.' 'Go where you like,' I said: 'but you won't catch me again with women at the play or in a restaurant.'

He retired to sleep and dream of the blonde. I went to bed with thoughts gnawing and a tempest in my soul, which kept me wide-awake all night. Early next morning my friend took his walks abroad, and at dinner-time he returned to inform me with amazement that the blonde was an inhuman tigress; all his artifices had not succeeded in subduing her. 'She may thank heaven,' he continued, 'that I must quit Venice tonight.

The prudish chatterbox has put me on my mettle. I should like to see two days pass before I stormed the citadel and made her my victim.' He went away, leaving me to the tormenting thoughts which preyed upon my mind.

I was resolved to break at once and for ever with the woman who had been my one delight through a whole year. Yet the image of her beauty, her tenderness, our mutual transports, her modesty and virtue in the midst of self-abandonment to love, assailed my heart and sapped my resolution. I felt it would be some relief to cover her with reproaches. Then the remembrance of the folly to which she had stooped, almost before my very eyes, returned to my assistance, and I was on the point of hating her. Ten days passed in this contention of the spirit, which consumed my flesh. At last one morning the pebble flew into my chamber. I picked it up, without showing my head above the window, and read the scroll it carried. Among the many papers I have committed to the flames, I never had the heart to burn this. The novel and bizarre self-defence which it contains made it too precious in my judgment. Here, then, I present it in full. Only the spelling has been corrected.

'You are right. I have done wrong, and do not deserve forgiveness. I cannot pretend to have wiped out my sin with ten days of incessant weeping. These tears are sufficiently explained by the sad state in which my husband has returned from Padua reduced to the last extremity. They will therefore appear only fitting and proper in the sight of those who may observe them. Alas! would that they were simply shed for my poor dying husband! I cannot say this; and so I have a double crime to make me loathe myself.

'Your friend is a demon, who carried me beyond my senses. He persuaded me that he was so entirely your friend, that if I did not listen to his suit I should affront *you*. You need not believe what seems incredible; yet I swear to God that he confused me so and filled my brain with such strange thoughts that I gave way in blindness, thinking I was paying you a courtesy, knowing not what I was doing, nor that I was

plunging into the horrible abyss in which I woke to find myself the moment after I had fallen.

'Leave me to my wretchedness, and shun me. I am unworthy of you; I confess it. I deserve nothing but to die in my
despair. Farewell—a terrible farewell! Farewell for ever!'

I could not have conceived it possible that any one should
justify such conduct on such grounds. Yet the letter, though
it did not change my mind, disturbed my heart. I reflected on
her painful circumstances, with her husband at the point of
death. It occurred to me that I could at least intervene as a
friend, without playing the part of lover any more. Yet I
dared not trust myself to meet the woman who for a whole
year had been the object of my burning passion. At the cost
of my life, I was resolved to stamp out all emotions for one
who had proved herself alien to my way of thinking and of
feeling about love. Moreover, I suspected that she might be
exaggerating the illness of her husband, in order to mollify
me. I subdued my inclinations, and refrained from answering
her letter or from seeing her.

The fact is that I soon beheld the funeral procession of her
husband pass beneath my windows, with the man himself
upon the bier. I could no longer refuse credence to her
letter.

This revived my sympathy for the unhappy, desolate,
beauty. I was still hesitating, when I met a priest of my
acquaintance who told me that he was going to pay a visit
of condolence to the youthful widow. 'You ought to come
with me,' said he. 'It is an act of piety towards one of your
neighbours.' I seized the occasion offered, and joined company
with the priest.

I found her plunged in affliction, pale, and weeping. No
sooner did she set eyes upon me, than she bent her forehead
and abandoned herself to tears. 'With the escort of this minister of our religion,' I began, 'I have come to express my sincere
sorrow for your loss, and to lay my services at your disposal.'
Her sobs redoubled; and without lifting her eyes to mine, she
broke into these words: 'I deserve nothing at your hands.'

Then a storm of crying and of sobs interrupted her utterance. My heart was touched. But reason, or hardness, came to my aid. After expressing a few commonplaces, such as are usually employed about the dead, and renewing my proffer of assistance, I departed with the priest.

A full month elapsed before I set eyes on her again. It chanced that I had commissioned a certain tailoress to make me a waistcoat. Meeting me in the road, this woman said that she had lost my measure, and asked whether I would come that evening and let her measure me again. I went, and on entering a room, to which she introduced me, was stupefied to find my mistress sitting there in mourning raiment of black silk. I swear that Andromache, the widow of Hector, was not so lovely as she looked. She rose on my approach, and began to speak: 'I know that you have a right to be surprised at my boldness in seeking an occasion to meet with you. I hesitated whether I ought or ought not to communicate a certain matter to you. At last I thought that I should be doing wrong unless I told you. I have received offers of marriage from an honest merchant. You remember what I told you about my father; and now he is moving heaven and earth to get me under his protection with my little property. I sought this opportunity of speaking with you, merely that I might be able to swear to you by all that is most sacred, that I would gladly refuse any happiness in this life for the felicity of dying in the arms of such a friend as you are. I am well aware that I have forfeited this good fortune; how I hardly know, and by whose fault I could not say. I do not wish to affront you, nor yet the intriguer whom you call your friend; I am ready to take all the blame on my own shoulders. Accept, at any rate, the candid oath which I have uttered, and leave me to my remorseful reflections.' Having spoken these words, she resumed her seat and wept. Armed as I was with reason, I confess that she almost made me yield to her seductive graces. I sat down beside her, and taking one of her fair hands in mine, spoke as follows, with perfect kindness: 'Think not, dear lady, that I am not deeply moved by your affliction. I am grateful to you for the stratagem by which you contrived this interview. What you have communicated to me with so much feeling not only lays down your line of action; it also suggests my answer. Let us relegate to the chapter of accidental mishaps that fatal occurrence, which will cause me lasting pain, and which remains fixed in my memory. Yet I must tell you that I cannot regard you, after what then happened, as I did formerly. Our union would only make two persons miserable for life. Your good repute with me is in a sanctuary. Accept this advice then from a young man who will be your good friend to his dying day. Strengthen your mind, and be upon your guard against seducers. The opportunity now offered is excellent; accept at once the proposals of the honest merchant you named to me, and place yourself in safety under his protection.'

I did not wait for an answer; but kissed her hand, and took my leave, without speaking about my waistcoat to the tailoress. A few months after this interview she married the merchant. I saw her occasionally in the street together with her husband. She was always beautiful. On recognizing me, she used to turn colour and drop her eyes. This is as much as I can relate concerning my third lady-love. It came indeed to my ears, from time to time, without instituting inquiries, that she was well-conducted, discreet, exemplary in all her ways, and that she made an excellent wife to her second husband.

25

Reflections on the matter contained in the last three chapters, which will be of use to no one

These three love-affairs, which I have related in all their details, and possibly with indiscreet minuteness, taught me some lessons in life. I experienced them before I had completed my twenty-second year. They transformed me into an

Argus, all vigilance in regard to the fair sex. Meanwhile I possessed a heart in some ways differing from the ordinary; it had suffered by the repeated discovery of faithlessness in women—how much I will not say; it had suffered also by the brusque acts of disengagement, which my solid, resolute, and decided nature forced upon me. The result was that I took good care to keep myself free in the future from any such entanglements.

I was neither voluptuous by temperament nor vicious by habit. My reflective faculties controlled the promptings of appetite. Yet I took pleasure in female society, finding in it an invariable source of genuine refreshment. With the exception of some human weaknesses, of no great moment, to which I yielded in my years of manhood, I have always continued to be the friend and observer of women rather than their passion-blinded lover.

The net result of my observations upon women is this. The love which most of them pretend for men, springs mainly from their vanity or interest. They wish to be surrounded by admirers. They are ambitious to captivate the hearts and heads of people of importance, in order to reign as petty queens, to take the lead, to exercise power, to levy contributions. Or else they ensnare slaves devoted to them, free-handed managers of theatres, men who will give them the means at balls, at *petits soupers*, at country-houses, at great entertainments, to eclipse their rivals, to acquire new lovers, and to betray their faithful servant, their credulous accomplice in this game of fashion. Again, they are sometimes spreading nets to catch a complaisant husband, who will support them in their intrigues.

I was not born to pay court. My position in the world was not so eminent as to secure a woman's triumph by my influence. I was neither wealthy enough nor extravagant enough to satisfy a woman's whims in those ridiculous displays which make her the just object of disdainful satire. I had no inclination to ruin myself either in my fortune or in my health. I had conceived a sublime and romantic ideal of the possibilities of love. Matrimony was wholly alien to my views of liberty. The consequence was that, after these three earliest experiences, I regarded the sex with the eyes of a philosopher.

I enjoyed the acquaintance of many women in private life, and of many actresses, remarkable for charm and beauty. Holding the principles I have described, I found them well contented with my manner of behaviour. They showed themselves capable of honourable, grateful, and constant friendship through a long course of years. In truth, it is in the main to men—to men who flatter and caress the innate foibles of women, their vanity, their tenderness, their levity—that we must ascribe the frequency of female frailties.

In conclusion, I will lift my voice to affirm this truth about myself. Without denying that I have yielded, now and then, but rarely, to some trivial weakness of our human nature, I protest that I have never corrupted a woman's thoughts with sophisms. I have never sapped the principles of a sound education. I have never exposed the duties and obligations of their sex to ridicule, by clothing license with the name of liberty. I have never stigmatized the bonds of religion, the conjugal tie, modesty, chastity, decent self-respect, with the title of prejudice—reversing the real meaning of that word, as is the wont of self-styled philosophers, who are a very source of infection to the age we live in.

Here, then, I leave with you the candid and public confession of my loves.[1] I have related the circumstances of my birth, my education, my travels, my friendships, my engrossing occupations, my literary quarrels, my amorous adventures. It is for you to take them as you find them. I have written them down at the dictation of mere truth. They are *useless*, I know, and I only *publish* them in obedience to the virtue of *humility*.

[1] Gozzi had a distinct object in writing these chapters on his love-affairs. Gratarol's accusation of his having been a hypocrite and covert libertine lay before him. He wished to make a clean breast of his frailties. The *Memorie* must always be read as an answer to Gratarol's *Narrazione apologetica*, first printed in Stockholm in 1779. (S)

26

On the absurdities and contrarieties to which my star has made me subject

If I were to narrate all the whimsical absurdities and all the untoward accidents to which my luckless star exposed me, I should have a lengthy business on my hands. They were of almost daily occurrence. Those alone which I meekly endured through the behaviour of servants in my employ, would be enough to fill a volume, and the anecdotes would furnish matter for madness or laughter.

I think that the following incident is sufficiently comic to be worth narration. I was living in the house of my ancestors, in the Calle della Regina at S. Cassiano. The house was very large, and I was its sole inhabitant; for my two brothers, Francesco and Almorò, had both married and settled in Friuli, leaving me this mansion as part of my inheritance. During the summer months, when people quit the city for the country, I used also to visit Friuli. I was in the habit of leaving the keys of my house with a corn-merchant, my neighbour, and a very honest man. It chanced one autumn, through one of the tricks my evil fortune never ceased to play, that rains and inundations kept me in Friuli longer than usual, far indeed into November. Snow upon the mountains, and the winds which brought fine weather, caused an intense cold. I travelled towards Venice, well enveloped in furs, traversing deep bogs, floundering through pitfalls in the road, and crossing streams in flood. At last, one hour after nightfall, I arrived, half-dead with the discomforts of the journey, congealed, fatigued, and wanting sleep. I left my boat at the post-house near S. Cassiano, made a porter shoulder my portmanteau, and a servant take my hat-box under his arm. Then I set off home, wrapped up in my pelisse, all anxiety to put myself into a well-warmed bed. When we reached the Calle della Regina, we found it so crowded with people in masks and folk of all sexes, that it was quite impossible for my two attendants with their burdens to push a way to my house-door. 'What the devil is the meaning of this crowd?' I asked a bystander. 'The patrician Bragadino has been made Patriarch of Venice today,' was the man's reply. 'They are illuminating and keeping open-house; doles of bread, wine, and money are being given to the people for three days. This is the reason of the enormous crowd.' On reflecting that the door of my house was close to the bridge by which one passes to the Campo di Santa Maria Mater Domini, I thought that, by making a turn round the Calle called del Ravano, I might be able to get out into the Campo, then cross the bridge, and effect an entrance into my abode.[1] I accomplished this long detour together with the bearers of my luggage; but when I reached the Campo, I was struck dumb with astonishment at the sight of my windows thrown wide open, and my whole house adorned with lustres, ablaze with wax-candles, burning like the palace of the sun. After standing half a quarter of an hour agaze with my mouth open to contemplate the prodigy, I shook myself together, took heart of courage, crossed the bridge, and knocked loudly at my door. It opened, and two of the city guards presented themselves, pointing their spontoons at my breast, and crying, with fierceness written on their faces: 'There is no road this way.' 'How!' exclaimed I, still more dumbfounded, and in a gentle tone of voice: 'Can I not get in here?' 'No, sir,' the terrible fellow answered; 'there is no approach by this door. Take the trouble to put on a mask, and seek an entrance by the great gate which you see there on the right hand, the gate

---

[1] The translator of this narrative has taken the trouble to make this tedious detour on foot. The quarter in which Gozzi lived remains exactly in the same condition as when he described it. His old palace has not altered; and the whole of the above scene can be vividly presented to the fancy by inspection of the localities. (S) This is still the case in 1962.

of the Palazzo Bragadino. Wearing a mask you will be permitted to pass in by that door to the feast.' 'But supposing I were the master of this house, and had come home tired from a journey, half-frozen, and dropping with sleep, could I not get into my own house and lay myself down in my bed?' This I said with all the phlegm imaginable. 'Ah! the master?' replied those truculent sentinels : 'please to wait, and you will receive an answer.' With these words they shut the door stormily in my face. I gazed, like a man deprived of his senses, at the porter and the servant. The porter, bending beneath his load, and the servant looked at me like men bewitched. At last the door opened again, and a majordomo, all laced with gold, appeared upon the threshold. Making many bows and inclinations of the body, he invited me to enter. I did so, and passing up the staircase, asked that reverend personage what was the enchantment which had fallen on my dwelling. 'So ! you know nothing then?' he answered. 'My master, the patrician Gasparo Bragadino, foreseeing that his brother would be elected Patriarch, and wanting room for the usual public festival, was desirous of uniting this house to his own by a little bridge of communication thrown across the windows. The scheme was executed with your consent. It is here that a part of the feast is being celebrated, and bread and money thrown from the windows to the people. All the same, you need not fear lest the room in which you sleep has not been carefully reserved and closed with scrupulous attention. Come with me, come with me, and you shall soon see for yourself.' I remained still more confounded by this news of a permission, which no one had demanded, and which I had not given. However, I did not care to exchange words with a majordomo about that. When I came into the hall, I was dazzled by the huge wax-candles burning, and stunned by the servants and the masks hurrying to and fro and making a mighty tumult. The noise in the kitchen attracted me to that part of the house, and I saw a huge fire, at which pots, kettles, and pipkins were boiling, while a long spit loaded with turkeys, joints of veal, and other meats, was turning round. The majordomo ceremoniously kept entreating me, meanwhile, to visit my bedroom, which had been so carefully reserved and locked for me. 'Please tell me, sir,' I said, 'how late into the night this din will last?' 'To speak the truth,' he answered, 'it will be kept up till daybreak for three consecutive nights.' 'It is a great pleasure to me,' I said, 'to possess anything in the world which could be of service to the Bragadino family. This circumstance has conferred honour on me. Pray make my compliments to their Excellencies. I shall go at once to find a lodging for the three days and three consecutive nights, being terribly in need of rest and quiet.' 'Out upon it!' replied the majordomo, 'you really must stay here, and take repose in your own house, in the room reserved with such great care for you.' 'No, certainly not,' I said. 'I thank you for your courteous pains in my behalf. But how would you have me sleep in the midst of this uproar? My slumber is somewhat of the lightest.' Then, bidding the porter and the servant follow me, I went to spend the three days and the three consecutive nights in patience at an inn.

Having slept off my fatigue that night, I paid a visit of congratulation to the Cavaliere Bragadino on the elevation of his brother to the Patriarchate. He received me with the utmost affability; expressed annoyance at what he had learned from his majordomo, and told me with the most open candour that the patrician Count Ignazio Barziza had assured him that he had dispatched a courier with a letter to me in Friuli, begging permission to use my mansion for the feast-days of the Patriarch, and that I had by my answer given full consent. To this I replied that in truth I had seen neither messenger nor letters, but that he had done me the greatest pleasure by making use of my poor dwelling. Wishing higher honours to his family, I added that if such should befall, without seeking the intervention of Count Barziza, he was at liberty to throw my doors and windows open and freely to avail himself of my abode. Take this affair as you choose, it earned for me the estimable goodwill of the patrician Bragadino, caused me to sojourn three days and three nights in an inn, and gave me occasion to relate one of my innumerable contretemps.

If I were to recount all the contrarieties that my pacific temper endured at the hands of my Venetian tenants, it would fill a volume.[1] In the hope of making my readers laugh, I shall select but two examples which I regard as rather droll.

One day a woman of respectable appearance came, and asked for the lease of an empty house I had on the Giudecca. I granted her request, and she paid the first instalment of her rent. After this first payment, all my clamours, demands for arrears, and menaces were thrown to the winds. She actually inhabited my house for three years, and discharged her obligations with the coin of promise and sometimes insults. I offered to make her a free present of her debt if she would only decamp. This roused her to a state of fury. Was she not a woman of honour? she exclaimed. She was wont to pay up punctually, and not to accept alms. At last I had recourse to the Avvogadori, one of whom sent for the woman, endured her chatter, and intimated that she must give the house up at the expiration of eight days. Accordingly, I went to take possession of my property; but no!—there was the woman, comfortably ensconced with her own family as though the house belonged to her. Again I applied to the court. Bailiffs were dispatched, who turned my tenants with their furniture into the streets. The keys of the house were placed in my hands, and I crossed over to the Giudecca to inspect the damaged tenement, of which, at last, I felt myself once more the owner. Vain error! That heroic woman, at the head of her family, had scaled the walls of the fortress by a ladder, entered through a window, and encamped herself in the middle of the conquered citadel. I need not add that I finally got rid of this tormenting gadfly. But what a state the house was in! No locks, no bolts, no doors, no windows; everything reduced to desolation.

[1] The following paragraphs, to the end of the chapter, are extracted and condensed from Part III, chap. 5 of the *Memorie*. (S)

On another occasion I happened to have a house empty at S. Maria Mater Domini. One morning a man, who had the dress and appearance of a gondolier, presented himself. He informed me that he was a gondolier in the service of a member of the Colombo family, a citizen of Venice who lived in the district of S. Jacopo dall' Orio. His own abode was at S. Geremia; and the great distance from his master's dwelling made his service difficult. My house at S. Maria would exactly suit him; the money for the first instalment of the rent was ready, if I would take him as a tenant. 'What is your name?' I asked. 'Domenico Bianchi.' 'Very well,' said I; 'I shall make inquiries of your master Signor Colombo; for I have so often got into hot water that I am even afraid of cold.' He urged me not to postpone matters; his wife was expecting her confinement every hour; it was of the utmost importance that he should be able to install her at once in their new abode. 'Well, well,' said I, 'you don't suppose that she will be laid-in this afternoon, do you? I will go to Signor Colombo after dinner; and if his report of you is satisfactory, you may take the keys as early as you like tomorrow.' 'You are right,' replied the fellow; 'although I know myself to be an honest man, I do not pretend that you should not inquire into my character. Only pray be quick about the business.'

With this he went away; but scarcely had I dined, when the gondolier re-appeared, leading by the hand a young woman. Half in tears, he began as follows: 'Here is my poor wife in the first pangs of labour. For the love of Jesus, let us into your house. I am afraid it is already too late, and that she will be confined upon the street.' As a matter of fact, the young person showed by her figure, and by the extraordinary contortions of her face and body, that what he said was the truth. Mortally afraid that she might give birth to her child in my house, I rushed to the writing-table, scribbled out an agreement, took the customary month's payment, and sent the couple off with the keys of my house.

Some weeks later on, the parish priest of S. Maria arrived all fuming with excitement, and cried out: 'To whom the devil

M

have you let your house in such-and-such a street?' 'To a
certain Domenico Bianchi, the gondolier of the Colombo
family, whose wife was on the point of being confined.' 'What
Domenico Bianchi? What Colombo? What gondolier? What
wife?' exclaimed he in still greater heat. 'The fellow keeps a
brothel; and she is one of his trollops. When they came to
you, she had a cushion stuffed beneath her clothes. The house
is inhabited by three prostitutes, who solicit the passers-by.
They sell wine, draw all the disreputable people of the quarter
together, and are the scandal of my parish. If you do not
immediately get rid of the nuisance, you will be guilty of a
mortal sin.' I calmed him down, and made him laugh by the
account I gave him of my interview with the *soi-disant*
married couple. Then I promised to dislodge the people on the
spot.

*This was sooner said than done. Gozzi first applied to the
Avvogadori, who washed their hands of the affair, claiming
that they were not competent to deal with it. He then
begged the priest to lay an information before the Venetian
watch-committee, the* Esecutori contro la Bestemmia. *He refused, explaining that prostitutes were powerfully protected
at Venice, and that he had already burned his fingers on a
previous occasion by proceeding against a notorious member
of the profession. In the end, Gozzi sought the help of a
patrician friend, Paolo Balbi, who found a summary but
efficacious remedy.*

'I informed Messer Grande of your affair,'[1] said Balbi, while
explaining his proceedings : 'he, as you are well aware, commands the whole tribe of constables and tipstaves; and I
begged him to find some way of ousting the *canaille* from
your house. Messer Grande dispatched one of his myrmidons,
one who knows these hussies, to tell them, under the pretext
of a charitable warning, that the chief of the police had orders
to take them handcuffed to prison. In their fright, the nest of
rogues dispersed and left the quarter.' After laughing heartily

[1] Messer Grande corresponded to the Bargello at Rome, and was the
chief of catchpoles and constables. (S)

over the affair, and thanking my good friend, I walked home, reflecting deeply on red tape in public offices, perversions of legal justice, and the high-handed proceedings of that generous and expeditious judge, *Messer Grande*.

27

A review of the origin and progress of the literary quarrels in which I was engaged—Also of the foundation of the Accademia Granellesca—A diatribe on prejudice—Father Bettinelli

The introduction to the first volume of my dramatic caprices (published in 1772) gave a sufficiently full account of the dates and origins of my ten *fiabe teatrali*, together with some notice of the literary quarrels which occasioned them.[1] Yet I find it necessary to pass these matters once more in review, since they concerned me not a little for the space of twenty-five years and more, and have consequently much to do with my Memoirs.

Here then are the steps which led me to bring those poetical extravagances on the stage—extravagances which I have never sought to value or have valued at more than their true worth—which never had, or have, or will have detractors among real lovers of literature—which always had, and have, and will have the entire population of great cities for their friends—which made, and make, and will for ever make a certain sort of self-styled *literati* mad with rage. Here then, as I said, are the steps which led me to their publication.

I must begin by confessing three weaknesses, which pertained to my ways of looking upon literature.

In the first place, I resented the ruin of Italian poetry, established in the thirteenth century, fortified and strengthened

[1] Gozzi alludes to the *Ragionamento ingenuo* prefixed to the first volume of Colombani's edition of his works. (S)

in the fourteenth, somewhat shaken in the fifteenth, revived and consolidated in the sixteenth by so many noble writers, spoiled in the seventeenth, rehabilitated at the end of the last and at the beginning of the present eighteenth century, then given over to the dogs and utterly corrupted by a band of blustering fanatics during the period which we are doomed to live in. These men, who have wrought the ruin I resent by their pretence to be original, by their habit of damning our real masters and institutors in the art of writing as puerile and frigid pedants—these men who lead the youth astray from solid methods and praiseworthy simplicity, incite them to trample under foot whatever in past centuries was venerated like the angel who conducted young Tobias, hurl them with hungry and devouring intellects into the gulf of entities which have no actual existence—these men, I say, have turned a multitude of hopeful neophytes, if only they were guided by sound principles, into mere visionary fools and the demoniacs of spurious inspiration.

In the second place, I resented the decadence of our Italian language and the usurpations of sheer ignorance upon its purity. Purity of diction I regarded as indispensable to plain harmonious beauty of expression, to felicitous development of thought, to just illumination of ideas, and to the proper colouring of sentiments, especially in works of wit and genius in our idiom.

In the third place, I resented the extinction of all sense for proportion and propriety in style, that sense which prompts us to treat matters sublime, familiar, and facetious upon various planes and in different keys of feeling, whether the vehicle employed be verse or prose. Instead of this, one monstrous style, now bombastically turgid, now stupidly commonplace, has become the fashion for everything which is written or sent to press, from the weightiest of arguments down to the daily letter which a fellow scribbles to his mistress.

Let it not be supposed, however, that my resentment against these literary curses of our century—for such I thought them—ever goaded me beyond my naturally jesting humour. All the compositions I have printed on the topics in dispute, regarding purity of diction, ancient authors, and the corrupters of young minds in Italy, witness to my joviality and coolness in the zeal and ardour of the conflict.

Finally, I must confess that all my endeavours in the good cause, joined to those of others, have been impotent to stem the tide of extravagance, the exaltation of heated brains, the absurdities of so-called philosophical reforms; also, as regards the purity of Italian diction, all that we have said and written has been thrown away. The charlatans have had the upper hand of us, by persuading the vast multitude of working brains that to seek purity in language is a waste of time and hide-bound imbecility, and that to spare the pains of gaining it is a mark of free and liberal talent. The remedy must be left to time and to the inscrutable ebb and flow of fashion, which makes the world at one time eager for the true, at another no less eager for the false, in spite of any human efforts to control it.

It was about the year 1740, when an Academy was founded in Venice by some people of gay humour, versed in literary studies, and amateurs of polish and simplicity and nature. Caprice and chance brought us together. But we followed in the wake of Chiabrera, Redi, Zeno, Manfredi, Lazarini, valiant predecessors in the warfare against those false, emphatic, metaphorical, and figured fashions, which had been introduced like plague-germs by the *Secentisti*.[1] This Academy imbued the minds of young men with higher ideas, and fostered the seeds it planted by a generous emulation.

The lively and learned little band happened to alight upon a simpleton called Giuseppe Secchellari, who had been bamboozled by his own vanity and the cozenage of merry knaves agog for fun into thinking himself a man of profound erudition, and who accordingly blackened reams of paper with ineptitudes and blunders so ridiculous that nobody could

[1] That is, the authors of the seventeenth century, during which an extravagant and affected style prevailed in Italy. (S)

listen to them without fits of laughter. It was decided to elect this queer fish Prince of the Academy. The election took place unanimously amid shouts of merriment. He was dubbed Arcigranellone, and received the title of Prince of the Accademia Granellesca, by which names he and the club were henceforth to be known.[1]

A solemn coronation of this precious simpleton with a wreath of plums followed in due course. All the Academicians were grouped around him, and nothing could be more burlesque than his proud satisfaction at the honours he received, the air and grace with which he thanked us for some thirty odes and rigmaroles, which were really witty squibs and gibes upon our princely butt, and which he took for panegyrics.

A large arm-chair of antique build and very high, so high that the dwarfish Prince had to take two or three jumps before he leaped into it, was the throne from which he lorded over us. There he sat and swaggered, having been gulled into thinking it the chair of Cardinal Pietro Bembo, that renowned and illustrious author. An owl with two balls in its right claw stood over him, and was the object of his veneration as the crest of the Academy. Perched there aloft, he used to draw from his bosom a roll of papers, and recited in a quavering falsetto some preposterous gibberish or other which he styled a dissertation. After a few lines had been declaimed, the clapping of hands and mocking plaudits of his audience brought him to a pause. Fully persuaded that he had entranced his hearers, he then handed his manuscripts with majestic condescension to the secretary, and bade him enroll them in the archives of the Academy.

[1] These names require explanation. *Granelli*, *coglioni*, and *testicoli* are words for the same things, and have the secondary meaning of *simpleton*. Thus *Arcigranellone* is the Arch-big-simpleton. The crest of the Academy carries an allusion to the same things. Apropos of this not very edifying topic, it is worth mentioning that the canting arms of the noble Bergamasque family of Coglioni consisted of three *granelli* counterchanged upon a field party per fesse gules and argent. I cannot recall a parallel instance in heraldry. (S)

When we met together in the heat of the summer, ices were handed round to the members; but the prince, to mark his superiority, received a bowl of boiling tea upon a silver salver. In the depth of winter, on the other hand, hot coffee was served out to us and iced water to the Prince. The venerable Arcigranellone, puffed up with this distinction, swallowed the tea in summer and the water in winter, dissolving into sweat or shivering with cold according to the season.

I could not reckon all the pleasantries, for ever new and always witty, which we played off upon our Prince, and which his stupid vanity made him accept as honours. Each time the Academy met, these diversions acted like an antidote to melancholy. And since he never would admit that he was ignorant of anything a member asked, at one time he was made to rhyme extempore, at another to sing a song, and sometimes even to descend and strip to the shirt and fence with a master in the noble art, who rained down whacks with the foil upon his hide and sent him spinning like a peg-top round the room. Arcigranellone as he truly was, the man essayed everything, and never failed to triumph in the deafening derisive plaudits which he raised.

This novel kind of Calandrino,[1] of whom I am sketching a mere outline, served chiefly as a lure to young men who cared more for mirth than serious scholarship, and drew them to enroll themselves with zeal beneath the banner of the owl.

When we had amused ourselves enough, at the commencement of our sessions, with the marvellous diatribes, wholly unexpected answers, and harlequinesque contortions of our Arcigranellone, we left him up there alone upon the chair of Bembo, and drew from our portfolios compositions in prose and verse, serious or facetious as the theme might be, but sensible, judicious, elegant in phrase, varied in style, and correct in diction. An agreeable reading followed, which entertained the audience for at least two hours. Each reader, when he had finished his recitation, turned to the Arcigranel-

[1] Calandrino was a famous fool and butt in the *Decameron* of Boccaccio. (S)

lone, whose whimsical opinions and distorted reasonings renewed the clatter of tongues and laughter.

This serio-comic Academy had for its object to promote the study of our best old authors, the simplicity and harmony of chastened style, and above all the purity of the Italian tongue. It drew together a very large number of young men emulous of these things; and few foreigners of culture came to Venice without seeking to be admitted to its sessions. I shall not attempt to catalogue the names of innumerable members. But I may observe that many names might be found upon our books whose owners had no inkling of the fact; for the following reason. Some of our merriest wags used to amuse themselves and the company by inflating the Arcigranellone's vanity with burlesque epistles addressed to him by very exalted personages. These great people wrote to say that, induced by the renown of his learning, wise rule, and sublime administration of his principality, they begged to be inscribed by him upon the list of his fortunate subjects, the Academicians. In this way it came about that Frederick II of Prussia, the Sultan, the Sophy of Persia, Prester John, and other notables of like eminence, appeared among us on paper. All the members, I ought to mention, had an academical name assigned to them and published by his Magnificence the Prince. I was dubbed the Solitary.

The compositions produced in our Academy were candidly exposed to criticism; and, after receiving polish at the hands of accomplished scholars in the club, many works of style and value, in all kinds of verse and prose, went forth to the world. Serious poems, humorous poems, satires in the manner of Berni, Horatian satires with the masculine and trenchant phrase of ancient Rome, orations on occasions of importance in the State, dissertations in defence of the great masters of Italian literature, commentaries upon Dante, novelettes in graceful diction, familiar letters, volumes of occasional and moral essays, Latin verses and prose exercises, translations from choice books in foreign languages; all these, after passing the review of the Academicians, were sent to press. I need not speak further about what has become common property through publication.

Perhaps I shall be accused by modern innovators of seeking to attach importance to frivolities. That will not hurt me. Those are far more hurt and wounded who allow themselves to be seduced into believing that the works of these same innovators contain things better worth their notice than frivolities—uncouth frivolities, ill-thought, unnatural, and written in a monstrous jargon.

Who could have imagined that a single word, wrested from its proper sense, made common in the mouths of boys and women to denote what does not suit their inclinations, should have the power to turn established rules—based on the experience of sages, and confirmed by ancient usage—all topsy-turvy? This word is nothing more nor less, in naked truth, than—*prejudice*.[1]

I have just said that the word in question has been wrested from its proper meaning; and I am prepared to maintain this proposition. According to my principles, which will have to bear the shame of being stigmatized as *prejudices* by the innovators, it is impossible to apply the term 'prejudice' to things which are not only harmless, but beneficial, nay, necessary to the totality of mankind.

Now I am bound to believe that religion and its accessories are beneficial to society and nations. But our new-fangled philosophers have dubbed all these things the prejudices of intellects enfeebled and intimidated by seductive superstition. Consequently, religion, that salutary curb on human passion, has languished and become a laughing-stock.

I am bound to believe that the gallows is beneficial to

[1] What follows in the text above might be largely illustrated. It is curious to find Casanova, for example, agreeing with Gozzi on a point of morality: 'Une méchante philosophie,' he says, 'diminue trop le nombre de ce qu'on appelle préjugés.' Compare the ludicrous account of the rogue Squaldo-Nobili, who shared Casanova's prison at S. Marco, and who had purged himself of prejudice by reading *La Sagesse de Charon*. (S) See J. Casanova, *Histoire de ma vie*, ed. Brockhaus, Wiesbaden–Paris, 1960, i. 83, ii. 230.

society, being an instrument for punishing crime and deterring would-be criminals. But our new-fangled philosophers have denounced the gallows as a tyrannical prejudice, and by so doing have multiplied murders on the highway, robberies and acts of sacrilege, a hundred-fold.

I am bound to believe that heroism, probity, good faith and equity are beneficial to society. But our unprejudiced philosophers, who identify felicity with enjoyment and getting hold by any means of what you can, call these virtues mere romantic prejudices. Accordingly, justice has been sold with brazen impudence, knaveries and tricks and treachery have triumphed, and a multitude of simple, innocent, downtrodden creatures, poor in spirit and impoverished in substance, have wept tears of blood.

It was pronounced a musty and barbarous prejudice to keep women at home, for the supervision of their sons and daughters, their hirelings, their domestic service and economy. Immediately, the women poured forth from their doors, storming like Bacchantes, screaming out 'Liberty! Liberty!' The streets swarmed with them. Their children, servants, daily duties, were neglected. They meanwhile abandoned their vapoury brains to fashion, frivolous inventions, rivalries in games, amusements, loves, coquetries, and all sorts of nonsense which their own caprices and their counsellors, the upstart sages, could suggest. The husbands had not courage to oppose this ruin of their honour, of their substance, of their families. They were afraid of being pilloried with that dreadful word, prejudice.

The law which punishes infanticide with death was styled a prejudice. Good morals, modesty, and chastity received the name of prejudice—enforced, so ran the tale, by bugbears of the Levites and the foolish training of poor superstitious females. What the result was, I blush to record. The infinite advantages conferred upon society and families by these fine philosophical discoveries, and by their triumph over prejudices of the sort I have described, had better remain unwritten.

The few who stood aloof and mocked at fashions—fashions which fade and fall each year like autumn leaves—were quizzed as ignoramuses, blockheads, zanies tainted with the leprosy of prejudice. They passed for stolid, coarse-grained creatures, void of thrill, of sentiment, of taste, of culture, delicacy, and refined perception. Women and men, in one vast herd, became illuminated visionaries. They piqued themselves upon their intuition and originality. They discovered endless harmonies and discords, all imaginary; endless comforts and discomforts, all imaginary; endless imaginary savours, insipidities, depravities in things about them, in furniture, in dress, in colours, in decorations, in the kitchen, in food, in wine, in dressing of the table, all imaginary. They detected elegance or inelegance in every dumb and senseless object: down to chamber-pots and night-commodes there was nothing which escaped the epithet of elegant. Let thus much be said for truth's sake, with the patience which is needful nowadays in speaking truth to folk infected by the real and not the spurious leprosy of prejudice.

Well, when all the so-called prejudices which I have just described had been put to flight and dissipated by the piercing sunbeams of the innovators, many great and remarkable blessings appeared in their room. These were the blessings of irreligion, of respect and reverence annulled, of justice overturned, of law-courts made the play-ground for flagitious vices, of criminals encouraged and bewept, of heated imaginations, sharpened senses, animalism, indulgence in all lusts and passions, of imperious luxury, with her brood of violent insatiable desires, deceits, intrigues, oppressions, losses of faith and honesty and humour, swindlings, pilferings, bankruptcies, pecuniary straits, base traffickings in sexual bargains, adulteries, the marriage-tie made unendurable and snapped by force or cold collusion.

After such wise, but turning the innocent word 'prejudice' into a weapon of attack against everything which restrained vice, crime, illicit pleasure, violence, and social profligacy—against whatever, in short, rationally deserves to be called prejudice—the human race plunged willingly and universally into a pitiable and apparently immedicable state of pure unvarnished prejudice. And this has been effected by the flattering enthusiasm for curing us of prejudices! Indeed it is fine to notice how that poor word 'prejudice' is bandied about. The folk who suffer from the real disease, and who complain most loudly of its miserable consequences, declare themselves atheists, declaim against what they call prejudice in their sophisticated jargon, while they bless the legitimate, veracious prejudice, which is the font and source of all the evils over which they weep, lament, and shriek.

Compared with these weighty topics, what follows may appear a trifle hardly worthy of consideration. I allude to the revolution in literary taste attempted by the Jesuit Father, now the Abbé Saverio Bettinelli, together with some other restless spirits. Twisting that unfortunate word 'prejudice' to suit their purpose, they scouted sound studies, established models, correctness of style, and the authority of acknowledged masters. All such things were reckoned prejudices by these iconoclasts, who would fain have burned down the temple of Diana in their insolent ambition to be stared at as new stars, original thinkers, independent writers.

Bettinelli, a man not destitute of parts, fecundity, and eloquence, began by preaching to our youth that it was a prejudice to keep gazing at and slumbering over our old authors. What good could the study of Dante, Petrarch, and Boccaccio do us now? How could the imitation of their successors in Italian poetry and prose be profitable to us in the middle of the eighteenth century? Students of the good old type he derided as arid word-mongers, who had lost their wits by poring over languid, prosy, frigid models of an antiquated style. To Dante, without understanding him, he condescendingly allowed a few fine verses, a few felicitous images, amid that vast ocean of scurrilities and repulsive barbarisms—the Divine Comedy!

This would-be innovator was possibly justified in his contempt for the fashionable keepsake books of poetry which we call *raccolte*.[1] I will not defend them, though much might plausibly be urged in favour of a custom which does no harm, reflects lustre on noble families, encourages the young to practise and excel in the art of literary composition, and affords the rich an opportunity of succouring needy men of letters. However that may be, Bettinelli wrote and published a satire entitled *Le raccolte*, which was intended to crush them, and to serve as a specimen of his originality in works of fancy. The Granelleschi had always watched with humorous attention Signor Bettinelli's pranks and gambols, and they now resolved on doing something to sober him down a bit. Two of the best scholars in the Academy, Signor Marco Forcellini and the Abbé Dottor Natale dalle Laste, undertook the task of examining his poem. They had little difficulty in proving that its author, while seeking to pass for a giant of original genius, was nothing better than the servile plagiarist of Ariosto and Boileau. This conclusion they put forth in an essay, entitled 'A criticism of the little poem *Le raccolte*.' It seemed to us, however, that the essay was somewhat serious in style for an Academy which aimed at playfulness. Accordingly, I was commissioned to enliven it with an epistle in a lighter strain. This epistle I wrote, as my poor brains dictated, but with perhaps too much of boldness and asperity. The essay and the epistle were published together in one volume. Meanwhile, my brother Gasparo, indignant that Dante, whose resplendent genius had shed the light of glory upon Italy through so many centuries, should become the butt of a mere seeker after notoriety, wrote his *Defence of Dante*, which was also printed. Intelligent judges allow that this book is full of truth, and that its arguments are convincingly victorious over Bettinelli's arrogant and puerile scoffings. I am therefore at liberty to say that my brother's *Defence of Dante* is a really fine work.

What good came of these polemics? Very little, I am bound to say. Novelties, whether they are really new or only seem to be so, have the power of seducing and exciting innumerable intellects among the mass of those who cannot grasp the

[1] See above, p. 94.

truth, but who respond at once to clamorous fanaticism. In number such folk infinitely exceed the small minority who, remaining loyal to truth, seek her even at the bottom of the well into which imposture plunges her.

I have always shared the hardihood of politicians, who dare to raise their minds aloft, and look down from a height upon the lowly vale in which humanity resides. But with this difference: they regard the valley as inhabited by a swarm of insects, whom it is their art to sway, oppress, and drive about in their own interest; nor do they stoop to fraternize with these same insects until death reduces all to one brotherhood. I regard the valley as peopled by creatures of my kith and kindred, making observations on them, laughing at their grotesque gestures, motions, and contortions; then I descend to their level, associate once more with my neighbour, assure him that we are all alike ridiculous, and try to make him laugh at himself no less than at me by the proofs I give him of my proposition.

I do not need to study astronomy in order to discover whether there are planets which control the course of human thought. The natural seeds of levity, inconsistency, ennui, thirst for new sensations, with which our brains are crowded, when they begin to germinate, suffice to change the thoughts of mortals, and occasion fits of fashion, which not all the cables of all the dockyards in the world can check before their course is run. When one fashion is exhausted, the seeds I have described above set others in motion; and without inter-rogating the stars—unless indeed it be the vogue to do so—any patient student of past history may easily arrive at the con-clusion that an unbroken chain of such manias and fits of fashion, due to the same natural causes, has always swayed, and will always sway, the stupidity of man; and man in his stupidity is always blind, always possessed of the assurance that his glance is eagle-eyed.

What our forefathers saw, we see, and our posterity is doomed to see—a constant ebb and flow of opinions, deter-mined in some part by a few bold thinkers, who publish to the world discoveries now useful and now useless, now frivolous and now pernicious. Let not, however, these thinkers flatter themselves that when they have contrived to set a fashion going, their most clamorous supporters will take and stick to it more firmly than they do the vogue created by the opening of some new magnificent coffee-house or by Blondi's magazine of novelties, that very phœnix of fashion-makers in things our butterflies of human frailty think the most important.

As regards literature, in the middle of this century, and under the rising sun of Signor Bettinelli, we were condemned to behold a decided change for the worse. All that had been done to restore purity and simplicity, after the decadence of seventeenth-century taste, was swept away by a new and monstrous fit of fashion. The Granelleschi cried out in vain for sound principles and cultivated taste; contended in vain that, Italy being a nation which could boast a mother-language, with its literary usage, its vulgar usage, and its several dialects, reason bade us hold fast by the Della Cruscan vocabulary, and seek to enrich that, instead of disputing its authority. We cried to the winds, and were obliged to look on while the world was deluged with fanatical, obscure, bombastic lucubrations—laboured sophisms, rounded periods with nothing in them, the flimsy dreams of sick folk, sentiments inverted and distorted—and the whole of this farrago indited in a language mixed of all the vernacular dialects, with interlarded bits of the Greek tongue, but above all with so many French words and phrases that our own Italian dictionaries and grammars seemed to have become superfluous.

The great French poet Boileau[1] used to say that, although real merit may be choked and obscured for a time by malicious impostors with their noisy cavilling, it is like a piece of wood that is held under water by force. Someone may think that he has submerged it for ever, but the day will come when

---

[1] Gozzi had the highest regard for Boileau, who is mentioned several times in the Memoirs, always with respect. The sixth volume of Gozzi's works (Venice, Colombani, 1772–92) contains his translation of Boileau's twelve satires and a biography of the French writer.

he takes away his restraining hand, and it rises to the surface again for all to see and recognize. For my part, I must leave it to posterity to see the great tradition of Italian literature re-emerge in all its former glory.

28

Sequel of my literary quarrels—Goldoni and Chiari— My resolve to amuse my fellow-citizens with fantastic dramatic pieces on the stage

This new fashion of unlicensed freedom and of sheer en- thusiasm made rapid strides, because it was convenient and comfortable. Intellects, misled and muddled, lost the sense of what is good and bad in writing. They applauded the worst and the best without distinction. Little by little, common- place and transparent stupidities on the one hand, stupidities sonorous and oracular upon the other, were adopted in the practice of literature. Pure, cultivated, judicious, and natural style took on the aspect of debilitated languor and despicable affectation.

The contagion spread so rapidly and so widely, that even men like Doctor Carlo Goldoni and the Abbé Pietro Chiari were universally hailed and eulogized as first-rate Italian authors. Their original and incomparable achievements were lauded to the skies. To them we owed a fit of fashion, which lasted some few lustres, and which helped to overthrow the principles of sound and chaste expression.

These rivals, both of them dramatic poets, and each the critic of the other, were strong enough to heat the brains of our Venetian folk to boiling-point, so that the public formed two stormy parties, which came well-nigh to fisticuffs over the sublimities of their respective idols.

A whirlwind of comedies, tragi-comedies, and tragedies, composts of imperfections, occupied the public stage; the one genius of inculture vying with the other in the quantity he could produce. A diarrhoea of dramatic works, romances, critical epistles, poems, cantatas, and apologies by both the Vandals poured from the press and deluged Venice. All the youth were stunned, distracted, and diverted from good sense by din and tumult. Only the Granelleschi kept themselves untainted by this Goldonio-Chiaristic epidemic.

We did not shun the theatres. We were not so unjust as to refuse his share of merit as a playwright to Goldoni. We did not confound him with Chiari, to whom we conceded nothing, or but little. Yet we were unable to glance with other eyes than those of pitying derision upon the toilet-tables of fine ladies, the writing-desks of gentlemen, the stalls of booksellers and artisans, the hands of passers in the street, the rooms of public and private schools, colleges, even convents— all of which were loaded with Goldoni's comedies, Chiari's comedies and romances, the thousand trivialities and absurdities of both quill-drivers—while everything the scribblers sent to press was valued as a mirror of reform in literature, a model of right thinking and good writing.

I hope that no one will be scandalized if I report a saying which I heard with my own ears. There was a certain Abbé Salerni, Venetian-born, a preacher of the gospel. He was in the habit of thundering forth Lenten-sermons from the pulpits, and had a multitude of eager listeners. This man announced one day, with an air of frank and sturdy self-conceit, that he had arrived at composing his oratorical masterpieces upon sacred themes by the unremitting study of Goldoni's comedies.

I ought to render a candid account here of the impression made upon me by those two deluges of ink, Goldoni and Chiari. To begin with Goldoni. I recognized in him an abundance of comic motives, truth, and naturalness. Yet I detected a poverty and meanness of intrigue; nature copied from the fact, not imitated; virtues and vices ill-adjusted, vice too frequently triumphant; plebeian phrases of low double meaning, particularly in his Venetian plays; surcharged characters;

N

scraps and tags of erudition, stolen Heaven knows where, and clumsily brought in to impose upon the crowd of ignoramuses. Finally, as a writer of Italian—except in the Venetian dialect, of which he showed himself a master—he seemed to me not unworthy to be placed among the dullest, basest, and least correct authors who have used our idiom.

In spite of all the praise showered upon Goldoni, paid for or gratis, by journalists, preface-writers, romancers, apologists, Voltaires, I do not think that, with the single exception of his *Beneficent Grumbler*,[1] which he wrote at Paris, which suited the French theatre, but which had no success in its Italian translation here, he ever produced a perfect dramatic piece. At the same time I must add that he never produced one without some excellent comic trait. In my eyes he had always the appearance of a man who was born with the innate sense of how sterling comedies should be composed, but who, by defect of education, by want of discernment, by the necessity of satisfying the public and supplying new wares to the poor Italian comedians through whom he gained his livelihood, and by the hurry in which he produced so many pieces every year to keep himself afloat, was never able to fabricate a single play which does not swarm with faults.

In the course of our playful and airy polemics—polemics which had more the form of witty squibs than formal criticisms—polemics which we Granelleschi never deigned to aim directly, in due form of siege, against the outpoured torrents of Goldoni and Chiari, but which we meant to act as sinapisms on the minds of sluggish youths, besotted by that trash and froth of ignorance—I once defied the whole world to point out a single play of Goldoni's which could be styled perfect. I confined myself to one, because I did not care to be drowned in an ocean; and I felt confident that I could fulfil my part of the challenge by making even boys and children see how the public had been taken in. No one stooped to take my glove up, and to name the perfect comedy. The goad and lash of pleasantry, with which I exposed Goldoni's stupidities,

[1] *Le Bourru bienfaisant.*

only elicited the following two verses, which he wrote and printed, and which exactly illustrate the stupidity I accused him of :

> *Pur troppo so che buon scrittor non sono,*
> *E che a' fonti miglior non ho bevuto.*

> Too well I know that I am no good writer,
> And that I have not drunk at the best fountains.

Proceeding next to the Abbé Chiari. In him I found a brain inflamed, disordered, bold to rashness, and pedantic; plots dark as astrological predictions; leaps and jumps demanding seven-league boots; scenes isolated, disconnected from the action, foisted in for the display of philosophical sententious verbiage; some good theatrical surprises, some descriptions felicitous in their blunt *naiveté;* pernicious ethics; and, as for the writer, I found him one of the most turgid, most inflated, nay, the most turgid, the most inflated, of this century. I once saw a sonnet of his, printed and posted on the shops in Venice; it was composed to celebrate the recovery from illness of a patrician, and began with this verse :

> *Sull' incude fatal del nostro pianto.*
> Upon the fatal anvil of our tears.

Nothing more need be said. With such monstrosities in metre, he had the courage to proclaim himself a modern Pindar. Goldoni he looked down upon like some gull of the lagoons. Yet, such as he was, Chiari succeeded in mystifying a thousand empty brains, who admired him without understanding a line he wrote.

It is not to be wondered at if a Goldoni and a Chiari, with a few disciples and adherents, were able to create a temporary **furore**, when we consider that this furore flamed up in the precincts of the theatres. Here all the population was divided into hostile camps, and each party was so blind and bewitched as not to recognize the infinite superiority of Goldoni as a comic playwright over his rival.

What is the force of righteous indignation when a vogue of this sort has been launched on its career? That of Goldoni and Chiari was bound to run its natural course, and when it died away, the other, which I have described in the foregoing chapter, the vogue of immoderate, unnatural, incorrect enthusiasts, so-styled sublime philosophers, came in, who discovered new worlds in literature, and who are fawning now upon the young men of our days, threatening new vocabularies, nay, new alphabets, treating antiquity as a short-sighted idiot, and involving humanity in an undistinguishable chaos of literary follies.

With regard to the mania created by Goldoni and Chiari, as may easily be imagined, I looked upon it as a fungus growth upon opinion, worthy at the best of laughter. I deemed that, at any rate, I had the right to be the master of my own thoughts; and a trifle in verse which I wrote for my amusement, without the intention of sending it to press, was the accidental cause of obliging me to maintain my views against these poets by a series of good-natured *jeux d'esprit*. My real friends know that I harboured no envy, no sentiment of rivalry against them and their swamps of volumes in octavo. Anyone who has the justice to remember that I was a mere amateur in literature, giving away gratis whatever issued from my pen, will agree with my friends, and acknowledge that I was prompted by a disinterested zeal in the cause of pure and unaffected writing. May Heaven pardon those, and there are many of them, who have held me up for detestation as a malignant satirist, seeking to found my own fame and fortune upon the ruin of others! The players and publishers would be able to disabuse them of this notion. But I do not choose to beg for testimonials to my generosity; and perhaps I have not told the whole truth about it in the chapter already written upon my own character.[1]

It was in the year 1757 then that I composed the little book in verse which I have mentioned, closely following the style of good old Tuscan masters, and giving it the title of *The*

[1] See above, chap. 21.

Tartane, an Almanac of Influxes for the Leap Year 1756.[1] This little work contained a gay critique in abstract on the uses and abuses of the times. It was composed upon certain verses of that obscure Florentine poet Burchiello, which I selected as prophetic texts for my own disquisitions. It took the humour of our literary club, and I dedicated it to a patrician of Venice, Daniele Farsetti, to whom I also gave the autograph, without retaining any copy for my own use. This Cavaliere, a man of excellent culture, and a Maecenas of the Granelleschi, wishing to give me an agreeable surprise, and thinking perhaps that he would meet with difficulty in getting the poem printed at Venice, sent it to Paris to be put in type, and distributed the few copies which were struck off among his friends in Venice.

This trifling volume might have gone the round of many hands, affording innocent amusement by its broad and humorous survey over characters and customs, if a few drops of somewhat pungent ink, employed in lashing the bad writers of those days, had not played the part of venomous and sacrilegious asps. Goldoni, besides being a regular deluge of dramatic works, had in him I know not what diuretic medicine for composing little things in verse, songs, rhyming diatribes, and other such-like poems of a very muddy order. This gift he now exercised, while putting together a collection of panegyrics on the patrician Veniero's retirement from the rectorship of Bergamo, to vent one of his commonplace *terza-rima* rigmaroles against my *Tartane*. He abused the book as a stale piece of mustiness, an inept and insufferable scarecrow; treating its author as an angry man who deserved compassion, because (he chose to say) I had wooed fortune in vain. Many other polite expressions of the same stamp adorned these triplets.

Meanwhile, the famous Signor Lami, who at that time wrote the literary paper of Florence, thought my *Tartane* worthy of notice in his journal, and extracted some of its stanzas on the decadence and corruption of the language.

[1] *La Tartana degl'influssi per l'anno bisestile, 1756.*

Father Calogerà, too, who was then editing the *Italian Literary Journal*,[1] composed and published praises on it, which were certainly above its merits. I flatter myself that my readers will not think I record these facts out of vanity. I was not personally acquainted with either Lami or Calogerà. It is not my habit to correspond with celebrated men of letters in order to manufacture testimonials out of their civil and flattering replies. I do not condescend to wheedle journalists and reviewers into imposing on the credulity of the public by calling bad things good and good things bad in my behoof. I have always been so far sensible as to check self-esteem, and to appreciate my literary toys at their due worthlessness. Writers who by tricks of this kind, extortions, canvassings, and subterfuges, seek to gratify their thirst for fame, and to found a reputation upon bought or begged-for attestations, are the objects of my scorn and loathing. For Lami and Calogerà I cherished sentiments of gratitude. I seemed to find in them a spirit kindred to my own, and a conviction that I had uttered what was useful in the cause of culture.

As a matter of fact, although the *Tartane* was written in strict literary Tuscan, although its style was modelled upon that of antiquated Tuscan authors, especially of Luigi Pulci, and was therefore 'caviare to the general', the book obtained a rapid and wide success. The partisans of Goldoni and Chiari took it for a gross malignant satire.

Possibly the rarity of copies, and the fact that it came from Paris, helped to float the little poem. Anyhow, it created such a sensation, raised so much controversy, and brought so many young students into relations with myself and membership among the Granelleschi, that I almost dared to hope for a new turn of the tide in literature.

It was this hope which made me follow up the missile I had cast into the wasp's nest of bad authorship by a pleasant retort against Goldoni's strictures on my *Tartane*. Goldoni was a good fellow at bottom, but splenetic, and a miserable writer. Having begun life as a pleader at the bar of Venice, he never

[1] *Giornale de' letterati d'Italia.*

succeeded in throwing off a certain air of professional coarse-
ness and a tincture of forensic rhetoric. I seized upon this
point of weakness, and indited an epistle, which he was supposed to have written me, larded with all the jargon of the
law-courts. The object of the letter was to introduce his tercets
to my notice. I gave it the following title: *Letter of Contestation
against the Rig of the Tartane, an Almanac of Influxes printed
in Paris in the year 1757.*[1] After this I set myself to examine his
terza-rima poem, and had no difficulty in exposing a long
list of stupidities, improprieties, puerilities, and injustices.
Without altering the low and trivial sentiments expressed in
it, I rewrote the whole in a style of greater elegance and
elevation, so as to prove that even the most plebeian thoughts
may acquire harmony and decent grace by choiceness of diction. Finally, I dissuaded him from sending his unhappy
pamphlet to the press, and concluded by addressing some
octave stanzas to the public, in which I begged them to set him
free in future from his self-imposed obligation of composing
in verse.

I did not stop here. My *Tartane* contained some satirical
sallies against the comedies in vogue upon our stage; and
Goldoni had appropriated these to himself. In his invective he
inserted a couple of forensic lines against me, which conveyed
a kind of challenge. Here they are :

> *Chi non prova l'assunto e l'argomento,*
> *Fa come il cane che abbaia alla luna.*

> He who proves not both theme and argument,
> Acts like the dog who barks against the moon.

This excited me to write another little book, in which I
proved the proposition and the argument, and at the same
time afforded my readers food for mirth.

I feigned that the Granelleschi were assembled one day
during Carnival, to dine at the tavern of the Pellegrino,

[1] *Scrittura contestativa al taglio della Tartana degl'influssi stampata
a Parigi l'anno 1757.*

which looks out upon the Piazza di S. Marco. My comrades gathered round the windows to observe the passing masqueraders, when a monstrous creature, wearing a mask of four strongly-marked and different faces, entered the inn. They entreated it to come up into our room, in order that they might examine it at leisure. This mask of the four faces and four mouths represented the Comic Theatre of Goldoni, personified by me in the way I shall explain. As soon as it caught sight of me, the author of the *Tartane*, it turned to fly off in a rage, but was forced to stay and sustain an argument with me upon the theme of its dramatic productions.

In the dialogue which ensued, I maintained and proved that Goldoni had striven to gain popularity rather by changing the aspect of his wares than by any real merit which they possessed. After scribbling plots in outline for the old-fashioned comedy of improvisation, which he afterwards attacked and repudiated, he had begun by putting into written dialogue certain motives neglected by that kind of drama. Then seeing that this first manner began to pall, he dropped his so-called Reform of the Stage, and assailed the public with his *Pamelas* and other romances. When this novelty in its turn ceased to draw, he bethought himself of those Venetian farces, which were indeed the best and longest-lived of his dramatic hashes. In time they suffered the fate of their predecessors, because such vulgar scenes from life could not fail to be monotonous. Accordingly, he tried another novelty, tickling the ears of his audience with rhymed Martellian verses and semi-tragic pieces, stuffed out with absurdities, improprieties, and the licentiousness of Oriental manners. These *Persian Brides*, brutal *Hircanas*, with their dirty eunuchs, and unspeakable *Curcumas*, by the mere fact of their bad morality, monstrosity, and improbability, raised Goldoni's fame among a crowd of fools and fanatics, who learned his long-winded Martellian lines by heart, and went about the alleys of the town reciting them aloud, to the annoyance of people who knew what good poetry really is.

I maintained and proved that he had rashly essayed

tragedy of the sublime style, but had prudently fallen back
on such plebeian representations as *Women's Gossip, Signora
Lucrezia and the Jealous Women, The Respectable Girl, The
Good Wife, The Tyrants*, and *Theodore the Grumbler*.[1] The
arguments of comedies like these were well adapted to his
talent. He displayed in them a really extraordinary ability for
interweaving dialogues in the Venetian dialect, taken down
by him with pencil and note-book in the houses of the common people, taverns, gaming hells, *traghetti*, coffee-houses,
places of ill-fame, and the most obscure alleys of our city.
Audiences were delighted by the realism of these plays, a
realism which had never before been so brilliantly illustrated,
illuminated, and adorned, as it now was by the ability of
actors who faithfully responded to the spirit of this new and
popular type of farce.

I maintained and proved that he had frequently charged
the noble persons of his plays with fraud, absurdity, and
baseness, reserving serious and heroic virtues for personages
of the lower class, in order to curry favour with the multitude,
who are always too disposed to envy and malign the great.
I also showed that his *Respectable Girl* was not respectable,
and that he had incited to vice while praising virtue with the
dulness of a tiresome sermon. With regard to this point, the
four-mouthed Comic Theatre kept protesting that it wished to
drive the time-honoured masks of improvised comedy off the
stage, accusing them of imposture, immodesty, and bad example for the public. I, on the other hand, clearly proved that
Goldoni's plays were a hundred times more lascivious,
more indecent, and more injurious to morals. My arguments were rendered irrefutable by a whole bundle of ob-
scene expressions, dirty double-entendres, suggestive and
equivocal situations, and other nastinesses, which I had collected and textually copied from his works. The monstrous mask
defended itself but poorly, and at last fell to abusing me

---

[1] *I pettegolezzi delle donne, Le femmine gelose della signora
Lucrezia, La putta onorata, La bona muger, I rusteghi, Sior Todero
Brontolon.*

personally with all its four mouths at once. This did not serve it; and when I had argued it down and exposed it to the contempt of the Granelleschi, it lifted up its clothes in front, and exhibited a fifth mouth, which it carried in the middle of its stomach. This fifth allegorical mouth raised up its voice and wept, declaring itself beaten and begging for mercy. I admit that my satire here was somewhat harsh and broad; but it had been provoked by an expression of Goldoni's, who twitted me with being *a man out of temper with fortune.*

As a preface to these two little works, I composed an epistle in blank verse, in which I dedicated them to a certain well-known poverty-stricken citizen of Venice, called Pietro Carati. The man used to go about the streets, wrapt in a ragged mantle, with a rusty periwig, and black stockings, mended in a thousand places with green, grey, or white silk (the surest signs of beggary), modestly demanding from his acquaintances some trifle to support his dignity as *cittadino.*

In this epistle I repeated that I was not out of temper with fortune, that I sought no favours from that goddess by my writings, and that my only object was to carry on the war against bad authors, and to uphold the rules and purity of literature. These two little pamphlets became the property of the public before I had time and opportunity to print them. The stir they made while yet in manuscript occasioned a series of events which I will now relate.[1]

The noble gentleman, Giuseppe Farsetti, who was a member of our Academy, came to me one day, and told me that he and another patrician, Count Ludovico Widiman, would take it very kindly if I consented to withdraw my little works from publication. I was somewhat surprised, because I knew that the Cavaliere Farsetti was a lover of good literature. Count Widiman, on the other hand, had declared himself a partisan of Goldoni. Nevertheless, I readily assented to their request,

---

[1] I have to say that what follows in this chapter has been very considerably abridged from Gozzi's text. Apology is owed to him by the translator for condensing his narrative and confining it to points of permanent interest, while retaining the first person. (S)

and promised to bury my two pamphlets in oblivion. I added, at the same time, that I felt sure that Goldoni, when he was aware of this act of generosity on my part, would begin hostilities against me, trusting to his numerous and enthusiastic following.

I was not mistaken when I made this prophecy. It soon became evident that Goldoni intended to carry on the war against us lovers of pure writing in all the *Raccolte* which appeared from time to time in Venice. He also introduced affected and unpleasant types of character upon the stage under Florentine names, and otherwise jeered at us in the coarse little poems which he styled his *Tavole Rotonde*. Confiding in his popularity and the influence of those fine gentlemen whom he called his 'beloved patrons', he hoped to revenge himself on me and to suppress my *Tartane*.

To break my promise given to the two Cavalieri, and to publish the satirical pieces I have described above, was out of the question. So I prepared myself for a guerrilla warfare, something after Goldoni's own kind, but more witty and amusing. I judged it better to fight the quarrel out with short and cutting pieces, which should throw ridicule upon my adversary and amuse the public, than to begin a critical controversy in due form. Squibs and satires were now exchanged daily between Polisseno Fegeio (such was Goldoni's high-sounding title in the Arcadia of Rome) and my humble self, the Solitario in our modest Academy of the Granelleschi.

To meet Goldoni's lumbering diatribes in verse, I brought out a little burlesque poem, which I called *Labours of Hymen*.[1] It was printed on the occasion of a wedding, and created a revolution among the wits which exceeded my most sanguine expectations. At this distance of time I find it impossible to render a precise account of the innumerable compositions which I produced in this controversy. They were read at the time with avidity, because of their novelty and audacity. I never cared to keep a register of my published or unpublished writings in prose and verse. If I were asked where these trifles

[1] *Sudori d'Imeneo.*

could be found, I should reply : 'Certainly not in my hands.' Some of my friends, however—among them the Venetian gentleman, Raffaelo Todeschini, and Sebastiano Muletti of Bergamo—thought it worth while to form complete collections of such pieces from my pen.

It must not be imagined that the Abbé Chiari escaped without blows in this battle of the books. It so happened that an unknown writer subjected one of his prologues to a scathing satire in an essay called *Five Doubts*. The piece was mistakenly attributed to me; and Chiari answered it by six cowardly, filthy, satirical sonnets, which he circulated in manuscript, against myself and the Granelleschi. Upon this there arose a whole jungle of pens in our defence. The five doubts we remultiplied by four, by six; and the Abbé was argued and twitted out of his wits. In these straits, he condescended to extend the kiss of peace to his old foe Goldoni, and Goldoni abased himself to the point of accepting the salute. Drowning their former rivalries and differences, they now entered into an offensive and defensive alliance against the Academy and me.

Meanwhile our party grew steadily in numbers. The headquarters of the Granelleschi as a belligerent body were at this time established in the shop of the bookseller Paolo Colombani. Every month we issued here in parts a series of critical and satirical papers, which drew crowds of purchasers round Colombani's counter. The papers appeared under the title of *Atti Granelleschi,* and were prefaced with an introduction in octave stanzas from my pen. The noise they created all about the town was quite remarkable, and young men eagerly enrolled themselves under our standard of the owl. Chiari and Goldoni, on their side, were not idle; but the alliance they had struck took off considerably from their vogue. This depended in no small measure on their former rivalry. The dropping fire which had been exchanged between their partisans kept their names and fames before the public. Now that they were fighting under one flag against us, the interest in their personalities declined.

Without pursuing the details of this literary war, which raged between the years 1757 and 1761, I will only touch upon those circumstances which led me to try my fortune on the stage as a dramatic writer. Both Goldoni and Chiari professed themselves the champions of theatrical reform; and part of their programme was to cut the throat of the innocent *Commedia dell'arte*, which had been so well supported in Venice by four principal and deservedly popular masks: Sacchi, Fiorilli, Zannoni, and Darbes. It seemed to me that I could not castigate the arrogance of these self-styled Menanders better than by taking our old friends Truffaldino, Tartaglia, Brighella, Pantalone, and Smeraldina under my protection. Accordingly, I opened fire with a dithyrambic poem, praising the extempore comedians in question, and comparing their gay farces favourably with the dull and heavy pieces of the reformers.[1] Chiari and Goldoni replied to my attacks and those of my associates by challenging us to produce a comedy. Goldoni, in particular, called me a verbose wordmonger, and kept asserting that the enormous crowds which flocked together to enjoy his plays constituted a convincing proof of their essential merit. It is one thing, he said, to write subtle verbal criticisms, another thing to compose dramas which shall fill the public theatres with enthusiastic audiences. Spurred by this continual appeal to popularity and vogue, I uttered the deliberate opinion that crowded theatres proved nothing with regard to the goodness or the badness of the plays which people came to see; and I further staked my reputation on drawing more folk together than he could do with all his scenic tricks, by simply putting the old wives' fairy-story of the *Love of the Three Oranges* upon the boards.

Shouts of incredulous and mocking laughter, not unnaturally, greeted this Quixotic challenge. They stung my sense of honour, and made me gird up my loins for the perilous adventure. When I had composed the scheme of my strange drama, and had read it to the Granelleschi, I could see,

[1] This poem (*La Tartana degl'influssi*) is printed in vol. viii of Colombani's edition of Carlo Gozzi's Works. (S)

by the laughter it excited, that there was stuff and bottom in the business. Yet my friends dissuaded me from producing such a piece of child's-play before the public; it would certainly be hissed, they said, and compromise the dignity of our Academy.

I replied that the whole public had to be attacked in front upon the theatre, in order to create a sensation, and to divert attention from our adversaries. I meant to give, and not to sell this play, which I hoped would vindicate the honour and revenge the insults of our Academy. Finally, I humbly submitted that men of culture and learning were not always profoundly acquainted with human nature and the foibles of their neighbours.

Well, I made a present of *The Love of the Three Oranges*[1] to Sacchi's company of comic players, and the extravaganza was produced in the theatre of S. Samuele at Venice during the Carnival of 1761. Its novelty and unexpectedness—the surprise created by a fairy-tale adapted to the drama, seasoned with trenchant parodies of both Chiari's and Goldoni's plays, and not withal devoid of moral allegory—created such a sudden and noisy revolution of taste that these poets saw in it the sentence of their doom.

Who could have imagined that this twinkling spark of a child's fable on the stage should have outshone the admired and universally applauded illumination of the two famous talents, condemning them to obscurity, while my own dramatized fairy-tale throve and enthralled the public for a period of many years? So wags the world!

[1] *L'amore delle tre melarance.*

29

---

*My plan of campaign for assailing Goldoni and Chiari
through the militia of actors I had chosen—The four
Fiabe: The Raven, The King Turned Stag, Turandot,
The Lucky Beggars*

In the long course of my observations upon human nature
and the different classes into which chance or force have divided mankind (so that the gospel term 'neighbour' may not
be used again legitimately until the last judgment day), I had
not as yet enjoyed an opportunity of studying the race of
actors. I was curious to do so, and the time had come.

With the view of attacking my two poet-adversaries in the
theatre, I made choice of the comic troupe of Sacchi, the
famous Truffaldino.[1] It was composed for the most part of
close relatives, and bore the reputation of being better behaved and more honest than any others. Professionally, they
sustained our old national comedy of improvisation with the
greatest spirit. This type of drama, as I have said above, Goldoni and Chiari, under the mask of zeal for culture, but
really with an eager eye to gain, had set themselves to ruin
and abolish.

Antonio Sacchi, Agostino Fiorilli, Atanagio Zannoni, and
Cesare Darbes, all of them excellent players in their several
lines, represented the four masks, Truffaldino, Tartaglia, Brighella, and Pantalone. Each of these men could boast of perfect practice in their art, readiness of wit, grace, fertility of
ideas, variety of sallies, byplay, drollery, naturalness, and
some philosophy. The soubrette of the company, Andriana

---

[1] I may remind my readers that Truffaldino was the specific form
invented for the mask of Arlecchino by Sacchi. Truffaldino was originally a character in Boiardo's *Orlando innamorato*, where he played
the part of a consummate rogue, traitor, and coward, and was killed by
the paladin Rinaldo (Bk. i. Canto 26). (S)

Sacchi-Zannoni, possessed the same qualities. Its other members, at the time when I took up their cause, were old men and women, persons of good parts but unattractive physique, lifeless sticks, and inexperienced children. Some time earlier, the troupe had been extremely well-to-do and popular in Italy. But the two playwrights in question, after having lived in partnership with them, had turned round and taken the bread out of their mouths. Sacchi, in these circumstances, withdrew his company to the Court of Portugal, where they prospered, until a far more formidable enemy than a brace of poets assailed them. The terrible earthquake of Lisbon put a stop to all amusements in that capital; and our poor players, having lost their occupation, returned to Venice after an absence of some four years, and encamped in the theatre of S. Samuele.

Upon their arrival, they met with a temporary success. Many amateurs of the old drama, who were bored to death with Martellian verses and such plays as the *English Philosophers*, *Pamelas*, *Faithful Shepherdesses*, *Plautuses*, *Molières*, *Terences*, and *Torquato Tassos*, then in vogue, hailed them with enthusiasm. During the first year the four masks and the soubrette, with some other actors of merit in the extempore style, took the wind out of Goldoni's and Chiari's sails. Little by little, however, the novelties poured forth by these two fertile writers, who kept on treating the clever fellows as contemptible mountebanks and insipid buffoons, prevailed, and reduced them to almost total neglect.

It seemed to me that I should be able to indulge my humour for laughter if I made myself the colonel of the regiment. I also hoped to score a victory for the insulted Granelleschi by drawing crowds to Sacchi's theatre with my dramatic allegories based on nursery-tales. The fable of *The Love of the Three Oranges* made a good beginning. My adversaries were driven mad by the revolt it caused among playgoers, by its parodies and hidden meanings, which the newspapers industriously explained, describing many things which I had never put there. They attempted to hoot it down by clumsy abuse, affecting at the same time disgust and contempt for its literary triviality. Forgetting that it had been appreciated and enjoyed by people of good birth and culture, they called it a mere buffoonery to catch the vulgar. Its popularity they attributed to the co-operation of the four talented masks, whom they had sought to extirpate, and to the effect of the transformation scenes which it contained, ignoring the real spirit and intention of this comic sketch in a new style.

Laughing at their empty malice, I publicly maintained that art in the construction of a piece, well-managed conduct of its action, propriety of rhetoric and harmony of diction, were sufficient to invest a puerile fantastic motive, if taken seriously, with the illusion of reality, and to arrest the attention of the whole human race—excepting perhaps some thirty confirmed enemies, who would be sure, when my contention had been proved before their eyes and ears, to accuse a hundred thousand men of ignorance, and to renounce their sex rather than admit the truth.

This proposition was met with new gibes; and I found myself committed to make good my bold assertion. The fable of *The Raven*, extracted from a Neapolitan story-book, *The Tale of Tales*,[1] and treated by me in the tone of lofty tragedy, wrought the miracle. I must add that I assigned some humorous passages to the four masks, whom I wished to keep upon the stage for the benefit of hypochondriacs, and in contempt of misunderstood and falsely applied rules from Aristotle.

The success of *The Raven*[2] was complete. The public wept and laughed at my bidding. Multitudes flocked to hear this old wives' tale, as though it had been solemn history. The play had a long run; and the two poets were seriously damaged in their interests, while the newspapers applauded and extolled the allegory as a splendid example of fraternal affection.

I wished to strike while the iron was hot. Accordingly, my third table, *The King Turned Stag*,[3] appeared with similar results of popularity and sympathetic criticism. A thousand

[1] *Lo cunto de li cunti overo lo trattenemiento de' peccerille.*
[2] *Il corvo.*   [3] *Il re Cervo.*

O

beauties were discovered, which I, who wrote it, had not seen. Folk regarded its allegory as a mirror for those monarchs who allow themselves to be blinded by their confidence in ministers, and are in consequence transformed into the semblance of monsters. Meanwhile, my opponents persisted in ascribing the great success of these three pieces to stage decorations and the marvellous effect of magic metamorphoses, neglecting the writer's art and science, the charm of his verse, and his adroit employment of rhetoric, morality, and allegory. This impelled me to produce two more fables, *Turandot* and *The Lucky Beggars*,[1] in which magic marvels were conspicuous by their absence, while the literary art and science remained the same. A like success clinched my argument, but did not disarm my antagonists.

However, they were beginning to flag, and every time they staged a new play I answered it with one of my poetic extravaganzas. These were based on pure fantasy, but thanks to the qualities I have already mentioned and the abundance of other ingredients, which were assuredly 'things of substance, not mere verbiage', my plays reduced the takings at the theatres supported by 'cultured' playgoers and swelled Sacchi's revenues by a like amount.

I had formed the habit of conversing with my family of players in our hours of leisure; and very racy did I find the recreation of their society. In a short space of time I learned to understand and see into the characters and talents of my soldiers, with insight so perfect that all the parts I wrote for them and fitted, so to speak, upon their mental frames, were represented on the stage as though they issued naturally from their hearts and tempers. This added hugely to the attraction of the spectacle. The gift of writing for particular actors, which does not seem to be possessed or put in use by every dramatist, is almost indispensable while dealing with the comic troupes of Italy. The moderate payments which are customary in our theatres prevent these people from engaging so large a number of actors and actresses as to be able to select

---

[1] *I pitocchi fortunati.*

the proper representatives of all the varied characters in nature. To the accident of my possessing this gift, and the ability with which I exercised it, must be ascribed a large part of my success. Goldoni alone devoted himself with patience to the study of the players who put his premeditated pieces on the boards;[1] but I defy Goldoni and all the writers for our stage to compose, as I did, parts differing in character, containing jokes, witticisms, drolleries, moral satire, and discourse in soliloquy or dialogue, adapted to the native genius of my Truffaldino, Tartaglia, Brighella, Pantalone, and Servetta, without lapsing into languor and frigidity, and with the same results of reiterated applause.

Other playwrights, who attempted to put written words into the mouth of extempore actors, only made them unnatural; and obtained, as the reward of their endeavours, the abuse and hisses of the public at the third representation of their insipid pieces. It is possibly on this account that they revenged themselves by assuming comic airs of grave and serious criticism, treating our miracles of native fun and humour as contemptible buffoons, all Italy as drunken and besotted, myself as the bolsterer up of theatrical ineptitudes, and my prolusions in a new dramatic style as crumbling relics of the old *Commedia dell'arte*. So far as the last accusation goes, everybody will allow that the masks which I supported as a *tour de force* of art and for the recreation of the public who rejoiced in them, play the least part in my scenic compositions; my works, in fact, depend for their existence and survival on the sound morality and manly passion, which formed their real substratum, and which found expression on the lips of serious actors.[2]

[1] This passage indicates Gozzi's justice, his habit of conceding the *suum cuique*, however grudgingly. Goldoni, as we learn from his Memoirs, piqued himself upon the study he made of actors like Darbes, Golinetti, and Collalto. (S)

[2] A singular piece of self-criticism. Gozzi appeals to posterity on points which seem to us the least noteworthy in his work. Nothing is needed beyond the above sentences to dispel the illusion of his having been a free romantic genius. (S)

For the rest, the players whom I had taken under my wing looked up to me as their tutelary genius. Whenever I appeared, they broke into exclamations of delight, and let the whole world know that I was the propitious planet of their resurrection. They professed themselves indebted to me for benefits which could not be repaid, except by an eternal gratitude.

30

The actors and actresses of Italy in general, considered with regard to their profession, their characters, and their manners; written from the point of view of a philosophical observer

Among all sorts and conditions of human beings who offer themselves to a philosophical observer, none are so difficult to know in their real nature as actors and actresses.

Educated in deception from the cradle, they learn the art of masking falsehoods with an air of candour so completely, that it requires great gifts of penetration to arrive at their true heart and character. Journeyings from place to place, affairs of business, accidents of all sorts, experience of common life, examples furnished by their commerce with the world, the constant exercise of wit and intellect in rivalry, wake their brains up, and subtilize their comedians' nature.

In another chapter I intend to paint a special picture of Sacchi's company, with whom I fraternized, and whom I helped for about a quarter of a century. At present I shall confine my remarks to Italian players in general, who are, I think, in no essential points of moral quality different from those of other nations.

It may be laid down as an axiom, to be accepted with closed eyes, that the chief idol of all actors is their venal interest. Expressions of politeness, acknowledgments of obligation, terms of praise, humanity, sympathy, courteous welcome, and

so forth, have no value among actors, except as parts of a
fixed system of deception which they consider necessary in
the worship of this idol. If that idol of pecuniary interest is
attacked (with justice it may be and the best reasons), you
will not find in them a shadow of these fine sentiments. The
merest scent of coming profit makes them disregard and
blindly sacrifice the persons who have done them good; the
reputation of the whole world is as nothing to them then;
they take no thought of the damage they may have to suffer
in the future, blinded by greediness, lulled into security for
the time being, and hoping to avoid impending disaster by
address and ingenuity. The present moment is all that actors
think of.

Hot and choleric temperaments reveal their true selves more
readily among this class of people. The cool-headed are more
difficult to fathom. Their system of cozenage is not only
applied to persons outside the profession, from whom they
expect material gains; it is always at work to take in and de-
lude the members of the guild. Of course they find it less easy
to checkmate the initiated in their own devices. But if they
have attained to the position of being necessary to their comrades in the trade, there is no sort of impropriety, pretence,
injustice, swindling, tyranny, which they do not deem it law-
ful to employ.

These arts, which the progress of our century has extended
to many kinds of persons who are not of the profession, have
a certain marked character among the tribe of actors. Other
people, when detected, show some sense of shame and self-
abasement. The unmasked comedian, after all his turns and
twists have been employed in vain, is so unprejudiced and
candid that he laughs good-humouredly in the face of his
detective, and seems to exclaim with indescribable effrontery:
'You are a great fool if you flatter yourself that you have
made a notable discovery.'

Such is my experience. But of course it is possible that
among the innumerable actors, male and female, whom I
have known, conversed with, and studied, some phœnix of

the one or the other sex may have escaped my observation.

In what concerns the practice of their art, all that these people know is how to read and write; one better, and one worse. Indeed, I have been acquainted with both actors and actresses who have not even had the minimum of education, and yet they carried on their business without flinching. They got their lines read out to them by some friend or some associate, whenever a new part had to be impressed in outline on their memory. Keeping their ears open to the prompter, they entered boldly on the stage, and played a hero or a heroine without a touch of truth. The presentation of such characters by actors of the sort I have described abounds in blunders, stops and stays, and harkings back upon the leading motive, which would put to shame the player in his common walk of life.

Barefaced boldness is the prime quality, the chief stock-in-trade, the ground-element of education in these artists. Assiduous use of this one talent makes not a few of them both passable and even able actors.

These are the reasons why a civil war is always raging in our companies about the first parts in new pieces. The conflict does not start from an honest desire to acquire or to manifest theatrical ability. The players are actuated wholly by ambition, by the hope of attracting favourable notice through the merit of their rôle, by the wish to keep themselves continually before the public, performing ill or well as their blind rashness prompts them.

Notwithstanding all these disadvantages, Italy would be able to make a good show in comparison with other nations if our theatres were better supported and remunerated. There are not wanting persons of fine presence, of talent, sensibility, and animation. What we do want are the refinements of education, solid protection, and emoluments sufficient to encourage the actor in his profession.

I have observed that the best artists of both sexes are those who have some higher culture; but I have also observed that the support of themselves and their families, and the inevitable expenses of their wardrobe, render their professional salaries inadequate. They make up for these deficiencies by sponging upon credulous tradesmen and besotted lovers; and thus they bring discredit on the whole profession.

I have always laughed at those who depreciate the influences of the pulpit, and think they can instil sound morality into the people by the means of scenic shows. When Rousseau maintained that the precept *Do what I tell you, and not what I do,* is worthless without a good example from the man who gives it forth, he uttered one of the truest things that can be said. I leave people to meditate upon the inverted morality which is being now diffused in our most recent dramas, the dramas of so-called culture, from the lips of players in the place of preachers.

3I

A description of Sacchi's company in particular—I continue the tone of a philosophical observer

Having recorded the impression made upon me by Italian actors and actresses in general, I shall now attempt a description of Sacchi's company, which I had good opportunities of studying through some twenty-five years.

Though I read with sufficient ease into the hearts and characters of these my protégés, and could supply them with sentiments, dialogues, and soliloquies adapted to their inmost natures, I found it difficult to penetrate the motives of their moral conduct, which were far more closely fenced about from prying gaze than either their intellectual or their physical peculiarities.

There is no doubt that at least seven members of this troupe were excellent artists in the national *Commedia alla sprovveduta*—a species of comedy which has always afforded innocent recreation to the public when performed with taste and spirit, but which is utterly insufferable when badly executed. This much I concede to the persecutors of the species—little talents, more ridiculous and useless with their ostentation of gravity than are even bad harlequins.

Sacchi's company enjoyed general respect in so far as their personal conduct was concerned. On this point they differed widely from the majority of our actors, who are for the most part very badly looked upon. This excellent reputation weighed strongly with me, when I sought their society, and entered into fraternal relations with them. The way they held together, the harmony which reigned among them, their domesticity, studious habits, severity in moral matters, their rules against visits being paid to women, the abhorrence the women themselves displayed for those who took presents from seducers, the regularity with which they divided their hours between household duties, religious exercises, and charitable attentions to the indigent among their members, gratified my taste. I may incidentally mention that if any of the salaried actresses or actors exceeded the prescribed bounds of decent conduct, they were quickly sent about their business; and such offenders were replaced by others, whose moral character had been subjected to stricter inquiry than even their professional ability.

I am sufficiently unprejudiced and free from scruples; I have never evaded opportunities of studying human nature, which brought me into passing contact with all sorts of men; yet it is certain that I should not have entered into familiar relations and daily converse in my hours of recreation with these people, for upwards of the space of twenty years, if it had not been for their exceptional good character.

I not only composed for them a long series of theatrical pieces, novel in kind and congenial to their talents, but I also furnished them with a new arsenal of stock passages, essential to the *Commedia dell'arte*, and which they call its *dote*, or endowment.[1] I could not say how many prologues and epi-

---

[1] Gozzi uses the word *squarci* for these stock passages. The expression is explained by what follows in the paragraph. See Bartoli's *Scenari*, pp. lxxv. *et seq*. (S)

logues in verse I wrote, to be recited on the first and last evenings of the run of some play by the leading lady for the time
being; nor how many songs to be inserted in their farces; nor
how many thousand pages I filled with soliloquies, sallies of
despair, menace, reproach, supplication, paternal reprimand,
and such-like matters appropriate to all kinds of scenes in
improvised comedy. The players call such fragments of
studied rhetoric *generici*, or commonplaces. They are vastly
important to comedians who may not be specially gifted for
improvisation; and everything of the sort I found in their
repertory was vitiated by the turgid mannerisms of the
seicento.

I was godfather at the christening of their babies, author-
in-chief, counsellor, master, and mediator to the whole company; all this without assuming the pretentious airs of a
pedant or a claimant on their gratitude; but always at their
own entreaty, while I preserved the tone of disinterested,
humane, and playful condescension.

Some of the girls of this dramatic family—none of whom
were ugly, and none without some aptitude for the profession—begged me to help them with support and teaching.
I consented, provided them with parts adapted to their characters, taught them how they ought to act these parts, and put
them in the way of winning laurels. At their entreaties I
devoted some hours of my leisure to giving them more
general instruction. I made them read and translate French
books suited to their calling. I wrote them letters upon divers
familiar themes, calculated to make them think and develop
their sentiments under the necessity of composing some reply
or other. I corrected their mistakes, which were frequently of
the grossest and most unexpected kind, and laughed heartily
while doing so. This afforded me sprightly amusement and
gave them a dash of education.

When they left Venice for the customary six months,[1] I ran

[1] After the Carnival, until the following October. The theatrical
year in Venice began at the end of October, and ended with the next
Ash-Wednesday.

no risk of not receiving letters from them, written in rivalry with one another—sometimes real love-letters—arriving by each post from Milan, Turin, Genoa, Parma, Mantua, Bologna, all the cities where they stopped to act. Nor were answers wanting upon my side; playful, affectionate, threatening, derisive; taking any tone which I judged capable of keeping these young creatures wide-awake. It seemed to me that such an active correspondence and exchange of sentiments was the most appropriate and profitable school for a comedian.

Let no man deceive himself by supposing that it is possible to converse with actresses without love-making. You must make it, or pretend to make it. This is the only way to guide them to their own advantage. Love moulds and kneads them in flesh, bones, and marrow. Love begins to be their guiding-star at the age of five or six. In this respect, I soon discovered that the austerity of Sacchi's company was a barren formula; just as I had previously noticed that strictness in private families, beyond a certain point, had ceased to be accounted of utility or value.

Among actresses, the term friendship is something fabulous and visionary. They immediately substitute the word love, and do not attend to distinctions. Their idea of friendship only serves as the means of mutual deception between women, accompanied by deluges of endearing phrases and Judas kisses.

I ought, however, to declare that the actresses of Sacchi's company carried on their love-affairs with prudence and without indecency. The ideal of severity which prevailed there bore at least these fruits of goodness; and the ideal of honesty produced notably different results from those which other systems in the trade of love elicited elsewhere. How many actresses lay siege deliberately and in cold blood to their lovers, despoil them of their property, and do their very best to suck them dry! Catching at the locks of what they call their fortune and I call their infamy, these women do not stop to see whether the path before them be clean or filthy. They worship wickedness and abhor good living, if they hope to fill their purse or gratify their cupidity by the former. Though they strive to cloak their baseness with the veil of verbal decency, and do all in their power to preserve external decorum, in their souls they trample on shame and sing this verse :

> *Colla vergogna io già mi sono avvezza.*
> With infamy I long have been at home.

For the actresses of Sacchi's company, it is only justice to assert that they were far removed from harbouring such sentiments of vile and degrading venality.

There are two phrases in the slang of the profession; one is *miccheggiare*, which means to cozen folk out of their money by wheedling; the other is *gonzo*, gull or cully, the foolish lover who believes himself an object of affection, and squanders all his fortune under the influence of this impression. I must declare that the women of Sacchi's company never put the arts which these words imply into practice. They made love by instinct, inclination, and hereditary tradition.

This does not mean that they were not eager to get lovers who could support them on the stage, or who would be likely to marry them, and withdraw them from a calling which they always professed, hypocritically I believe, to abhor.

In what concerned myself, I looked upon their love-intrigues as duels of wit and comic passages, which furnished me amusement. Closely related to each other, and ambitious for advancement in their art, they regarded me as a bright shining star, worshipped by the leading members of the troupe, and capable of securing them success upon the stage. Their mutual rivalry, which I made use of for their own advantage, the profit of the company, and the success of my dramatic works, turned their brains. They would have done anything to gain my heart. Possibly some matrimonial projects entered into their calculations; but on this point I was always careful to disabuse them in the clearest terms. Meanwhile, their attentions, protests, fits of rage, jealousies, and tears on my account had all the scenic illusion of an overwhelming passion.

In the cities where they passed the spring and summer, the same comedy was re-enacted with a score of lovers. On their return to Venice, the correspondence which they carried on with these admirers, and which they vainly strove to hide from me, betrayed their inconstancy. By cross-examination and adroit suggestive questionings, I always brought them to make a clean breast of it, and their avowals furnished me with matter for exquisite amusement. They protested that the letters they received were written by young merchants or rich citizens, sometimes by gentlemen of the Lombard towns, who entertained the liveliest intentions of an honourable kind, and were only waiting for the death of an uncle or a father or a mother, all upon the point of dying of apoplexy or consumption or dropsy, to offer them their hands and fortunes. Finally, in order to reveal the sincerity of their hearts, when lying could no longer help them, they offered me these precious epistles. Probably they hoped to excite jealousy in my own breast. This opened a new chapter of diversion. I read the love-letters, and found that the vaunted admirers were either bombastic lady-killers or romancers or libertines, or sometimes, to my astonishment, dull Lombard hypocrites upon the scent of goatish pleasure.

I enlightened them, so far as this was possible; advised them not to waste their time in such perilous fooleries, which distracted their attention from the serious concerns of their profession; bade them look out for young comedians of talent, with whom they might marry and propagate the breed of actors. They never failed to express that loathing for the trade which all actresses profess, remaining actresses, however, in the utterance of their repugnance. In order to open their eyes to the real state of the case, I then dictated answers to these lovers, affectionately urging them to declare themselves on the essential point. Cold replies came with the next post, and after a short exchange of letters the correspondence dropped. In this way, they were brought to see their error, remaining always ready to resume it on the next occasion.

Their sentiments for me, according to their own showing,

were the most enduring and substantial; and my incredulous laughter wounded them. They bullied and maligned each other, complained, and accused their comrades at my judgment-seat. I pronounced sentence against them all; but the most persecuted were always the object of my heartiest protection. When I wrote parts adapted to their characters, they were lifted to the heavens. What obligations! What gratitude! What vows of love! I cannot deny that in certain moments they were justified in thinking they had gained my affection. The next day they found me quite another man, indifferent and icy cold. *Amour propre* then made them fly into a rage, and grow the angrier the more they saw me laugh at their frenzies.

All things considered, it is very difficult to frequent the society of young actresses, who harbour in their breast six books upon the art of love beside those of Ovid, to be their daily guide, philosopher, and friend, to make their fortunes in the theatre, and not to fall into some low matrimonial scrape, which would be called a solemn act of folly by the world. I use such terms as scrape, baseness, folly here, in order to adopt the language of people in general; although I am persuaded by personal observation, and by philosophical study of the current training given to girls, that it is easier to find a good wife on the stage than in private families. People in general are not philosophers enough to recognize and confess this truth; but the opinion of the general is always respectable.

My temperament, my abhorrence of ties, my partiality for study, the pity for human woes which I derived from knowledge of my neighbours, and the thirty-five years which I counted at the period in question, were my faithful counsellors. I have already written a chapter on my love-affairs, which sufficiently explain my sentiments.[1]

In the midst of these feminine intrigues and rivalries, it is impossible to distribute protection with perfect impartiality among all claimants. The girl who is most persecuted by her

[1] Translated in chaps. 22–24.

comrades, most looked down upon, and reckoned stupidest in her profession, will always be chosen out by me for support and advancement, without regard for hostile gossip bred by envy.

In the course of time I saw all these young women married, thanks to the fame they acquired through my efforts on their behalf. Some of them found husbands in the theatre, and some outside it. Without withdrawing my assistance from married actresses, I took care, from the moment of their nuptials, to cause no shadow of disturbance in their home. This I did by persistently refusing to visit them, which made them know me in my true principles apart from pleasantry. My conduct astounded them, and they affected notable displeasure at my withdrawal from their intimacy.

With regard to the chief men in this commonwealth of comedians, they were always most attentive lest I should receive annoyances. Above all things, they begged me not to take notice of any indiscretions prompted by levity, professional jealousy, touchiness on points of honour, pretensions to leading parts in my forthcoming plays, which might issue from the steaming brains of their women. I used to reply that, so long as the company maintained its good reputation, and so long as such quarrels and idle chatterings were confined to the women, I should never deign to be annoyed or to withdraw my aid and friendship from their troupe; but that if the men took to the same follies and dissensions as the women, I should have to think otherwise.

It was a comfort to me to pass my hours of leisure among those lively-witted, humorous, civil, merry people. It gratified me to observe that the men were eagerly sought after and invited to the tables of the quality and honest folk, while the women received similar attention from gentlefolk of their own sex, a thing almost unheard of with respect to others of their calling. Finally, I was pleased to see them thriving in their business and making profits by their theatre, which I had revived and continued to sustain by a long series of new and successful dramatic pieces. If prejudice or malignity were to cast it in my teeth that I had evil motives in this choice of my companions through so many years, I might easily turn the satire back against what is commonly called the respectable society of *casini*, assemblies, and coffee-houses. In order not to incur hatred by describing inconvenient facts, I will, however, confine myself to begging my critics to reflect and to be indulgent for differences of taste.

Returning to my comic protégés, I have yet to say that the insinuation of so-called culture into our theatres gradually corrupted the customs of this well-regulated family of actors, much in the same way as the advance of culture into private families corrupted domestic manners. Outsiders, hired at wages to swell the ranks and to take serious parts in tragedies or comedies, introduced a new freedom of thinking and behaving. The old habits of the troupe, which may perchance have only worn a feigned appearance of respectability, altered for the worse. The time has not arrived for describing this change, which I shall have to do in its proper place, since it was closely connected with important occurrences in my own life.

Some weaknesses are so entwined with our instincts as to be incurable. Such, in my case, are good faith and compliance, which often degenerated into silliness. During the whole course of my life, as my writings prove, and as is well known to my friends and acquaintances, I have always scourged hypocrisy. I cannot, however, deny the fact that the apparent honesty, piety, and good behaviour, in which my protégés persevered for so long a period, was convenient to their friends and extremely profitable to their pockets; whereas the freedom of thinking and acting introduced among them by the science of this depraved century and by so-called culture, brought them to the condition of the builders of the Tower of Babel.

I have seen them pass from ease to indigence, forget that they were relatives and friends—all at war together, all suspicious, each man of his neighbour; all irreconcilable and hostile—in spite of frequently renewed attempts on my part to bring them into harmony again; so that, at the last, I had to withdraw from their society, as will be stated in the sequel of these Memoirs.

32

The end of the rage for Goldoni and Chiari—I go on amusing my fellow-citizens with plays—Make reflections, and perhaps catch crabs

We had arrived at the year 1766, when it became evident that my band of comedians, by this time well established in their theatre, and supported by the public, who flocked eagerly to see the pieces I provided for them, were about to win a decisive victory over our adversaries. Chiari's works stood revealed in all their native nakedness; the glamour of enchantment had departed. Those of Goldoni, in spite of their real merit, did not make the same effect as in the past. People noticed that he repeated himself; they discovered poverty of ideas, flaccidity, and faults of construction in his later pieces. They said that he was played out.

The truth is that a rage so vehement and fanatical as that created by Chiari and Goldoni was bound to die away. They had been so much spoken and quarrelled about that their very names began to pall upon the ear. In Italy, moreover, there is no well-founded and intelligent respect for authors.[1] Dramatists in particular are merely regarded as purveyors of ephemeral amusement. Perhaps Venice exceeds every other capital in this way of thinking. A Venetian citizen, to take a single instance, was congratulating Goldoni on the success of one of his comedies; then, as though ashamed of condescending to so trivial a theme, he added: 'It is true that works of this sort are trifles, which do not deserve our serious attention;

[1] From the beginning of the chapter down to this point Symonds freely paraphrases the Memoirs.

and yet I can imagine that you may have been gratified by the reception of your play.'

Goldoni, with true business-like prudence, had compelled the shabby Italian comedians to pay him thirty sequins for every piece, good, bad, or indifferent, which he supplied them. I gave my dramatic fancies away gratis. It is very probable that, finding themselves eclipsed by what their rivals got for nothing, Goldoni's paymasters waxed insolent against him.

Chiari stopped writing when he saw that his dramas ceased to take. Goldoni went to Paris, to seek his fortune there, whereof we shall be duly informed in his Memoirs. Sacchi's company remained in possession of the field and earned a handsome competency. A few dramatists of small intelligence, self-styled purveyors of culture, tried to ape Goldoni and suffered the fate that was to be expected, considering the staleness of their vein and the lifeless pedantry of their feeble talents.

It became a necessity, a sort of customary law dictated by my friendship, to present these actors every year or two with pieces from my pen. The ability with which they had interpreted my fancies deserved gratitude; and the sympathy of the Venetians, who had so warmly welcomed them, called for recognition. Accordingly, I added the *Snake Woman*, *Zobeide*, and the *Blue Monster* to those dramatic fables which I have already mentioned. This brought us down to the year 1766.[1]

The new *genre* which I had brought into fashion, and which, by being confined to Sacchi's company, inflicted vast damage on their professional rivals, inspired other so-called poets with the wish to imitate me. They relied on splendid decorations, transformation scenes, and frigid buffooneries. They did not comprehend the allegorical meanings, nor the

---

[1] This is not quite accurate. The *Mostro turchino (Blue Monster)* was first performed on 8 December 1764, whilst the *Donna serpente* and *Zobeide* were performed earlier still, in October 1762 and November 1763 respectively. The last of the ten *fiabe* was *Zeim re de' geni (The King of the Genii)*, performed on 25 November 1765.

P

polite satire upon manners, nor the art of construction, nor the conduct of the plot, nor the real intrinsic force of the species I had handled. I say they did not comprehend the value of these things, because I do not want to say that they were deficient in power to command and use them. The result was that their pieces met with the condemnation which their contempt for me and for the public who appreciated me richly deserved.

You cannot fabricate a drama worthy to impress the public mind for any length of time by heaping up absurdities, marvels, scurrilities, prolixities, puerilities, insipidities, and nonsense. The neglect into which the imitations of my manner speedily fell proves this. Much the same may be said about those other species—romantic or domestic, intended to move tears or laughter—those cultured and realistic kinds of drama, as people called them, though they were generally devoid of culture and of realism, and were invariably as like each other as two peas, which occupied our stage for thirty years at least. All the good and bad that has been written and printed about my fables; the fact that they still hold the stage in Italy and other countries where they are translated in spite of their comparative antiquity; the stupid criticisms which are still being vented against them by starving journalists and envious bores, who join the cry and follow these blind leaders of the blind—criticisms only based upon the titles and arguments I chose to draw from old wives' tales and stories of the nursery—all this proves that there is real stuff in the fabulous, poetical, allegorical *genre* which I created. I say this without any presumptuous partiality for the children of my fancy; nor do I resent the attacks which have been made upon them, for I am humane enough to pity the hungry and the passion-blinded.

Goldoni, who was then at Paris, vainly striving to revive the Italian theatre in that metropolis, heard of the noise my fables were making in Italy, and abased himself so far as to send a fabulous composition of his own fabrication back to Venice. It was called *The Good Genius and the Evil Genius*, and appeared at the theatre of S. Giovanni Grisostomo, enjoying a long run. The cause of its success lay in the fact that his piece displayed dramatic art, agreeable characters, moral reflection, and some philosophy. I conclude, therefore, that allegorical fables on the stage are not so wholly contemptible.

At the same time, just as there are differences between the different kinds of dogs, fishes, birds, snakes, and so forth, though they all belong to the species of dogs, fishes, &c., so are there notable differences between Goldoni's *Good and Evil Geniuses* and my ten *Fiabe*, though all are grouped under the one species of dramatic fable. Goldoni, who has deserved renown for his domestic comedies, had not the gifts necessary for producing poetic fables of this kind; nor could I ever understand why my ridiculous censors cast the ephemeral success of his two *Geniuses* in my teeth, with the hope of mortifying a pride I did not feel.

The dramatic fable, if written to engage the interest of the public and to keep its hold upon the theatre, is more difficult than any other species. Unless it contains a grandeur which imposes, some impressive secret which enchants, novelty sufficient to arrest attention, eloquence to enthral, sententious maxims of philosophy, witty and attractive criticisms, dialogues prompted by the heart, and, above all, the great magic of seduction whereby impossibilities are made to seem real and evident to the mind and senses of the audience—unless it contains all these elements, I repeat, it will never produce a firm and distinctive impression, nor will it repay the pains and perseverance of our poor actors by its permanent pecuniary value. It may be that my fables possess none of these qualities. Yet the fact remains that they contrived to produce the effects I have described.

In the year 1766, Gozzi reinstituted proceedings against Marchese Terzi of Bergamo. He threw himself heart and soul into the battle and settled down to make a personal study of the legal documents. He writes :

I procured one of those licences, which are technically called courtesies, from Signor Daniele Zanchi, the defendant's advocate, to study the documents at his chambers, and set myself down with imperturbable phlegm to peruse millions of lines in antique characters, faded, half-effaced, semi-Gothic, and for the most part hieroglyphical. I selected those which seemed to the purpose, and had forty-two volumes of transcripts filled at my cost by Signor Zanchi's copyist.

Painful circumstances leave ineffaceable impressions on the memory. The examination of those vast masses of manuscript, word by word and letter by letter, so different from delightful literature in prose or verse, taxed every nerve and fibre. I well remember that my study of them lasted over more than two months, in the dead of a hard snowy winter. Signor Zanchi, taking pity on my shivering wretchedness, kindly furnished me with a brazier of live coals; and yet I thought, what with the irksome labour and the cold, that I should have to breathe my last between the walls of the fortress of my enemies.

After three years of exhausting litigation and the expenditure of the sum of 17,000 lire (part of which was supplied by the loyal and generous Massimo) the case was settled in Gozzi's favour. The effort had taxed his health, but had not prevented him from writing more pieces for the theatre. As he says:

It is not to be wondered at that I fell ill at last. But what will seem more wonderful, nay, almost incredible, is that I sought distraction during my few leisure hours in planning and composing dramatic pieces. I used to take sheets of paper, on which I had sketched the outlines of scenes, in my pocket down to a coffee-house on the Riva degli Schiavoni. There I engaged a room facing S. Giorgio, had coffee brought, and ordered pen and ink. Thus furnished, I forgot my troubles for a while in the elaboration of soliloquies and dialogues. It was in this way that, while my suit dragged on through three tempestuous years, I produced the *Green Bird*, the *King of the Genii*, the *Vindictive Woman*, the *Fall of Donna Elvira*, and the *Open Secret*.[1] I flatter myself that none of these plays be-

---

[1] *L'augellin Belverde, Zeim re de' geni, La donna vendicativa, La caduta di donna Elvira, Il pubblico secreto.*

trayed the melancholy and distraction of a harassed brain. They were welcomed with enthusiasm by the public, and brought fame and profit to my friends the actors.

33

The beginning of dissensions in Sacchi's company—My attitude of forbearance and ridiculous heroisms

Having spent ten years of serene recreation among my professional friends, the time had come for clouds to gather on the horizon. *Two Nights of Tribulation*,[1] my last dramatic venture, was the source of much profit to Sacchi. But the company, while gaining strength from actors hired to sustain serious parts, began to degenerate in their behaviour. Though they professed the same severe morality as formerly, I noticed signs of change and of dissension. Differences between relatives spread the seeds of future dissolution. The imported actors helped the theatre, but introduced pernicious ideas into this previously happy family. They criticized the administration of the property; accused the managers of injustice, tyranny, even fraud; sympathized with those who thought themselves oppressed; threw stones, and carefully concealed the hands which launched them. Pluming themselves upon their sapience, they contrived to persuade the troupe that the plays I gave for nothing were not so beneficial as the latter blindly believed. They ascribed the crowds which filled the theatre to the attraction of stage decorations and their own spirited performance. Not unlike the fly in Aesop's fable, they exclaimed: 'Look at the dust which we are raising!' By artfully reckoning the cost of putting my fables on the stage, and by insinuating calumnies against the managers, they brought some of the sharers into a state of mutiny, made them depreciate my services, and stirred up anger and suspicion against

[1] *Le due notti affannose.*

Sacchi. Finally, they got them to think it would be more advantageous to exchange their shares for salaries, and prepared them for hating one another cordially.

The older and more sagacious comedians still continued to pay me court and beg for my poetical assistance. I thought it, however, wiser to suspend my collaboration for a year or two, without showing annoyance, or letting it be known that I was aware of what was being said against me. I could not take a better way of bringing them back to reason; and my private engagements provided me with a good pretext for withdrawing my assistance.

In the first year after my retirement, the public began to grumble at the lack of new pieces. In the second, it began to growl. The audiences thinned, and Sacchi's theatre became a desert. There were not wanting folk who from the boxes shouted insults at the actors. Their dejection increased daily; and then they all with one accord broke into protestations of affection and fervent entreaties for my help.

I had accustomed the public to novel kinds of drama, and the company had seconded my efforts. I did not think it right to assist them for ten years and then to drop them. To condescend to take affront at what comedians say or do is utterly impossible for me. I could, indeed, have laughed in their faces and turned my back. But I preferred to laugh in my sleeve while once more coming to their aid with the energy and good results which I shall presently describe.

The owners of the other theatres in Venice, finding themselves extremely injured by the plays I gave to Sacchi, kept making me proposals to write for their houses; and the pretty actresses who worked there seconded these misplaced endeavours by spreading snares to catch me with their charms. Though my old protégés would have richly deserved it, I had the burlesque heroism not to desert them.

Sacchi often complained of having to remain in theatres out of the way and inconvenient for the people, such as S. Samuele and S. Angelo, where only striking novelties like mine could draw large houses. He was always sighing to get the lease of S. Salvatore,[1] a most popular theatre, since it is situated at the centre of the town, within easy reach of its densely inhabited quarters. Now it so happened that this theatre was occupied by a company which performed pieces in the fashion introduced by Chiari and Goldoni. I have already said that the vogue of such things had declined; and the proprietor, his Excellency Vendramin, was anxious to secure me in the interest of his failing house. He sent a priest of my acquaintance, a certain Don Baldassare, as envoy, offering me his cordial regards, together with considerable emoluments, if I would pass from Sacchi's company to that which occupied S. Salvatore. I draped myself in the dignity of Attilius Regulus, and replied that I did not write for money, but for pastime. As long as Sacchi's troupe kept together and remained competent, I did not mean to give away my work to any other. If his Excellency had the fancy to see plays of mine performed at his theatre, he could indulge it by placing the house at Sacchi's disposal. Not many months passed before I was chosen by that gentleman as arbitrator between him and Sacchi. I acted the solicitor, drew up a lease, and installed my manager in the theatre his heart was set on.

I should have liked to devote myself entirely to my private studies; but the responsibility I had taken by transferring Sacchi's company to S. Salvatore, together with the informal engagement I felt under to Signor Vendramin, made me resume my task of writing for the stage. I ought to add that my old habit of associating with actors weighed strongly with me in this circumstance. Therefore a new chapter of some fourteen years of my life was opened, the principal events of which I mean to write with all the candour and piquancy I can.

[1] This theatre was also called S. Luca. (S)

34

Dangerous innovations in Sacchi's company—My attempts to arrange matters, my threats, prognostications, and obstinate persistence on the point of honour to support my protégés—Things sufficent to move reasonable mirth against me

The grant of the theatre at S. Salvatore for the next year had hardly been handed over to Sacchi, when the other troupe, who were expelled to make room for him, engaged the theatre at S. Angelo, which he was leaving, and began at once to plot revenge. They tried, by flatteries and promises of money (always needed by Italian comedians), to circumvent the best actors of the company, among whom were Cesare Darbes, the excellent Pantalone, and Agostino Fiorilli, the famous Tartaglia. In fact, they did seduce these two champions of impromptu comedy to desert Sacchi's ranks and join their squadron, more with the object of weakening our forces than of strengthening theirs, since their own members were unfit for any performances but those of the so-called cultivated drama.

This desertion mortified the sharers in Sacchi's company, and they whispered their misfortunes in my ears. For my own part, I was sorry to think that the quartette of masks, real natural wonders, who made such pleasant mirth in concert, should be scattered. I determined, therefore, to try whether I could not dissuade these two actors from the somewhat shabby step they had resolved on. When I remonstrated with Darbes, who was my gossip, the answer he gave me ran as follows: Precisely because I feared that you would attempt to separate me from my new comrades, and because I know my inability to refuse you anything, I concealed the agreement from your eyes, and signed it in secret, so that I might not have it in my power to comply with your request. It grieves me that I am no longer able to meet your wishes.' On hearing this preposterous excuse, I lost my humour for a moment, and burst into serious reproaches. He assumed a theatrical air of sorrow, and defended himself by repeating the complaints which were current among the disaffected members of Sacchi's troupe. I contented myself with prophesying that he would find himself without place or part in his new company, adding by way of menace that I should well know how to make him repent of his desertion to the enemy.

Then I repaired to Fiorilli with as much solicitude as though I were bent on averting some grave disaster from myself. Him I found more tractable. He had not signed his agreement; and I was able to reconcile him with his old comrades, and to make him subscribe a paper, by which he promised to remain with them for the next three years.

A bad system of etiquette divides the actors and actresses of every troupe in Italy into first, second, third, and so forth. It happened at this time that Sacchi had dismissed his first actress, Regina Cicucci, a very able artist, but one who had not won great fame with Venetian playgoers. 'What a fine stroke of business it would be,' said he to me one day, 'if we could rob our rivals of their first actress, Caterina Manzoni! The revenge would be complete and just, and I should be provided with a leading lady. I am afraid, however,' he added, 'that my company would not suit her.' Signora Manzoni was my good friend. I appreciated her talents, her personal attractions, her cultivated manner and her educated mind. She had often asked me whether I could not introduce her into Sacchi's company; and though I did not usually mix myself up with such affairs, the present occasion and Sacchi's speech inclined me to attempt a negotiation.

Accordingly, I made proposals to the lady, which she welcomed with great delight and profuse expressions of gratitude. Some differences with regard to appointments and other details arose. These I settled, like an able broker, and brought the bargain to an agreement. When I presented the papers for her signature, the beautiful young woman met me with an air of sadness, which added to her charms. She looked as though she had not the courage to address me. I did not understand what this meant, and strove to hearten her up. At length she told me, dropping a few lovely tears, that her former friends and comrades, when they got wind of her meditated desertion, had come to her weeping violently, and had flung themselves at her feet imploring her not to abandon them to certain ruin. Moved by a spirit of compassion, she had signed a paper which obliged her to remain with them for some years to come.

Although I knew the tenderness of her heart, I did not think her capable of such a breach of promise through mere sensibility. She must have had stronger reasons for breaking the engagement she had entered into with me; and if she ever writes her Memoirs, we shall hear of them.[1] Perhaps I ought to have lost my jovial humour, as I did with Darbes. I could not do so in the face of so much beauty. I only told her, with a smile upon my lips, that she was her own mistress; Sacchi might get a first actress of any sort he could; I should have wit enough to make the person as able an artist as my fair renegade. With these words I engaged myself to a new point of honour.

I have never regretted that I treated Signora Manzoni in this courteous fashion. She has always shown me the attentions of delicate and cordial politeness; and it is only justice to declare that she possesses qualities which would be estimable in a gentlewoman. A few years after the events related here she married, retired from the profession, and devoted herself to the education of her two little boys in sound moral and religious principles.

When I reported the failure of my negotiation to Sacchi, he replied roughly: 'I knew that the person in question could never have adjusted herself to my company.' Then he pushed

---

[1] This looks as though Gozzi had reason to believe that Caterina Manzoni would write her autobiography. . . . The remark shows how popular and common self-indited Memoirs had become. (S)

forward his correspondence for the engagement of another prima donna.

I should like my readers to believe that my intervention in the affair I have described was due principally to my regard for the Cavaliere[1] who granted his theatre at my request to Sacchi's company. Really afraid that their internal dissensions, rivalries, and intrigues might reduce them to a state of impotence, and that his interests would suffer in consequence, I wished to avoid having any share in this disaster. A barren and old-fashioned delicacy!

35

Sacchi forces me to give advice—Teodora Ricci enters his company as first actress—An attempt at sketching her portrait—The beginnings of my interest in this comedian

Whenever Sacchi had to engage a prima donna, all the other actresses rose up in tumult. Why they should have done so, when the engagement was merely temporary, remains a mystery. That they were connected among themselves by blood or marriage does not explain their conspiracy. The newcomers had to endure a martyrdom of criticism, depreciation in their art, and gross calumny in their morals. Who knows whether the prospect of such imminent tribulation did not form one reason of Signora Manzoni's defection? These details do not appear to have any bearing on my Memoirs; but it will soon be seen that they have only too much.

Sacchi always affected, out of prudence, to consult with me on his affairs, especially at this time, when the change of theatre had disorganized his system of management. Accordingly, he informed me one day that he was in treaty with two

[1] That is, the Venetian noble Antonio Vendramin. (S)

first actresses, and asked for my advice. One of them was Signora Maddalena Battagia, a Tuscan by birth, talented, but no longer in her prime, incapable of taking part in the *Commedia dell'arte*, and extremely exacting with regard to precedence, etiquette, and a substantial salary. The other was Signora Teodora Ricci; from what he heard about her, she was a beginner, young, full of spirit, with a fine figure and voice, who had been applauded in every city where she had appeared; moreover, she was accustomed to act in the *Commedia dell'arte*. She had a husband of some distinction as a player; and Sacchi could get them both at a salary of only 520 ducats a year.

I had never heard before of either. But after weighing and comparing their testimonials and correspondence, I gave a laconic answer: 'Engage Signora Ricci with her husband.' This is precisely what Sacchi had resolved in his own mind on doing; and his appeal to me for counsel was only a comedian's way of feigning esteem and sense of dependence.

Signora Ricci and her husband were bound over under articles for three years at a salary of 520 ducats. This was a wretched stipend for a poor actress, who had to provide herself with a decent wardrobe on the stage, to meet the expenses of frequent journeys, and to maintain a husband and a son; and who, moreover, was expecting her confinement, and was about to expose herself to all the calumnies, criticisms, and venomous detractions of the allied women of the company.

My new protégée reached Venice in the Lent of 1771. I received an invitation from Sacchi to meet her and her husband at his house one evening, on their arrival from Genoa. He wanted me to hear her recite a passage from some tragedy, in order that I might form an estimate of her manner, her talent, and her disposition. I saw at once that she was a young woman of fine figure, though her pregnancy took off from its appearance. Her face with pitted with the small-pox; but this did not prevent it from being theatrically effective at a distance. The abundance of her beautiful blond hair made up for some defects of feature. Her clothes, which betrayed a scanty purse, were well put on; and she carried them with such an air and grace that no one stopped to think whether they were of silk or wool, new or worn. She seemed to be somewhat constrained by the unfamiliar society in which she found herself. I could not make my mind up whether her reserve and shyness were the result of timidity or cunning. Yet I detected in her something of habitual impatience. She chafed because her husband did her little honour in our conversation. He, good man, slept sweetly, in spite of the clandestine nudges which she gave him.

She recited the fragment of a tragic scene in verse, with a fine and powerful voice, sound sense, intelligence, and a fire which gave good hopes of her in her profession, especially in fierce vituperative parts. I noticed a trifle of hardness and monotony in her declamation, and some other defects which could be remedied. One incurable fault she had; this was the movement of her lips, which often amounted to what is called making a wry face. Her mouth, not small by nature, had been relaxed and ravaged at its angles by the small-pox, so that the poor young woman could not overcome the involuntary fault of which I speak. I must add a physiological observation I have made, which bears upon this point. When we feel disgust for any object disagreeable to our senses, we naturally express it by a writhing of the mouth. Signora Ricci, through prejudice, or through something proud and wayward in her temper, was always hearing and seeing things which she felt nauseous and repulsive, and this repugnance stamped itself upon her features in a contortion of the lips. Enforcing and stereotyping the physical blemish in question, it became an ineradicable habit, or rather second nature.

When the trial-piece was finished, I paid her some deserved compliments, and sought to inspire her with a courage which seemed lacking in her demeanour. The other actresses hung upon my words; but Sacchi, more attentive to his interests than to what I was saying, turned towards me and spoke: 'Signor Conte, I have engaged this young woman at your advice; pray bear in mind that you have a duty to perform—

that is, of making her useful to our company.' I replied that I would do the utmost in my power, both for him and for her, as soon as I had made myself acquainted with her real gifts for comedy and tragedy. On the faces of the other actresses I read a sullen sadness and a disposition to squirt poison.

The company was bound for Mantua. Signora Ricci begged for my assistance in studying the new parts assigned to her during the few days which remained before they left Venice. I complied; and hardly a day passed without my going to her lodgings, and giving her the instructions I thought needful. Feeling my honour pledged by what I had said to Darbes and Signora Manzoni, and wishing to establish a strong troupe in Cavaliere Vendramin's theatre, I had pronounced a good opinion of young Teodora Ricci's future, and I was sincerely anxious not to find it faulty. She received me with affability and an air of satisfaction. As the days went on, I discovered in her gifts above the average.

Sometimes I found her plunged in sadness; and on inquiring the reason, she told me that she saw certain ruin staring her in the face. She had entered a company of actresses and actors related by blood, and all allied against her. She was alone, without protection and support. Her mother had reproved and terrified her for having accepted this position, prophesying that she would be discredited and driven out of Venice, to the loss of all the fame which she had gained in other cities. I laughed at her fears and presentiments, although they were far from being mere phantoms of her imagination, and tried to make her believe the great falsehood that real merit always ends by overcoming obstacles. I promised to write pieces adapted to her talents. If she could but once make herself necessary to the company by winning the favour of the public, all her difficulties would vanish. But this could only be achieved by conquering her trepidation and steeling her mind against untoward circumstances.

The respect I enjoyed in Sacchi's troupe for past favours conferred and future benefits expected impressed her mind; and she resolved to cultivate my friendship as her only stay.

Her poverty moved my compassion; and I liked her civil hearty ways of greeting me, which seemed sincere. I wanted to study her disposition in order to compose parts suited for her; but time was short, and I could not do much. Meanwhile, my visits and attentions roused the jealousy of the other actresses. They used to question me with affected nonchalance upon Signora Ricci's talent; confessed they saw great faults in her, and doubted whether she could ever be of service to the company; but ingenuously added that they hoped they were mistaken. Seeing through their artifice, I repeated my favourable prognostications, and engaged myself to secure the fulfilment of my prophecies.

It was then that calumnies began to fly abroad against my poor new pupil's moral character. That was only what had to be expected. Everybody knew the reports for facts, and nobody had set them going. I have said that my habit of protecting the persecuted amounted to a vice. Now that she was attacked in her honour, I vowed with greater fervour to defend and rehabilitate her.

The troupe departed in due course of time for Mantua; thence they passed to Verona, where Teodora Ricci was delivered of a baby, which Heaven in kindness removed from this world. Letters arrived from these cities depreciating her talents, accusing her of invincible defects, and prejudicing the public mind against her. Meanwhile, the partisans of two able actresses in the rival company at S. Angelo were not idle; and I foresaw that I should have formidable obstacles to overcome before I succeeded in establishing her reputation. This only made me the more obstinate.

Not being thoroughly acquainted as yet with her character and special gifts, I composed a drama called *The Woman Who Was Truly in Love*.[1] My object was to place her in different lights, and to give her the opportunity of hitting the public taste in one point or another. She had to play the part of a lady in love, exiled, forced to disguise herself as a waiter, then

[1] *La donna innamorata da vero*, printed in vol. ix of the *Opere*, ed. cit. (S)

as a gipsy, then as a soldier, then as a gentleman of quality, in order to hide from the pursuit of justice and to remain faithful to her passionate attachment. At the least I hoped that great pains in the performance of this rôle might win for her indulgence and favour. I had reason to see that I was mistaken in my expectations and my judgment. The piece, though it proved successful in itself, was not adapted to Signora Ricci. Sacchi, however, wrote about it and the actress enthusiastically from Mantua, where it was exhibited.

I shall now have to describe the début of this young artist at Venice, the difficulties we met with, the triumph which finally confirmed my prophecies, and the friendship which I maintained with her for the space of six years. Many of my friends have asked for the real history of this friendship. It was always my habit to waste no breath in talking, but to use up several pens without fatigue in writing. I shall, therefore, very likely be too long and prolix in my narrative of a friendship, which folk are quite at liberty to call love if they like. Since it occupied six years of my life, I cannot omit it; but every one is at liberty to skip the following chapters if they find them tedious.[1]

---

[1] It cannot be denied that Gozzi has spun out the history of his liaison with Teodora Ricci to a tedious length, giving the episode of Pietro Antonio Gratarol an importance which it is far from deserving. I intend therefore to abridge the chapters which he invites his readers to skip. But, with the view of preserving unity of style, I shall not drop the first person singular, and shall select, so far as this is possible, nothing but phrases of Gozzi to translate. (S) From this point, in fact, the English text becomes progressively less a literal translation and more a free paraphrase of the Italian. The highest degree of condensation occurs between chapters 41 and 45, which reduce the corresponding section of Gozzi's text to a third of its original length.

36

Teodora Ricci makes her début at Venice without marked success—My reasons for feeling engaged in honour to support her

My histrionic phalanx returned to Venice, and took possession for the first time of the theatre at S. Salvatore, deprived of one of their best actors, Darbes. The managers of the company wished to keep the public in suspense about the new actress for the first few nights. This is the common policy of such people. They reason thus: 'We are all of us novelties at the beginning of the season. Let us keep the new actor in reserve to stimulate the public when our own attractions fall off. Come what may, we are sure to have our purses full that night at least.' Desire of gain is their only motive principle.

At last the time came for poor Teodora Ricci to be exhibited. The flaming announcement of *new actress, new play*, drew a full house. My piece was well received; but Signora Ricci was voted a barely tolerable artist. This pleased the other actresses of the troupe and amused me, who had formed a very decided opinion of her real ability. She next appeared as the Queen of England in the old play of the *Earl of Essex*.[1] Poorly dressed, she raised no applause, although she acted well; and her capital sentence seemed to be irrevocable.

About this time Sacchi asked me to translate a French play called *Fayel*,[2] in which he proposed to give the part of Gabrielle to the débutante Teodora Ricci. I remember that I scribbled off this version in the small rooms of the theatre while my friends were acting; an earthen pipkin with some ink in it and a dirty stump of a pen, supplied by the green-room man, helped me through it in a few evenings.

[1] *Il Conte d'Essex* (probably the tragedy by Thomas Corneille).
[2] By the playwright François-Thomas-Marie de Baculard d'Arnaud (1718–1805).

Q

Before it appeared I chose to have my translation published, together with an essay inveighing against the habit of importing plays from France. The stir caused by this essay, together with other circumstances, drew a large house on the first night of *Fayel*. Teodora Ricci sustained the part of Gabrielle admirably; but it so happened that Signora Manzoni had recently been acting a nearly identical rôle[1] at the theatre of S. Angelo, and her partisans determined to crush the débutante, whom they considered a presumptuous rival. This third failure made her ruin palpable to every eye.

Fervid and impetuous by nature, proud as Lucifer, and intensely ambitious, she chafed and wept, took to her bed, and raged there like a lioness, cursing the hour when she had joined Sacchi's troupe and set her foot in Venice. As far as possible, she concealed the true cause of her fury, and dwelt on family difficulties, her poverty, and a new confinement in prospect. To my attempts at consolation, though flattering and reasonable, she turned a deaf ear.

It was then that, having gained a perfect knowledge of her character, I composed my *Philosopher-Princess*,[2] precisely with a view to her. When I read it to the company, they broke forth into their usual extravagant laudations. But just at this time they were plotting the removal of Signora Ricci; and the actresses most interested in expelling her from the troupe raised obstacles against the *Princess* being put upon the stage. They buzzed about from ear to ear that my drama was languid and tiresome. I had omitted the four masks, and had constructed the piece with the sole object of bolstering up an actress already out of credit and rejected by the public. Teodora Ricci chafed with rage; while I continued to laugh, knowing well that I should find the means of bringing these passion-blinded creatures back to reason.

Just then it happened that the patrician of Venice, Fran-

---

[1] The title-rôle of *La Gabriella*, an Italian translation of *Gabrielle de Vergy*, a tragedy by the French playwright De Belloy (Pierre-Laurent Buyrette, 1727–75).

[2] *La principessa filosofa*, printed in vol. v of the *Opere*, ed. cit. (S)

cesco Gritti, one of our best and liveliest pens, translated Piron's tragedy of *Gustavus Vasa* from the French.[1] At my request, he gave this play to Sacchi, assigning the part of Adelaide to Teodora Ricci. New difficulties and new intrigues arose among the jealous actresses. These I put down with a high hand, the play in question being not my own, but my distinguished friend's donation to the company. Signora Ricci learned her part with diligence and ease. Her chief anxiety was about her costume; for the managers refused to make her any advances on this score, and her rivals, who took subordinate parts in the tragedy, were straining all the resources of their lengthier purse to outshine her by the wardrobe. I amused myself enormously at their ill-founded expectations. When the night arrived, the play was very decently got up, and Signora Ricci entered on the scene far better dressed than any of her comrades. *Gustavus Vasa* had a decided success; and Teodora Ricci, who played Adelaide well, but certainly not better than the three parts which had well-nigh ruined her, was encouraged by a fair amount of applause. I could see how much good this little gleam of sunshine did her.

Meanwhile days flew by without anything being said about my *Philosopher-Princess*. I thereupon determined to try what a little artifice could do. I began by confiding to some of our actors that I could not resist the wish to see this piece upon the stage; and that appreciating Sacchi's reasons for not venturing to take the risk of it, I was thinking of offering my *Princess* to the company at S. Angelo. Signora Manzoni, I added, seemed to be admirably fitted for the leading part. No sooner was it whispered that I intended to follow Darbes to the rival camp, than marvellous alacrity began to be displayed. Sacchi, always violent and excessive, insisted that the

---

[1] Francesco Gritti (1740–1811) came of an ancient patrician family. He is best known for his satirical poems in Venetian dialect, the *Apologhi* (published posthumously in *Poesie*, Venice, Alvisopoli, 1815). Apart from Piron's tragedy, he also translated tragedies by Voltaire and Ducis, Voltaire's *Pucelle d'Orléans*, and Montesquieu's *Temple de Gnide*.

Philosopher-Princess should be got up and ready for representation in the course of a few days. In fact, this piece appeared on 8 February 1772. Teodora Ricci, carefully coached by me, sustained the title-rôle with astonishing spirit. She was welcomed with thunders of applause; and a run of eighteen nights to overflowing houses established her reputation as an artist of incomparable energy and spirit. This joint triumph of author and actress made the latter necessary to Sacchi's company. Yet some of her comrades persisted in regarding her with covered rancour. They never acknowledged her talents, and ascribed her success to the rôle I had composed for her.

37

A pliant disposition is apt to neglect the dictates of reflection—I proceed with my narrative regarding Signora Ricci and myself

If the company loaded me with gratitude, Teodora Ricci was not behindhand with the same sweet incense. She professed herself wholly and simply indebted to my zeal, good management, and friendship for her victory. She did everything in her power, and laid herself out in every way to secure my daily visits. So long as I frequented her house, she felt safe from her persecutors; and her main ambition was to commit me to an open and deliberate partiality. She did not, however, know the true characters of her comrades, nor yet my fundamental principles and temperament; nor, what was worse, did she know herself.

Had I declared that open partiality which she desired, it is certain that I should have exposed her to still more trying enmities and persecutions. The managers of the troupe, governed exclusively by calculations of interest, would have felt themselves compelled to curry favour with me by indulging her in all her whims, demands, breaches of discipline, and a thousand feminine caprices. Nothing could be more alien to my real character than to make myself the proud and domineering protector of one actress to the injury of her companions. Besides, her views and mine were so fundamentally at variance upon some elementary points of conduct, that I doubted whether a liaison between us could ever be of long duration. Light-headed, vain, and sensitive to flattery, she had no regard for prudence and propriety; nor did she recognize those faults in herself which were always involving her in difficulties. I knew, moreover, that characters like hers must sooner or later incline to those who caress their foibles and pervert their judgment, while they come to regard their real friends and honest counsellors as tiresome pedants. She had no grounds for believing that I was in love with her. Yet, such was her self-assurance, that she interpreted my kind offices on her behalf into signs of submission to her charms. Finally, though I was far from believing all she said about her affection for my person, I determined to extend to her a cordial friendship.

There are two classes of sinners, whom the world, however dissolute, will always hold in abhorrence—the shameless cynic and the hypocrite. Libertines invariably attempt to confound prudent and respectable friends of women with the odious tribe of hypocrites.[1] I delighted in the theatre. I was known, appreciated, and courted by actors and actresses of all sorts, composers, singers, ballet-dancers. They came to me for advice and support on all occasions. I had to write pieces for them, prologues, epilogues, and what not. I was consulted about the arrangement of pantomimic scenes, dances, words for music. If the innumerable actresses with whom I conversed were to give their testimony, it would appear that I never took advantage of these opportunities to play the part of a seducer or a libertine. These Memoirs I am writing, together with the whole tenor of my life through a long course of years, suffice to clear me from the imputation of hypocrisy.

[1] Gozzi is here answering Gratarol, who had called him a hypocrite in his *Narrazione*. (S)

Some of my readers will probably suppose that I am making a vain parade of philosophy in order to gain credit for virtues I did not possess. Others will call me a simpleton for not availing myself more freely of my exceptional position among the beauties of the stage. What I am going to relate concerning my friendship for Signora Ricci will show that I erred upon the side of simplicity and folly. It was my fixed intention to benefit her, and at the same time to benefit the troupe I had taken under my protection, by making her an able artist and verifying my own opinion of her talents in the teeth of jealousy and opposition.

She had spirit, a good voice, a retentive memory, extraordinary rapidity of perception, and a fine figure, which she knew how to set off to the best advantage. On the other hand, she was inattentive to the conduct of a dialogue, deficient in naturalness and in real sensibility for the rôles she undertook. These defects, which are fatal to scenical illusion, proceeded from lack of intelligence, want of real heart for her business, and all kinds of feminine distractions. Some literary culture would have been of service to her; but, like all Italian actresses, she was deficient in such culture. According to her own account, she had been the most neglected of five or more sisters. After taking some lessons in dancing, she abandoned that branch of the profession because of a physical weakness in her knee-joints. Her mother, poor, and with a drunken husband, then made her the domestic drudge. Since she showed some talent for acting, however, a certain Pietro Rossi begged this woman to let her enter his company of players. She made no difficulties; and signing the girl's forehead with a large maternal cross, sent her out into the world with this practical injunction : 'Go and earn your bread; do not come back to be a burden to the family, where there are too many mouths to feed already.' Throwing herself with courage and closed eyes into her new career, Teodora won applause by her natural aptitude for acting, and by the charm of her youth. The piece I wrote for her placed her well before the public, and I was not at all doubtful of her future success. Yet I could not but apprehend that her defective moral education, her inflammable and reckless disposition, might make me one day repent of my cordiality and intimacy.

In conversation with this young woman I enjoyed no exchange of wit or sentiment, no perspicacity of intellect, no piquant sallies and discussions. On the other hand, her way of meeting me was always frank and open; she showed much decency and neatness in her poverty; told anecdotes with comic grace; mimicked her comrades, the actresses, with spirit; evinced a real repugnance for immodesty; betrayed the ingenuousness of her nature by a hundred little traits. What above all attracted me towards her was that she could not tell a lie without showing by involuntary blushes how much the effort cost her. Time taught me that I ought to mistrust her apparent ingenuousness. The artless sallies with which she turned old friends and benefactors into ridicule made me reflect that she might come to treat me in like manner. Her blushes, when she told a fib, did not spring from a dislike of lying, but from anger with herself for not being able to distort the truth more cleverly. Yet self-love is a weakness so ingrained in human frailty, that men are always ready to believe that they will fare better than their neighbours, because they think they have deserved better, or fancy themselves preferred by the woman on whose very faults they put an indulgent interpretation. This was my case with Teodoro Ricci.

I was never able to induce her to sacrifice even a few hours a day to reading good books or exercising her mind by writing. Arguments, entreaties, reproaches were all thrown away. She excused herself by pleading her domestic duties; and though I was ever anxious to spend our time together in useful studies, as I had done with other actresses, I could not bring her to do more than con the parts she had to play upon the stage. Probably she thought that her native pluck and talent were sufficient to sustain her without troubling her brains by serious work. The duties which she always pleaded consisted in sitting at her toilet-table before the eternal looking-glass, arranging laces, changing ribands, altering the folds of veils, matching colours, and such-like frivolities. All these things are useful with a view to stage effect; but exclusive devotion to them distracts the mind from the higher exigencies of dramatic art, leads an actress to court applause by illegitimate means, and brings her in course of time to mere posing and peacocking upon the boards before the eyes of voluptuaries in the boxes. Teodora Ricci was only too prone to such faults; and besides, her purse could not stand the expense of her toilette.

When I ventured to express my fears upon these points, she betrayed her real way of thinking by replies to the following effect: 'If we do not earn more than our fixed wages, how on earth are we poor actresses to hold out in a profession like ours?' I did not conceal my abhorrence of the principles implied in such remarks; and she professed that she had only spoken in jest. At the same time, her behaviour was so good, she ruled her house with such economy, paid her debts so regularly, and conducted herself with such propriety, that I hoped, by good advice and by getting her salary increased, to save her from the evil influences of a misdirected early training. Vain illusion to flatter oneself that one can ever cure an actress of the faults instilled in her from childhood! I was perhaps blinded by the partiality I felt for her; and no man, face to face with a woman, can trust the clearness of his insight. Six years of continual assiduity, friendship, benefits, were not worth one straw against the poison she had imbibed. The woman who, with a sound education, might have become a person of true culture and a real friend, gave herself up to flattery and her own perverted inclinations; so that in the end she brought upon me troubles which the world has judged of serious importance and public gravity.

38

I publicly avow my friendship for Signora Ricci—
Efforts made to secure her advancement—I become
godfather to her child, and indulge in foolish hopes
about her future

Before entering into those open and formal ties of friendship
which in Italy carry something of the nature of an obligation,
I thought it right to warn Signora Ricci with regard to certain
matters.[1] I pointed out that she was a member of a company
renowned for its good character, and that she had already
been exposed to calumny by her detractors. This ought to
make her circumspect in repelling the advances of men of
pleasure who might compromise her reputation. For myself, I
meant to be her avowed friend, her daily visitor, and
cavalier in public; but she must not think I wanted to play the
part of a lover, far less of a flatterer. My age, which bordered
upon fifty, and my temperament were enough to prevent me
from making any foolish pretensions to her favours. Should
she find herself in need, through the failure of her monthly
salary to meet expenses, she might count upon my purse. If,
in spite of my good counsels, she increased her reputation for
light conduct, I should be obliged to break with her at once
and for ever. On the other hand, if my principles were distaste-
ful to her, she had only to speak the word, and I would leave
her absolutely at liberty. So long as I supported her in public
and championed her honour as a woman and her fame as an
artist, I had the right to expect conduct from her conformable
to my avowed philosophy of life.

To these Quixotical discourses she replied by saying that
all honest folk congratulated her upon acquiring my favour.
They urged her to do all in her power to strengthen our
alliance, and to avoid everything which could make me leave

[1] Gozzi means that he had assumed the rôle of *cicisbeo* to Teodora
Ricci. (S)

her. Nay, more : her spiritual director, in the course of confession, had exhorted her to remain by me, a man whom he
regarded as a marvel of our century. This I thought a little
exaggerated; it smacked of the stage.

Teodora Ricci's husband was a good sort of fellow, who had
been a bookseller, and had acquired a kind of literary fanaticism in that business.[1] All day and night he scribbled volumes,
which were sure, he said, to be the source of vast profit to
himself and his heirs. Absorbed in these barren studies, he
abandoned the household to his wife, philosophically making
no claims on her attention. Shoes in holes and muddy stockings never troubled him. But meanwhile his health was being
ruined. He grew as lean as a corpse and spat blood from the
lungs, while bending over his beloved desk. His wife vainly
scolded him, predicting that he was sure to fall into a consumption, which might infect his family. He pitied her gross
ignorance, and continued to immolate himself upon the altar
of learning. How this ill-assorted couple ever came together
I cannot imagine. They appeared, however, to like each other,
and lived on fairly good terms.

An income of 500 ducats was wholly insufficient for man
and wife and child, with an expected confinement, and the
expenses of a theatrical wardrobe to be met. I represented the
case to Sacchi, who agreed to add a sum of 130 ducats
annually, remarking, however, that each year Teodora would
be sure to clamour for a further rise in wages. He was right.

[1] This man was called Francesco Bartoli. We owe to his pen a
valuable collection of biographical notes on Italian actors and
actresses : *Notizie istoriche dei comici italiani che fiorirono intorno al
MDL fino ai giorni presenti* (Padova, Conzatti, 1782). This work contains a life of Teodora Ricci and the author's own autobiography.
After the events of 1777 he separated from his wife, and only acknowledged the first of her three children. Critics may pause to wonder, at this point, whether Gozzi's relations to Teodora Ricci were as
Platonic as he painted them. In 1782 Bartoli retired from the stage and
lived at Rovigo. On Teodora's leaving the profession in 1793, he took
her back, and endured her hysterical tempers until the date of his own
death in 1806. She died mad about the year 1824 in the asylum of
S. Servilio at Venice. (S)

In proportion as she grew more necessary to the company, she augmented her threats of leaving it and her demands for better appointments.

On the days when she was not on duty at the theatre, I used to accompany her openly to the opera and playhouses and other places of diversion. She had her cover laid at my house, and she frequently dined there in company with her husband, whom I liked for his modesty and civil manners. I also managed to introduce her into society. Many of the noble or wealthy families of Venice took pleasure in receiving members of Sacchi's troupe at their houses. At first Teodora Ricci was excluded from such invitations, so cruelly had her character been blackened by female jealousy and malice. I made myself responsible for her good behaviour, and removed the prejudices which placed her at this disadvantage. Under my protection, she went to fashionable dinner-parties and polite assemblies; I also introduced both men and women of good manners to her at her own home. Acting with reckless or stupid good faith, I did not foresee how soon the hidden mines of her perverted inclinations and bad early training would explode and cover me with confusion.

Meanwhile her condition improved in other ways. She exchanged the dark, ill-smelling apartment she first occupied for a small but convenient abode. Perhaps I ought to touch upon those material services which she may have from time to time received from me; but if she can forget them, it is easier for me to do so also. I must add that, while I was never blindly enamoured of her, I never found her grasping or rapacious.

The time arrived when my friends the actors were about to leave Venice for the theatres of Bergamo and Milan. Before parting from Teodora, I begged her to remember that she had to some extent my honour in her keeping. She was going into danger, among a crowd of envious persons who would enjoy nothing better than to see her compromise herself and me by levity of conduct. She replied that her wishes and intentions were so firmly bent on abiding by my counsels, that she should like to ratify our alliance by a bond of religion. Would

I hold her expected infant at the font? I said that I should be very willing to do so, but that I could not promise to leave Venice to be present at the christening. To this I added jestingly: 'Your request is somewhat despotic in the condition it imposes on me. You are thinking more of your own interests than of my affections, which may perchance have been engaged for you. This bond of religion puts an insuperable barrier to my desires.' We laughed the matter over, and agreed upon it amicably.

She begged for letters of recommendation to Bergamo and Milan. Knowing how worse than useless such introductions are, I confined myself to one testimonial, addressed to my good friend Signor Stefano Sciugliaga, Secretary of the University at Milan, and to his wife, an estimable couple, full of kindness and distinguished by their virtues. Furnished with this letter, Teodora left me, and I felt the loss of her at Venice. She went to Bergamo, where she gave birth to a little girl, for whom Sacchi stood my proxy at the font. I discharged the usual duties to the Church, and did what was proper in the circumstances by the mother of my godchild. Teodora pursued her journey to Milan, whence she wrote me a full account of the kindness and courtesy she received from Signor Stefano Sciugliaga and his wife Lucia.

The weariness I feel in writing this chapter makes me measure what my readers must experience in reading it. I therefore cut it short and finish it.

By the end of the company's season in Milan, Teodora Ricci's husband was seriously ill with suspected consumption, and in order that the health of his wife and family should not be endangered he was sent off to his native town of Bologna for a period of convalescence at Sacchi's expense. It is from this period that Gozzi dates the beginning of the deterioration in his relations with the actress. A succession of episodes revealed her basic irresponsibility and convinced him that he must seize the first opportunity of breaking with her.

During the absence of Teodora's husband, Sacchi took advantage of the situation to press his attentions upon the actress. When Gozzi discovered that she was accepting expensive gifts from the director of the troupe, he threatened to withdraw his protection if she did not rebuff her admirer. Sacchi's presents were duly returned, with the result that for a while relations between the actor and the playwright were strained.

Teodora also displayed a degree of irresponsibility in her professional dealings. She was one of the actresses interviewed by Francesco Zannuzzi, premier amoureux at the Comédie Italienne, when he visited Italy to recruit fresh talent for the company in Paris. If Zannuzzi had found her suitable, she would have broken her engagement with Sacchi and gone to Paris. Not long after this, and within a short time of signing a five-year contract with Sacchi, she was again putting out feelers secretly with a view to securing an engagement in Paris, fully prepared to leave the company in the lurch and, if possible to avoid paying the stipulated penalty as well. She was again reprimanded by her protector, who was now more than ever determined to withdraw as tactfully as possible from his liaison with her.

39

Candid details regarding the composition and production of my notorious comedy entitled The Love-Potions *—More too about Signora Ricci, and her relations to Signor Gratarol*

Just about this time I had planned and partly executed a new comedy, which afterwards obtained a *succès de scandale* under the title of *The Love-Potions*.[1] The dust stirred up by this innocent piece in three acts obliges me to enter at some length into the circumstances which attended its composition and production.

[1] *Le droghe d'amore* printed at the end of the third volume of the *Memorie inutili di Carlo Gozzi*, Venice, Palese, 1797. (S)

Everybody is aware that, after the long series of my allegorical fables had run their course upon the stage, I thought fit to change my manner, and adapted several Spanish dramas for our theatre. Sacchi used to bring me bundles of Spanish plays. I turned them over, and selected those which seemed to me best fitted for my purpose. Taking the bare skeleton and ground-plot of these pieces, I worked them up with new characters, fresh dialogue, and an improved conduct of the action, to suit the requirements of the Italian theatre. A whole array of dramas—*The Woman Who Was Truly in Love, The Vindictive Woman, Donna Elvira, The Nights of Tribulation, The Philosopher-Princess, The Open Secret, Brother against Brother, The Moor with the White Body, The Metaphysician*, and *Bianca, Countess of Melfi*, all of which issued from my pen—attest the truth of these remarks.[1] I need say no more about them, because the prefaces with which I sent them to the press have sufficiently informed the public.

In pursuance of this plan, then, I had been working up Tirso da Molina's piece, entitled *Jealousy Cured by Jealousy*,[2] into my own *Love-Potions*. I was but little satisfied, made tardy progress, and had even laid aside the manuscript as worthless—condemning it, like scores of other abortive pieces, to the waste-paper basket. It so happened that after Christmas in this year, 1775, I was laid up with a tedious attack of rheumatism, which threatened to pass over into putrid fever, and which confined me to the house for more than thirty days. Signora Ricci kept up amicable relations with me during this illness; and even after Carnival began, she and her husband used to spend their spare evenings at my house. The society which cheered me through my lingering convalescence included the patrician Paolo Balbi, Doctor Andrea Comparetti, Signor Raffaello Todeschini, my nephew Francesco, son of Gasparo, Signor Carlo Maffei, Signor Michele Molinari, and an

---

[1] These will be found in Gozzi's *Opere*, ed. cit. The prefaces are printed before the plays. (S) The original titles of the last four plays in Gozzi's list are *I fratelli nimici, Il moro di corpo bianco, Il metafisico*, and *Bianca, contessa di Melfi*.

[2] *Celos con celos se curan.*

occasional actor from Sacchi's troupe. Wanting occupation
for my hours of solitude, I took up the *Love-Potions*, and went
on working at it; always against the grain, however, for the
piece seemed to me to drag and to want life. There is so much
improbability in the plots of Spanish dramas that all the arts
of rhetoric and eloquence have to be employed in order to
convey an appearance of reality to the action. This tends to
prolixity, and I felt that my unfinished piece was particularly
faulty in that respect. It was divided into three acts, and I had
brought the dialogue down to the middle of the third. Little
as I liked it, the fancy took me to see what impression it
would make upon an audience Accordingly, I read it aloud
one evening to Teodora Ricci, my nephew, Doctor Comparetti,
and Signor Molinari. They were interested beyond my expectation, and loudly opposed my intention of laying it aside. The
prima donna, in particular, urged me in the strongest terms
to finish what remained of it to do. The gentlemen I have just
named can bear witness to the sincerity of my coldness for
this play, which afterwards, by a succession of accidents,
came to be regarded as a deliberate satire on a single individual.

Some days after the reading, Signora Ricci asked me
casually if I was acquainted with Signor Pietro Antonio
Gratarol, secretary to the Senate. I answered that I did not
know him, which was the simple truth. I added, however,
that he had been pointed out to me on the piazza, and that
his outlandish air, gait, and costume struck me as very different from what one would expect in a secretary to the grave
Venetian Senate. 'Yet I have heard him spoken of as a man of
ability and intelligence.' 'He has a great respect for you,' said
she. 'I am obliged to him for his good opinion,' I replied. 'I
think him a man of breeding,' she went on, 'and I also think
him a man of honour.' 'So far as I am concerned,' I answered,
'I know nothing to the contrary, unless it be his unfortunate
notoriety for what is now called gallantry.' There was no
malice in thus alluding to what was universally talked about,
and had even come before the judges of the State. I only
intended to give a hint to my gossip, which I soon discovered

to be too late for any service. Having spoken, I immediately sought to soften what I said by adding: 'I do not deny that externals may expose a man to false opinion in such matters; and not being familiar with Signor Gratarol, I neither affirm nor deny what is commonly voiced abroad about him.' 'He is elected ambassador to Naples,' she continued, 'and I am anxious to appear upon a theatre in that capital. He may be of the utmost service to me.' 'Why,' said I, 'are not you thinking of going to Paris?' 'I must try,' she replied, 'to make my fortune where and how I can.' 'Do as you like,' I answered, and turned the conversation upon other topics.

It was clear to my mind that, during my long illness, Signora Ricci had struck up a friendship with this Signor Gratarol, and that she was beating about the bush to bring us together at her house. She had not forgotten my determination to cut short my daily visits if she received attentions from a man of fashion and pleasure. I, for my part, should have been delighted to meet Signor Gratarol anywhere but in the dwelling of the actress I had protected and publicly acknowledged for the last five years.

It now became my fixed resolve to procrastinate until the end of the Carnival, avoiding the scandal which would ensue from a sudden abandonment of Teodora Ricci. But when she left Venice for the spring and summer tour, I determined to drop our correspondence by letter, and to meet her afterwards upon the footing of distant civility. Events proved how useless it was to form any such plans with reference to a woman of her character.

Wearying at length of my long imprisonment, I ventured abroad against my doctor's advice, and found myself much the better for a moderate amount of exercise.[1] This en-

[1] From this point forward Gozzi relates the series of events which Gratarol had already described in his *Narrazione apologetica*. The two accounts agree in essentials, the fundamental difference between them being Gratarol's firm belief that Gozzi meant to satirize him in the *Droghe d'amore*, which Gozzi vehemently denies. It must be remembered that Gozzi had the *Narrazione* before him while writing these Memoirs. (S)

couraged me to seek my accustomed recreation in the small rooms behind the scenes of the theatre. There I was welcomed with loud unanimous delight by all the members of the company. But I was not surprised when, in spite of Sacchi's usual strictness with regard to visitors, I found Signor Gratarol installed in the green-room. He seemed to be quite at home, flaunting a crimson mantle lined with costly furs, and distributing candied citrons and Neapolitan bonbons[1] right and left. He very politely offered me some of his comfits, as though I had been a pretty girl, on whom such things are well bestowed. I thanked him for the attention, and took good care to utter no remarks upon the novelty of his appearance in that place.

I also went to see Signora Ricci at her house, but not every day as formerly, and always at times when I was certain not to meet with Signor Gratarol. He meanwhile continued to be a constant guest behind the scenes of the theatre.

In order to cast dust in my eyes, and not to lose the support of my protection, Signora Ricci took every opportunity of alluding to the good breeding and excellent behaviour of her new friend. He treated her with the respect due to a queen, she said, and greatly regretted that he was never fortunate enough to find me at her house. I reflected, perhaps unjustly, that Signor Gratarol would indeed have been delighted to meet me there. This would have suited his game; for when the flirtation had advanced to the stage of gallantry, his mistress would still have had her old friend and gossip to rely on. Anyhow, I responded to her suggestions in terms like these: 'I am much obliged to the gentleman in question. I believe all you tell me, although nobody else would believe it. You know my principles, and the position I have willingly assumed towards you. I am sorry to see you exposing yourself to fresh calumnies, and to be no longer able to defend you. With Signor Gratarol, much as I differ from him upon certain points, I should be glad to enter into social relations anywhere but

[1] *Diavoloni* is the Italian word. We hear of these comfits also from Gratarol. They are big sugar-plums containing liqueur. (S)

R

under your roof. You must have observed that I treat him with esteem and respect when we come together behind the scenes. It is impossible, however, that he can be ignorant of the open friendship I have professed for you during five whole years. All Venice knows it. I desire nothing more than that he should continue to treat you like a queen, as you say he does. But since I do not seek to oppose your liberty of action, I trust that you will not be so indiscreet as to impose conditions on my freedom.'

What report of this conversation she made to Signor Gratarol is known only to her and him. She was exasperated, and I do not think the picture she drew of me can have been very flattering. Probably I was described as weakly jealous— jealous, however, I had never been of other admirers, who did not compromise me in my intimacy with this actress.

A few weeks were left of the Carnival, when, entering the small rooms of the theatre one evening, I found Signor Gratarol as usual there. He addressed me courteously: 'Count, Sacchi here and Fiorilli and Zannoni have been invited to eat a pheasant with me at my casino in S. Mosè. I hardly venture to invite you also; yet knowing the kindly feeling you have for these persons, and the pleasure you take in their company, if you were disposed to join our party, I should esteem it an honour.' The invitation could not have been more politely given; and as the other guests had been named, I saw no reason to refuse. I added, however, that the state of my health prevented me from counting with certainty upon the pleasure he offered; anyhow, my absence would not be a great loss to his party. After a few compliments, the day was fixed.

On the following morning I met Sacchi upon the piazza. His eyes were starting from their sockets, and he told me he was in urgent need of my advice. What passed between us I will relate in dialogue. Sacchi began:

'A short time since, I met a gentleman who was dining last night at the house of a patrician, the President of the Supreme Tribunal.[1] He took me aside and said: "Such and such a noble-

[1] That is, Council of Ten with the *Inquisitori di Stato* at its head. (S)

man (and you know over what Tribunal he presides) was speaking last night about the theatres; in the course of his remarks he let these words fall :—I do not know how it is that Sacchi, who has the reputation of managing his troupe with strictness, and only allowing a few confidential friends to appear behind the scenes of his theatre, should receive secretaries of the Senate openly and every night in the green-room. —Dear Sacchi," this gentleman continued, "do not tell anyone that I have reported these words; my only object is to put you on your guard." You see, sir, that the communication forces me to take some active measures. If I neglect it rashly, I shall find myself in difficulties. I confess that I am puzzled, and come to you for counsel.'

'You have chosen an inappropriate adviser in this affair,' I answered. 'You are the master in your own theatre, and have always been severe upon the point in question. Why did not you civilly put a stop to the irregularity before it assumed so embarrassing an aspect? I was a whole month absent from your stage, owing to my illness. When I returned, I found Signor Gratarol installed, and hail-fellow-well-met with everybody. At any rate, it would not have befitted me to make remarks upon the sort of people you admitted.'

'I did not introduce the man,' said Sacchi. 'I noticed him one evening, and thought his visit might be accidental. When he came again and again, I made inquiries; and the whole troupe assured me with ironical malice that he came in the company of Signora Ricci, was introduced by her, and only came on her account.'

'That makes it still more difficult for me to advise you,' I replied. 'Yet I think I may tell you that I do not believe Signor Gratarol to be indiscreet. If you inform him privately, or let him know through Signora Ricci, what has been reported to you, I am certain that he will not show himself behind the scenes again.'

'I am aware,' rejoined Sacchi, 'that my way of talking is brusque, passionate, and awkward. Pray do me the kindness to speak to Signora Ricci.'

'Excuse me,' said I; 'I do not undertake commissions of this kind, and have no wish to be mixed up with what only concerns you.'

'Nay, I beseech you to do me this kindness!' exclaimed Sacchi once more. 'You need only hint at what I have communicated. I assure you, Count, that if I begin to give that woman a bit of my mind, I shall not be able to refrain from some gross insults.'

'Why do you not speak civilly to Signor Gratarol?'

'To tell you the truth, I have not the courage. He is always polite to me. I am afraid that he will take my remarks for an actor's scheming to expel him from the green-room. He might become my enemy, and Signora Ricci in her rage might do me some injury. You know that in our profession we are forced to keep on good terms with everybody.'

'Well,' said I, 'I see that you want me to put my paw into the fire to draw the chestnut out! Never mind! If the opportunity occurs, I will try to do what you request, and set things straight as cautiously as may be.'

In the course of one of my coldly ceremonious visits to Signora Ricci, I dropped these words before rising to take my leave : 'I was forgetting to tell you something, which I do not like to say, but which it would be unfriendly to leave unsaid. Sacchi has mentioned this and this to me, and asked me to give you a hint. You can see Signor Gratarol as much as you like in your own house. I hope that you will arrange matters so as not to incur further odium.' 'Gratarol does not come behind the scenes for me!' cried she, flaming up; 'what does it matter to me whether he comes or stays away? Sacchi can tell him to drop his visits.' 'I have reported to you a fact,' said I with perfect calm, 'at the request of an old acquaintance. Whether you, or Sacchi, or nobody tells Signor Gratarol, is all the same to me.' I left her fuming and chafing in a fury.

I perceived that my customary readiness to make myself of use had got me into a scrape. The viperish temper in which the woman was when I left her, made me feel sure that she would bite me behind my back; and what followed confirmed my apprehension. She saw with rage that my friendship for her was expiring. She wanted to hold her new friend fast. Incapable of acknowledging herself in the wrong, blinded by vanity and folly, she persisted in regarding me as the victim of jealousy. After the conversation I have just related, Signor Gratarol did not show himself again behind the scenes. What his feelings were towards me Heaven only knows.

On the evening before the famous banquet, I was in one of the small rooms of the theatre with Sacchi, Signora Ricci, a sister of hers named Marianna who danced in the ballet, and several other actresses and actors. Sacchi suddenly burst into the following tirade—'Tomorrow,' he began, 'we are to dine with Signor Gratarol. I thought that the guests were Count Gozzi, myself, Fiorilli, and Zannoni. Now it reaches my ears that certain actresses of my troupe have been invited, and that the sumptuous and splendid festivity is given solely in honour of Signora Teodora Ricci. It has never been my habit to act as go-between for the women of my establishment. Deuce take it all—&c., &c.—let him go who likes; I shall not, that is flat.' He followed up this flood of eloquence with the foulest invectives.

Signora Ricci's face burned; she did not know where to look, and fixed her eyes upon the ground. Everybody was staring at her. I confess that I felt sorry to see her pilloried in this way. 'Well,' said I to myself, 'the labour of five years has been cast to the winds by this vain woman's frivolous misconduct. The imbroglio is becoming so serious that I fear I shall not drag on to the end of the Carnival without some tiresome explosion.' Meanwhile Sacchi went storming on. I tried to calm him down. 'You say you do not want to make enemies, and yet you are ready to affront a gentleman who treats you with politeness. The whole affair may be quite harmless, and I do not see why you should lash yourself into a rage about it. You listen too much to idle or malignant gossip.' I succeeded in restoring peace, and Sacchi promised to keep his appointment.

I, for my part, feeling really indisposed, and having a rooted antipathy for banquets, especially when the host is no intimate friend of my own, excused myself next morning on the score of health, and received a letter of profuse compliments and expressions of regret in return.

40

A visit from Signor Gratarol—Notes of our conversation—Mutinous murmurs in the playing company—My weakly kindness towards Signora Ricci—Final rupture

On the morning after Signor Gratarol's superb banquet, I was still in bed when my servant announced a visit from that gentleman, whom I had only met before in passing at the theatre. He entered, walking more like an Englishman than a Venetian, elegantly attired, and uttering compliments which my humility forced me to regard as ill-employed cajoleries.

I begged him to excuse me for receiving him in bed. He inquired after my health, and then proceeded to business. A society of gentlefolk, he told me, had been formed, all of whom were amateur actors, and a theatre had been built at S. Gregorio for them to play comedies and tragedies. He was a member of this company; and he had suggested to his friends the propriety of electing a permanent chief, with full authority to control and dictate regulations, whose word should be implicitly obeyed. This suggestion having been unanimously accepted, he had taken the liberty to name me as the chief and manager in question, and my nomination had been received with general approval.

Besides the revolting flattery which underlay this speech, I was positively taken aback to hear a secretary of the august Venetian Senate, an ambassador-elect from the most Serene Republic to the court of a monarch of the Two Sicilies, discussing such a frivolous affair with so much seriousness and making such a fuss about it. I had much ado to maintain my gravity, and could not speak for a few seconds. He came to my relief by resuming his discourse. 'Such an institution,' he went on, 'will be extremely useful in Venice for developing and training the abilities of young men, for giving them, in short, a liberal culture. In my opinion it is admirable, of the greatest utility, and worthy of respect. What do you think, Count?'

I replied that I was far from disapproving of the well-established custom in schools and seminaries of making boys and young men act; and I thought that the same custom in families had many advantages. Besides sharpening and supplying the mental faculties of young people, and improving their elocution, it kept them to some extent aloof from those low sensual pleasures which were deplorably in vogue among them. It seemed to me, however, that persons of a mature age, holding offices and posts of public dignity, would do better to extend protection and encouragement to such perform-ances than to appear themselves upon the stage. Such was my private opinion. But I did not wish to set up for being a critic of my neighbours. For the rest, I thanked him for the honour done me by his amateur society, but begged to decline the office of director. I gave many reasons for not caring to under-take the responsibilities of such a post, and reminded him that my interest in the theatre served only as a distraction from many onerous and painful duties which I had voluntarily undertaken for the benefit of my numerous and far from wealthy relatives.

I do not know how far this candid answer was agreeable to Signor Gratarol. Much of it must certainly have gone against his grain, and a good deal he probably took for sarcasm. Nevertheless, he continued on the note of adulation which annoyed me. 'In truth,' he said, 'I hardly hoped for your acceptance, knowing how much you value a quiet life. Yet perhaps you will do me the favour of suggesting some one fit to undertake the duty.' 'In my opinion,' I replied, 'the Marchese

Francesco Albergati would be a very proper man.[1] He is an enthusiastic amateur, and has great experience in theatrical affairs. He has fixed his residence at Venice, and is sure to accept the post with pleasure.' 'Do you really think him capable?' asked Gratarol with the utmost gravity, as though we were discussing a matter of vast importance. 'Most capable,' I answered. 'Pray allow me then,' he continued, with the same ludicrous concern, 'to propose Marchese Albergati to my company of noble amateurs at your recommendation!' 'Certainly, if you think fit,' I replied, with difficulty repressing a yawn. The long conversation about nothing had almost tired my patience out. At length he rose to take his leave, drowning me in an ocean of compliments. I thanked him for his visit, and promised to return it, blessing Heaven for his departure.

After Signor Gratarol's banquet, which was described to me as regal in its pomp, the whole of Sacchi's troupe let their spite loose against Signora Ricci. It was a storm of innuendoes and equivocal allusions,[2] upon which my presence barely imposed a check. Some of the actresses went so far as to ask me in private whether I was not at last convinced of what they had always told me about that woman's character. I fenced with them as well as I could, sometimes pretending not to understand, sometimes rebuking their evil gossip, and sometimes turning my back with affected indignation. And so I rubbed on, always sighing for the arrival of Lent.

The last day of this most tedious Carnival at length arrived. It was the custom for the leading members of Sacchi's troupe, together with a numerous company of friends, to celebrate the evening with a supper at some inn. I had always accompanied Teodora Ricci on these occasions; and I now determined to put the final stroke to our friendship by acting as

[1] Francesco Albergati (1728–1804) was born in Bologna, but lived principally at Venice and at his country seat at Zola, where he had a famous private theatre, for which Goldoni wrote five of his comedies. He translated French tragedies and comedies. He was an admirer of Goldoni, and himself a prolific writer of comedies.

[2] It was rumoured that the actress sometimes spent the whole night at Gratarol's house.

usual. After a very festive supper, the whole party adjourned to the opera at S. Samuele. The performance began at midnight, and several boxes had been engaged beforehand. It chanced that I found myself alone in one of them with Signora Ricci. Thereupon, seeing that the Carnival was over, and the moment of my emancipation had arrived, I opened my mind to the young woman and informed her that my patience was exhausted. She tried to turn the matter off with a jest; her liaison with Gratarol had been a mere Carnival caprice, which would end with the Carnival. (As if that made any difference to me!) I replied with firmness that it was now too late. She had thrown away the fruits of my benefits conferred on her through five long years, and had repaid them by exposing me to shame and insult. I forgave her and left her at liberty; but abode by my decision to withdraw from her friendship.

'What!' said she, 'shall I not be your gossip[1] any more?' 'Please to forget that title,' I replied: 'a good woman does not turn her gossip into a simpleton or go-between. I shall not become your enemy, and have no petty thirst for vengeance. If I were wise, I should cut my old connexion with the troupe whom I have protected for twenty years. That would secure me against further annoyances and tittle-tattle. But I do not mean to take this step. And you may be very grateful to me; for were I to leave them, they would ascribe the loss of their great champion to you alone.' 'Oh, what will ever happen to me?' she exclaimed with an air of tragic desperation. 'Nothing,' I added laughing, 'except what you have sought and brought about.'

When the opera was over, I attended her home, and standing in the doorway, repeated that this was the last time she would be troubled with my company. 'Do you not mean then to visit me any more?' cried she. 'You certainly will not be exposed to that disturbance,' I replied. 'Oh, we shall see you here, we shall see you!' she answered with a cheerful air of

---

[1] The relation of gossip or *Compare di S. Giovanni* is reckoned sacred at Venice. (S)

security. I could not help laughing at her conceit. 'So you persist in looking on me as a hopeless victim of your charms! If I do come to visit you, you will see me, certes!' 'But I shall come to you,' she added. 'I hope that you will never give yourself the trouble,' said I; and with these final words I turned my back and walked away.

So ended the open and ingenuous friendship which I had carried on for five years with this woman.

41

The Love-Potions finished—Teodora Ricci's metamorphosis and my reflections on it—Sacchi entreats to have the Love-Potions, and I abandon it to him, in order to save myself from persecution—The play is read by me before the actors

My health remaining weak, I passed the greater part of this summer at a little country-house I had near Stra upon the Brenta. Here I rapidly recovered strength, more by open-air exercise and rational diet than by drinking the Cila waters recommended by my doctor. In the long idle days of this *villeggiatura*, I set hand once more to the *Love-Potions*, and finished it with indescribable aversion. Leaving Stra for Padua, I took the play with me, and read it aloud to my friend Massimo, under whose roof I was staying. He listened patiently all through the tedious declamation, praised certain passages of the comedy, and said he thought the chief objection to it was its prodigious length. When I returned to Venice, I made up my mind to put this abortion of my talent on the shelf; but Sacchi would not let it rest. He wrote so urgently upon the subject, that I begged my brother Gasparo to undergo the mortal tedium of hearing and pronouncing judgment on the play. His opinion was that, though it contained some excellent scenes, it too closely resembled my *Philosopher-Princess* in parts, and that its length would render it ineffective. The comedy was one of character and sentiments, and had no spectacular novelties to enliven it. However, he promised to read it through, and see whether judicious retrenchments could be made. After ten days or so, I received the manuscript again, with my brother's verdict that nothing could be omitted without breaking the warp on which the plot was woven. Accordingly, I wrote to Sacchi, saying that the *Love-Potions* would really not do, and promising some other piece instead. I had, indeed, already planned my *Metaphysician* and *Bianca, Countess of Melfi*, but had not had the time to dramatize them.

Autumn brought the actors back again as usual; and I composed a prologue for the opening of their theatre, which was recited by Signora Ricci. I used to meet that actress in the rooms behind the scenes, and was much struck by the singular change which had come over her. She continued to do everything she could to annoy me; and I kept wondering how it was that she had managed to conceal her true nature so cleverly during the five years of our friendship. Now she openly bragged about the presents she received; the wax-candles which gave light to her apartment; the exquisite wines, perfect coffee, boxes of bonbons, refined chocolate, and other dainties which furnished her repasts. She even went to the length of inviting that old satyr Sacchi to her house, adding in order to insult me: 'You will find no tiresome moral preachers on the *convenances* to frighten you away!' While as anxious as ever to lure me back, she piqued herself on letting it be understood that she had given me my dismissal. Indeed, I found it somewhat difficult to treat the woman with that reserved civility which I wished to preserve towards her in public.

The amusement I enjoyed in studying her new ways and manners compensated for these gnat-bites. She had become in six months shameless and affected, and meddlesome and garrulous as a magpie. She pretended to have learned all kinds of important sciences, and gravely informed us that the game *rocambol* was derived from two English words. She had left off wearing drawers, she said, because it was healthy to ventilate the body, adding details of the most comical indecency. Always dreaming about Paris, Venice had become a kind of sewer to her opinion. The Venetians and Italians in general were a race of stupid mediocrities, unenlightened and insupportable. 'I am dying to get to Paris!' she exclaimed; 'there the rich financiers fling purses full of *louis d'or* at actresses with as little regard as one flings a pear in Italy.' And then to show how well she had got rid of prejudices: 'Ah! blessed power of making love without the checks of a misguided education! To make love through our lifetime is the supreme happiness of mortals!' Not a word or a thought for her husband and two children.

Every evening she filled the theatre with such a potent smell of musk, that people complained and said it gave them the headache. 'What a prejudice!' she cried with a grimace in what she thought the French style. 'At Paris everything smells of musk, down to the very trees in the Tuileries gardens, against which ladies may have leant a moment.' She was taking French lessons; and her retentive memory made her catch up phrases, which she flung about with volubility. Paris entered into everything she said. She modelled her gait and action and tone of voice upon what she conceived to be the Parisian manner, producing a most laughable caricature which spoiled her acting. I felt really sorry for her, while observing this progressive deterioration in her art. She had been an excellent comedian in the Italian style, and would certainly have been appreciated on the stage at Paris. Now she had become an ape of the French race, surcharged with affectation, and unsuccessful in her travesty. It is impossible, I thought, that the Parisians, who require an Italian actress, and not a mongrel imitation of themselves, will put up with her. This prognostication, to my sincere regret, was verified when she appeared in that metropolis.

We had reached the first days of November in the year 1776, and Sacchi's receipts were languishing. He had been spoiled by getting gratis at my hands two or three pieces annually, which found favour with the public. This made him careless about supplying himself with novelties; while I was so engaged with law business that I had no time to dramatize my *Metaphysician* and *Bianca, Countess of Melfi*. In fact, I had nothing on hand but the *Love-Potions*. Pestered by perpetual applications for this comedy, in an evil moment I drew it from its sepulchre and tossed it over to the *capocomico*. I told him that he might take the manuscript as a gift, but that if the play failed before the public, as I thought it would, I should never exercise my pen again on compositions for the stage.

It was impossible to foresee that a chain of untoward circumstances would convert this harmless drama into an indecent personal satire upon Signor Gratarol. Mendacious and vindictive meddling on the part of an infuriated actress, false steps and ill-considered opposition on the part of the man whom she deceived, the pique of great folk who disliked him, and the ingenuity of comedians eager for pecuniary gains, effected the transformation. I was placed in a false light— shown up to public curiosity as the prime agent in a piece of vulgar retaliation, the victim of a weak and jealous fancy. If I could have divined what lay beyond the scope of divination, I swear to God that I should have flung that comedy into the flames rather than let it become the property of a *capocomico*.

Far be it from me to assert that Gratarol was not brought upon the stage in that very comedy of my creation. He certainly was. But he owed this painful distinction to his own bad management, to the credulity with which he drank the venom of a spiteful woman's tongue, to the steps he took for prohibiting my play which roused the curiosity of the whole city and gave it a *succès de scandale*, to the enmity of great people whom he had imprudently defamed, and finally to the artifices of an acting company who saw their way to making money out of these conflicting interests.

Well, soon after I had placed the manuscript in Sacchi's hands, he told me that it had passed the official revision and had been licensed for the stage. Only some eight or ten lines were struck out. This happens to every play which is referred to the censors of the State. Nothing occurred which called its character in question, or suggested that it was more than a comedy with traits of satire upon society in general.

Sacchi announced the new play to the public, and its capricious title whetted their interest. I distributed the rôles between the actors of the troupe; but later on, this assignment of parts was altered, without my knowledge or consent, as part of a base, malicious plot, hatched by the comedians, which I could not have foreseen.

After distributing the rôles, I had to read the comedy aloud. This is necessary; for players are so made among us that, unless they catch the spirit of their parts from the author, they are sure to spoil them by some misconception of their values. The reading took place at Sacchi's lodgings. Signora Ricci appeared in all her glory, and established herself at my right hand. I shall not enlarge upon the characters and plot of the *Love-Potions* because the play will be found among my works in print. Suffice it to say, that when I had toiled onward to the sixteenth scene of the first act, where Don Adone makes his appearance on the stage, Signora Ricci began to writhe upon her seat. One would have imagined that she had never heard the play before, and that this character took her by surprise. Yet more than a year ago she had been introduced to Don Adone, as I have said above, at my own house.[1]

I continued my reading. But whenever Don Adone turned up—and his part is merely episodical in the drama—Signora Ricci marked her agitation by still more extraordinary signs of impatience. She muttered between her teeth and moved about upon her chair, in a way which made me think that she was indisposed. At last I turned to her and said: 'Madam, you seem to be more bored than I am by this reading!' The only answer which I got was a shrug of the shoulders, a turn of the body to the side away from me, and an exclamation: 'Oh, 'tis nothing, nothing!'

The reading continued. At every word which Don Adone

[1] See above, p. 231.

uttered, Signora Ricci repeated her grimaces and contortions of the body. I bluntly reminded her that she knew all about this personage twelve months and more ago, and that she had urged me to complete the play. Forced to say something, she put on a sour sardonic smile, and murmured: 'Well, well! That Don Adone of yours, that Don Adone of yours!'

Like lightning, the truth flashed upon my brain. I saw what she was up to. In spite of having been, as it were, an accomplice in my comedy those many months before, she meant to fix the character of Don Adone upon Signor Gratarol. This was her plan for rousing his resentment against myself, for revenging herself for my indifference, and for stirring up a scandal worse than all the humdrum scenes my flat comedy contained.

I finished my reading, as may be imagined, in a perfunctory manner, flung the manuscript down upon the table, and told the assembled actors that I did not expect the piece to succeed. It was far too feeble and too prolix. All the same, I had given it away to them, and they must do as they liked with it.

Sacchi, on the spot, gave orders for the copying of the several parts, which were to be distributed as I had settled. The party then broke up, and I kept my eyes upon Signora Ricci. She seemed in a great hurry to get away, as though someone were waiting for her, and I saw that she was bent on mischief.

42

The history of the Love-Potions—*In spite of my endeavours to the contrary, Gratarol, by his imprudent conduct, forces it upon the stage—It is represented for the first time—The town talks, and a scandal is created*

The impressions left upon my mind after this night's reading were painful. I expected some disturbance of the peace through the malice of that woman, who had now become irreconcilably antagonistic. Meeting Sacchi next morning on the Piazza di S. Marco, I asked him whether he had noticed the strange conduct of Signora Ricci on the previous evening. He said that he had certainly been aware of something wrong, but that he could not ascribe it to any cause. Then I communicated my suspicion. 'The actress,' said I, 'means to persuade Signor Gratarol that he is being satirized under the character of Don Adone.' 'What is her object?' exclaimed Sacchi. 'That I will tell you briefly,' I replied: 'she wants to gain credit with her new friend, to inflict an injury on your troupe, and cause me annoyance by stirring up a quarrel between me and the gentleman in question.' 'It is not impossible,' said Sacchi, 'that she is planning something of the kind. But what are your reasons for thinking so?' 'If you had only been attentive to her mutterings and attitudinisings last evening, when the part of Don Adone was being read, you would not put that question,' I answered. 'I ask you, therefore, as a friend, to withdraw my play until the next season. Lent will soon arrive. Signora Ricci will go to Paris, and Signor Gratarol to Naples. You can make use of the *Love-Potions* later on, when its appearance will cause no scandal.' After some persuasion, he promised to fulfil my wishes; and next morning he told me that the play had been suspended.

Here the affair would have rested if Signor Gratarol, poisoned by his mistress's report, had not taken a step fatal for his own tranquillity. She returned, as I had imagined, from the reading of my play, and told him that he was going to be exposed upon the stage in the person of Don Adone. He set all his influence at work to prevent the public exhibition of the comedy. The result was that, four days afterwards, Sacchi came to me in great confusion and told me that Signor Francesco Agazi, censor of plays for the *Magistrato sopra la Bestemmia*, had sent for the *Love-Potions*. A new revision was necessitated by certain complaints which had been brought against the rôle of Don Adone.

'So then,' said I, 'you have given the manuscript to Signor

Agazi?' 'No,' he answered; 'I was afraid that I might lose it altogether. I told that gentleman that I had lent it to a certain lady.[1] He smiled and said that when she had done with it he expected to have it in his hands again. In fact, not wishing to be proved a liar in this matter, I took the play to the lady I have mentioned, related the whole story about Gratarol and Teodora Ricci, and recommended myself to her protection.' Sacchi could not have taken any step more calculated to give importance to this incident. I said as much to him upon the spot; predicted that the lady, who was known to have a grudge against Signor Gratarol, would do her best to circulate the scandal; assured him that the whole town would blaze with rumour, that I should be discredited, and that he might find himself in a very awkward position. 'The tribunals of the State,' I added, 'are not to be trifled with by any of your circumventions.'

Signor Gratarol had made a great mistake. Instead of listening to the gossip of an actress, and then setting the machinery of the State in motion by private appeals to persons of importance, he ought to have come at once to me. I should have assured him of the simple truth, and the *Love-Potions* would have appeared without doing any dishonour to either of us.

His manœuvring had the effect of putting all Venice upon the *qui vive*, and placing an instrument of retaliation against him in the hands of powerful enemies. The noble lady, Caterina Dolfin Tron, to whom Sacchi took my comedy, read it through, and read it to her friends, and passed it about among a clique of high-born gentlemen and ladies. None of them found any mark of personal satire in the piece. All of them condemned Gratarol for his self-consciousness, and accused him of seeking to deprive the public of a rational diversion,

[1] This lady was the celebrated Caterina Dolfin Tron, wife of the Procuratore Andrea Tron. Her husband exercised such influence in the State that he was called *Il Padrone*. A terrible portrait is drawn of her by Gratarol in his *Narrazione apologetica*, 2nd edn., Venice, Gatti, i. 23, 44. To him she certainly behaved with cruel tyranny. But she was a woman of brilliant talents and fascinating person, who gave tone to literary and political society in Venice. (S)

S

while moving heaven and earth to reverse the decision of the censors of the State.

In two days the town buzzed of nothing but my wretched drama, Gratarol, and me. It was rumoured that I had composed a sanguinary satire. Not only Gratarol, but a crowd of gentlemen and ladies were to be brought upon the scene. A whole theatre, with its pit, boxes, stage, and purlieus could not have contained the multitude of my alleged victims. Everybody knew their exact names and titles. Neighbours laid their heads together, quarrelled, denied, maintained, argued, whispered in each other's ears, waxed hot and angry, told impossible anecdotes, contradicted their own words, and, what was most amusing, everybody drew his information from an infallible source.

One thing they held for certain—that I had made Gratarol the protagonist of my satire. That became a fixed idea, which it only wanted his own imprudence to turn into a fact.

Knowing pretty well where the real point of the mischief lay, I determined to act, if possible, upon the better feelings of Signora Dolfin Tron.[1] I had enjoyed the privilege of her acquaintance for many years. But my unsociable and unfashionable habits made me negligent of those attentions which are expected from a man of quality. I did not pay her the customary visits; and when we met, she was in the habit of playfully saluting me with the title of *Bear*. By brother Gasparo, on the contrary, saw her every day, and she bestowed on him the tender epithet of *Father*. Such being our respective relations, I thought it best to apply to him.

I asked my brother, then, to do all he could to induce this

[1] Gozzi has not perhaps quite told the whole truth about his relations to Caterina Tron. They were certainly more intimate at one period than he here admits. He formed a member of the society whom she received on Monday evenings at the Casino di S. Giuliano, and dedicated his *Marfisa bizzarra* to her in terms of high compliment. At the same time he disagreed with Caterina Tron's liberal opinions, and disapproved of her philosophizing turn of mind. It is quite possible that before the date of 1776 their former intimacy may have cooled. Gratarol himself observes that Gozzi had not frequented her society during the seven years prior to these events. (S)

powerful lady to oppose the production of my comedy for at least the present season. Through the machinations of Signora Ricci, against my will, and much to my discredit, the piece was going to create a public scandal, with serious injury to a gentleman whom I had not meant to satirize. My brother, muttering a curse on meddlesome women in general and actresses in particular, undertook the office. He did not succeed. Signora Tron replied that I was making far too much fuss about nothing, and that my comedy had passed beyond my control. It had become the property of a *capocomico*, and was at the present moment under the inspection of the State.

Not many days elapsed before I received a visit from Francesco Agazi, the censor, as I have before observed, for the *Signori sopra la Bestemmia*.[1] He was clothed in his magisterial robes and he began as follows: 'You gave a comedy, entitled *The Love-Potions*, to the company of Sacchi. I perused it and licensed it for the theatre at S. Salvatore. The comedy has been passed, and must appear. You have no control over it. Pray take no steps to obstruct its exhibition. The magistracy which I serve does not err in judgment.' I could not refrain from commenting upon Signor Gratarol's action in this matter, and protesting that I had never meant to satirize the man. He bade me take no heed of persons like Gratarol, whose heads were turned by outlandish fashions. 'I made some retrenchments,' he added, 'in the twelfth scene of the last act of your comedy. They amount, I think, to about ten or twelve lines. These lines expressed sentiments such as are usually maintained by men of Gratarol's sort. You meant them to be understood ironically. But our Venetians will not take them so. What strikes their ear, they retain in its material and literal sense. And they learn much which is mischievous, unknown to them before.—May I parenthetically observe that certain gentlemen want to give orders where they have no right to speak?—I repeat to you that the magistracy which I serve does not err; and I repeat the decree which has been

[1] This magistracy exercised control over the morals of Venice. (S)

passed.' Having spoken these words, Signor Agazi bowed, and left me for his business.

What passed between me and the censor I repeated to friends of mine, who will bear me witness that I found myself stopped in my attempts to suppress the comedy. It had to appear; and Signor Gratarol owed this annoyance to his having powerful enemies.

Unfortunately he did his best to exasperate these enemies. Teodora Ricci, primed by him and parroting his words, went about libelling men and women of the highest rank, whom she had never seen. Phrases of the grossest scurrility were hurled at eminent people by their names. 'If Gratarol has committed himself in this way to an actress,' said I in my sleeve, 'what must he not have let fall to other friends and acquaintances? Such indiscretion marks him out as little fitted for the post of ambassador at Naples or elsewhere.'

I have said that I had lost all authority over my wretched drama. I only wanted to see it well hissed on its first appearance, and to bury the annoyances it caused me in a general overthrow. Yet I was obliged to be present at rehearsals. At the first which I attended, I noticed that two of the rôles had been changed. I had given Don Adone to an actor called Luigi Benedetti, and the jealous Don Alessandro to Giovanni Vitalba. Sacchi reversed my disposition of these parts, alleging that Benedetti was better fitted to sustain the character of a furious lover than Vitalba, who was somewhat of a stick. This seemed to me not unreasonable; and I was so accustomed to have my plays cut and hacked about by the actors, that I accepted his decision.

At the second rehearsal, Signora Ricci asked me negligently if I knew why this alteration had been made. I answered that Sacchi had explained it to my satisfaction. She held her tongue, thinking doubtless that I was well acquainted with certain machinations of which she had fuller knowledge than I.

At last the piece appeared—it was the night of 10 January 1777—at the theatre of S. Salvatore. I went there in good time, and found the entrance thronged with a vast multitude. For three hours people had been clamouring for seats, and the whole house was crammed. They told me that the boxes had been sold at fabulous prices. This might have swelled another playwright's heart with pride. I, on the contrary, was extremely dejected by finding my worst anticipations realized. Pushing my way through the press, which encumbered every passage, I reached the *coulisses* with much toil.[1] There I saw a swarm of masks begging for places anywhere at any price. 'What the deuce is the meaning of this extraordinary concourse?' I exclaimed. Signora Ricci answered me at once with: 'Don't you know? The town has come to see your satire on a certain person.' I put her down by saying bluntly that more than a year ago she heard my play, and knew that there was no personal satire in it. It was not my fault if diabolical intrigues and a succession of blunders had given it a false complexion. She dropped her eyes. I turned my back, and took refuge in a box I had upon the third row of the theatre.

Going up the staircase, I caught sight before me of Gratarol's unhappy wife, and heard her chattering to certain gentlemen she met upon the way: 'I wanted to see my husband on the stage.' These words of the poor deserted woman enlightened me as to the expectation of the public. Yet why was the whole house so intoxicated? Why did a wife look forward to the spectacle of her husband's caricature? I can only explain this phenomenon by remembering the corruption of our age. Women seduced and left to shift for themselves, rivals supplanted in their love-affairs, jealous husbands, wives abandoned and heart-broken, form an inflammable audience for such a piece as the *Love-Potions* under the notorious circumstances of its first appearance.

Sacchi joined me in my box; and casting my eyes over the sea of faces, I soon perceived Signor Gratarol with a hand-

[1] Gratarol gives a vivid picture of this throng. 'Many hundreds of persons were sent away from the doors, since the vast area of the theatre was crammed full. Boxes, which on ordinary nights were paid two pauls, this evening brought a couple of sequins, and not a single one was empty.'—*Narrazione*, ed. cit., i. 68. (S)

some woman at his side. He had come to air his philosophy, but I trembled for him. The curtain rose, and the play proceeded with great spirit. All the actors did their best. I was satisfied with their performance, and the audience applauded. At length, towards the close of the first act, Don Adone appeared. Then, and not till then, I understood the reason of the change of parts by which this rôle had fallen to Vitalba.[1] He was a good fellow, but a poor artist; and unfortunately he resembled Signor Gratarol pretty closely both in figure and colour of hair. The knavery of the comedians had furnished him with clothes cut and trimmed exactly on the pattern of those worn by Gratarol. He had been taught to imitate his mincing walk and other gestures. The caricature was complete; and I had to confess that Signor Gratarol had actually been parodied upon the stage in my comedy of the *Love-Potions*. Innocent as I was of any wish to play the part of Aristophanes in modern Venice, the fact was obvious; and the audience greeted Vitalba with a storm of applause and rounds of clapping which deafened our ears.

I turned sharply upon Sacchi, and complained bitterly of the liberty he had taken with my unoffending comedy. He only shrugged his shoulders, and said he was afraid that an exhibition which promised so well for his money-box might be suppressed as a public scandal. That was all I could extort from him; and the play advanced to the middle of the third act, accompanied with universal approval. Whenever Don Adone entered and spoke a line or two, he was greeted with thunders of applause. I still hoped for those salutary hisses which might have damned the piece. The audience had been crammed together now for full seven hours; they numbered some two thousand persons, and were largely composed of people from the lower ranks of life. It was no wonder that they began to be restless, fought together, tried to leave the house, and raised a din which drowned the voices of the

[1] Gratarol asserts plainly (*Narrazione*, i. 66) that Signora Tron induced Sacchi to change the rôles and to dress up Vitalba in clothes resembling his own. Gozzi tacitly admits the truth of this. (S)

actors. Don Adone made his last exit, and there was nothing to excite interest but the dregs of an involved and stationary plot. The hubbub rose to a tumult, and my hopes rose with it. The actors gabbled through the last scenes in helpless unintelligible dumb-show. At last the drop-scene fell upon a storm of cat-calls, howls, hisses, and vociferations. I turned to Sacchi and said: 'Your vile machinations deserved this retribution. Now you will admit that I prophesied the truth about my play.' 'Pooh!' he answered, 'the play took well enough up to a certain point. It is only necessary to shorten it a little, and we shall not have the same scene another night.' Then he left the box all in a heat, without waiting for my reply and without even bidding me good-night.

43

Gratarol tries to stop the performance of the play, which is no longer in my power—Intervention of Signor Carlo Maffei—Conference with him and Gratarol at my house—The worst hour I ever lived through

Next morning the actors came to me with joy beaming on their faces, and announced that the *Love-Potions* was going to be performed again. The town insisted on its repetition; and they had brought the manuscript, hoping I would condescend to make some alterations and curtailments.

Much as I disliked the news, I was glad at least to get my composition back. I made the players promise to modify Don Adone's costume, so that the effect of caricature might be reduced, and then sat down to hack away at the comedy. Besides shortening it at the expense of structure, plot, and coherence of parts, I carefully erased all passages which might seem to have some bearing upon Signor Gratarol. In this way, by mutilating my work and changing the costume of Don

Adone, I flattered myself that the illusion of the public might be dissipated. Vain hope! The cancer had taken firm hold, and was beyond the reach of any cautery.

The *Love-Potions* was repeated upon four successive nights to crowded audiences.[1] Don Adone, in spite of my endeavours, still formed the principal attraction. All I could do was to persuade Sacchi to replace it by another piece upon the fifth evening. I kept away from the theatre after the second representation; and on the morning of the fifth it gave me satisfaction, while crossing the Rialto, to read placards announcing an improvised comedy at S. Salvatore. 'Sacchi,' said I, 'has kept his word.' But this was not the case. Plenty of people stopped to tell me what had happened at the theatre the night before. Just as the curtain was going up and a full house was calling for the spectacle, a messenger arrived to say that Signora Ricci had fallen downstairs, hurting her leg so badly that she could not move. An indescribable tumult arose; shrieks, screams, curses, squabbles, hustlings—all the commotion of an eager audience deprived of its legitimate amusement.

When I reached the piazza, several actors of the troupe confirmed the news in all its details. They added that Signora Ricci's husband had to go before the footlights in order to assure the public of his wife's accident. But nobody believed that this was more than a ruse concocted by Signor Gratarol to stop the play. Surgeons were sent to Signora Ricci's house, who reported her in perfect health. Signor Vendramin forwarded an account of the disturbance at his theatre to the tribunals of the State, and they decreed that the comedy was to be repeated on the night of the 17th.

[1] Gratarol describes the public excitement of Venice. 'In the houses, the shops, the open squares, all sorts and conditions of folk were chattering about the play. When I entered the Piazza di S. Marco, the idle people who crowd the coffee-houses under the Procuratie Vecchie, lacqueys, barbers, players, spies, pimps, and baser beings, if such there be, came swarming out by tens and twenties to stare at me, walked in front, lagged behind, dogged my steps, jostled me, compared notes with each other as to my resemblance to the vile actor travestied to mimic me.'—*Narrazione*, i. 73. (S)

Thus Gratarol's unworthy stratagem made matters infinitely worse for us. I only discovered at a later date that he was seeking to gain time for dark and treacherous machinations against my person.

On 15 January I found myself, as usual, at S. Salvatore, expecting one of those old-fashioned improvised comedies which never fail to divert me. My excellent friend, Signor Carlo Maffei, stepped up, and begged for a few moments' serious conversation. I assented; we entered his box; he carefully secured the door, and made the following communication. But before proceeding to relate what passed between us, I must describe a few traits of this worthy gentleman's character. He is the very soul of honour, scrupulously upright in all his dealings, incapable of trickery or meanness, but gifted with such tenderness of heart and sensibility that he sometimes falls into mistakes of judgment about people who are not distinguished by his own sterling qualities. Signor Maffei only erred in admiring me and my writings beyond their merits. Yet he lived a very different life from mine. He was a prominent member of that society which is called *bon ton* and *the great world* at Venice. Partaking freely of its amusements, he had formed an intimacy with Signor Gratarol. Indeed, he must have known that gentleman several years before he became my friend. This accounts for the proposal which I shall now report.

'Gratarol's misfortunes,' he began, 'have made a deep and painful impression on my feelings. He came a little while ago to visit me, and literally drew tears from my eyes. He is in a state bordering on distraction. What he came to ask was whether I could undertake to arrange a conference between you and him apropos of that unfortunate comedy. It is indifferent to him whether we meet at my house or at yours.'

When I heard this, I felt sure that some scorpion must be concealed beneath so tardy an attempt at reconciliation. I told Maffei so, and asked why Gratarol had not sought me out at the commencement, when Signora Ricci was pouring her insidious venom into his ears. Now it was too late to do any good. I had lost the last thread of authority over my play. The Supreme Tribunal had taken cognizance of the affair, and we were both powerless to stir a finger. All the same, at Maffei's request, I was willing to meet Gratarol, although I could not conceive what object he had in ferreting me out.

If I had but known, while my friend was pleading for him, that this horned serpent had just presented an information to the Inquisitors of State, denouncing me in person, and deliberately aiming at my honour and my safety, I should have returned a very different answer.[1]

In the end, after enumerating all that had occurred in the long history of my unlucky drama, I gave my consent, suggesting at the same time that the meeting had better not take place in my house, and expressly begging Signor Maffei to let Gratarol clearly understand beforehand that I was utterly helpless with regard to the *Love-Potions*.

Maffei left the box at once, repaired to Signor Gratarol, and soon returned with the answer that his friend was absolutely determined to come to my house for the interview.

I spent a large part of the night in racking my brains to imagine what Gratarol could possibly hope to gain by this new step of his. Giving the problem up as insoluble, I laid a scheme of my own, the only one which seemed to me at all practicable, and which I resolved to propose to him upon the morning of the 16th. It was as follows. I should write a prologue addressed to the public, saying that my comedy was going to be stopped after the evening of the 17th, at my own request, because it had been turned to bad account and misinterpreted, to the injury of myself and persons whom I esteemed as friends. This prologue could be printed and distributed before the performance of the play. Then Signor Gratarol and I would go together, and take our places amicably side by side in a front box of the theatre. The whole world would see that we were not at enmity, and I should be

---

[1] *Gratarol has printed his petition to the Inquisitors (Narrazione, i. 81). It is not very injurious to Gozzi, if the document is really what he sent. (S)*

able to convince him, as the play proceeded, that Don Adone was not intended to be a personal satire on himself.

The plan approved itself to my judgment, and I went to sleep, persuaded that I had found a satisfactory way out of our worst difficulties.

Next morning, 16 January, I rose betimes, entered my study, and hurriedly composed a little prologue of twenty-four lines. Hardly had I finished the last verse, when my servant announced Signor Gratarol in a sonorous voice. Yes, there was the raging Cerberus Gratarol, accompanied by the gentle lamb Maffei! And all hopes of concealing this visit from the public had vanished. My servant had their names upon his lips, and Venice would soon be saying that my humiliated enemy had gone to prostrate himself at his persecutor's feet.[1]

Gratarol did not make his entrance like a suitor. He was closely masked, and came swaggering into my tiny work-room with the swaying gait which is called 'English style'. When he raised his mask, the steam from his face rose to the ceiling, and I could see by his rolling eyes, quivering lips, spasms of pain, and frenzied contortions, that the man suffered like the Titan with the vulture preying on his liver.

We all three took seats, and Signor Gratarol opened the conference by saying: 'I have come to visit you, not as a suitor, but as a reasoner upon the merits of this case. Pray do not interrupt the thread of my argument, but give me patient hearing to the end.' For upwards of an hour he thundered and declaimed like an infuriate Demosthenes against what he chose to call my 'vindictive comedy'. 'Not that the personage of Don Adone has the least resemblance to my character,' he added, 'but that you meant it to hurt and outrage me.' Starting on this note, he proceeded to dilate upon the splendour of his birth and education, his widespread

[1] This interview is related at length by Gratarol (*Narrazione*, i. 101–110). His account differs in several minor particulars from Gozzi's. But one can see that Gozzi had it before him while writing what follows above. (S)

celebrity, the offices of State he had discharged, his election as ambassador at Naples, and the magnificent career which lay before him. 'From the height of all this glory,' said he, 'I have fallen in a moment, and become the public laughing-stock through your comedy!' Then he touched upon his enemies among the great, and alluded significantly to a certain lady who had avowed his ruin. That led up to a moving picture of his present distress: 'When I pass along the streets or cross the piazza in my magisterial robes, the very scum and *canaille* swarm around me, leave their shops, and point me out as the secretary to the Senate who is being turned to ridicule in your *Love-Potions*.' He writhed upon his seat and tears fell from his eyes as he spoke these words, never reflecting that it was not *my* play, but *his own* bad management which had brought these tragi-comic woes upon him.

Resuming the thread of his discourse, he imprudently let out the fact that during the last few days he had presented a petition—to what tribunal he did not say—for the suppression of my piece. Then, hastily catching himself up, as though he had gone farther than he meant, 'In short,' he added, 'every door has been shut against me!' I was not so stupid as not to guess the awful tribunal to which an ambassador-elect had applied, and by which he had been rejected. Opening my eyes wide, I turned them meaningly on my worthy friend Maffei, as though to ask: 'What devil of a visitor have you brought here for my torment?'

At length the pith of the oration came to light. Admitting me to be susceptible of justice, humane feeling, religion, honour, magnanimity, and a host of other virtues, Gratarol laid it down as an axiom that I was able and that I ought to stop the performance of the comedy upon the evening of the 17th, and so long as the world lasted. '*Able* and *ought*,' exclaimed I to myself; 'when I have made it clear to Maffei that I cannot stir a finger to prevent the play, and have already been rebuked by a respectable magistrate for attempting to do so!' I perceived that Maffei had omitted to inform Gratarol of my powerlessness. However, I determined to hear his speech to the end in patience. He now proceeded to demonstrate my power by asserting that Sacchi was not in a position to refuse any of my requests:[1] Sacchi had declared he would be governed by me in the matter of the comedy; Sacchi was independent of the patrician Vendramin; it was consequently my duty to put pressure upon Sacchi; all I had to do was to go to Sacchi and forbid the performance. 'If you do not do so,' he continued, 'you will become deservedly an object of hatred to the Venetians; everybody regards you as the author of my misfortunes, and the public is on the point of turning round to take my side against you.' I knew that this was unluckily only too probable; but the painful position in which we were both placed had been created, not by my malice, but by his credulity and blundering.

When this oration came to an end, I replied as briefly and as calmly as I could. I began by observing that even if I had the power to stop the play, I should expose myself to the greatest misconceptions. Everybody would believe that it had been suspended by an order from the magistracy in consequence of its libellous character. But that was not the real question at issue. The question was whether I had or had not the power to do this. By a succinct enumeration of all the incidents connected with the revision of the comedy, I proved that neither myself nor Sacchi could interfere with a performance officially commanded and announced for tomorrow evening. Gratarol put in abruptly: 'What you are saying is irrelevant and inconsequential. My reasoning has made it certain that you can and ought to stop the play tomorrow and in perpetuity.' At this point I begged to remind him that he had recently applied to a supreme tribunal—by his own admission, let drop in the hurry of his cogent reasoning—and that 'the door had been shut in his face'. It was of little use to argue with Signor Gratarol. To every thing I said he kept

[1] Light is thrown on this paragraph by a passage in Gratarol's *Narrazione*, i. 99. He there says that Signor Maffei had reported Gozzi's great distress at the unexpected effect of his comedy, adding that Sacchi professed his willingness to abandon the play if Gozzi wished it and was able to arrange matters. (S)

exclaiming: 'Nonsense, nonsense! You can and must stop the performance.'

Wishing to cut matters short, but not without the greatest difficulty, and only by the assistance of Signor Maffei, I got him to listen to the plan I had devised that morning, and read him out my prologue. It was composed in a popular style, and ran as follows:

To the Respectable Venetian Public,

CARLO GOZZI.

This harmless drama, which hath won the grace
Of your most generous and kind applause,
Large-hearted men of Venice, at the prayers,
Repeated prayers, and not without effect,
Of him who wrote it, now has been withdrawn.

He knows not by what accidents or how,
The various characters, the actors too,
In this plain piece of stage-work, which he took
From an old Spaniard, Tirso da Molina,
Adapting it to our Italian taste,
Have lent themselves to satire, falsely felt,
On living persons whom the author loves.

Scandal, malignant rumours, which abuse
His frank and candid pen, incapable
Of setting snares for names whom all respect,
Have moved him to implore that from tonight
His play, Love-Potions, shall no longer run:
He meant it for amusement, not offence.

Warm thanks, dictated by his heart, he yields
To you, choice courteous public, who have deigned
To greet so poor a play with your applause;
And promises new works on other themes; and swears
That his sole object is to furnish sport
To you, dear countrymen, and keep your friend.

'Well, well!' cried Gratarol, rising from his chair with a contortion of impatience: 'all that is nothing but mere water,

water, water! I solemnly reject your prologue and your plan.[1] My cogent reasoning upon the merits of the case has proved that you can and must stop the play.' On my replying again and again that I was impotent to do so, his brows darkened, and he muttered with eyes wandering all round the room: 'I warn you, sir, that if the play comes on the stage tomorrow evening, I shall not value my own life at a brass farthing. Yes, yes, I mean what I am saying; I shall not care for my existence.'

The excellent Maffei was sitting all this while in a state of the greatest discomfort and distress. Seeing how pale and wretched he was, I rose to my feet, and addressed Gratarol in these words: 'Sir, I do not wish you to part from me under the impression that I am not your friend. All I can undertake is to use my influence by prayers and entreaties to prevent the performance of my comedy. This I promise to do. But I cannot engage to succeed, for I am not the master in this matter. You shall have a full and punctual report of my endeavours. Pray kiss me as a sign that we do not part in enmity.' The kiss was exchanged; and what I shall have to relate shortly will enable my readers to judge which of us two gave the kiss of Judas.

44

The several steps I took to meet the wishes of my blind and false antagonist—History of a long tedious day

How I spent the rest of the day after this painful scene may be told very briefly. I first sent a letter to the noble gentleman Signor Vendramin, entreating him in courteous but urgent

[1] In the *Narrazione* Gratarol gives a different turn to this incident. He does not represent himself as refusing the prologue; and indeed he asserts that on the night of the 17th he was extremely disgusted at not hearing it. See vol. i, p. 114. (S)

terms to sanction the suspension of the comedy. A polite and distant answer expressing his inability to do so was placed in my hands. Then I hurried to find Sacchi. He was dining at the house of the patrician Giuseppe Lini at S. Samuele. I sent for him into the antechamber, and explained my reasons for having the performance stopped. 'What can I do?' exclaimed the *capocomico*. 'Have you forgotten that the sublime tribunal has given orders for the play, and that Ricci is going to be brought to the theatre by one of its foot-soldiers? You are demanding the impossible—the ruin of myself and all my company.' 'But did not you yourself declare,' said I, 'that you would punctually fulfil my wishes in this matter?' 'To whom, and when, and where?' he answered in some heat; 'who has told these lies? I should like to be confronted with the man. Do you imagine I am such a donkey as to make ridiculous assertions of the kind? Nevertheless, if you can smooth away all obstacles, I am willing to submit to your demand.'

The noise we were making in the antechamber brought Signor Lini and his guests out of the dining-room. They protested with one voice that it was impossible to withdraw a comedy which was already the property of the public and under the protection of the Government. Gratarol had stirred up all the mischief by fitting the cap on his own head. It was too late to think of the misfortunes he had brought by his own madness on himself.

Furnished with Sacchi's conditional promise, I flew off at once to my friend Maffei. I told him what I had already done, and with what poor success. 'Nevertheless,' I added, 'there is yet another stone which I do not mean to leave unturned. I may find the noble Lady Caterina Dolfin Tron at home, if I go to her immediately. She certainly suggested and contrived the travesty which turned Vitalba into a caricature of Gratarol. She has availed herself of the latter's indiscretion and false steps, the excitement of the public, and the dust stirred up about my wretched drama, to wreak her vengeance for what crime against herself I cannot say. Tell Signor Gratarol what I have attempted up to the present moment, and come to meet me under the Procuratie Nuove at three hours after sunset.'

The January day in which I had to work was short; and I may parenthetically observe, although the fact is trivial, that I did not allow myself time to eat a mouthful of food.

It was already an hour and a half past sundown when I turned my steps to the palace of that noble lady. I wished to have a witness of our colloquy, and met with no one on the way more proper for the purpose than Luigi Benedetti, the actor, and Sacchi's nephew. We climbed the long staircase and asked if her ladyship were at home. 'Yes,' said the servant, 'she is receiving a company of ladies, senators, and men of letters.' I begged to be announced; and shortly afterwards Signora Dolfin Tron appeared, closing the doors of her reception-room behind her, from whence there came the sound of animated conversation. She saluted me cheerfully with her usual epithet of *Bear*, bade me take a chair beside her, and motioned to the actor to be seated.[1]

I unfolded the object of my visit in a few sentences, explained how urgently I desired the suppression of my comedy, and described the ineffectual steps which I had taken for securing it. 'Now I fling myself upon your powerful assistance, in the earnest hope that you will help me to suspend the performance of the *Love-Potions*.'

'What a request!' she cried: 'what has inspired you to make it?' I replied by describing my own bitter annoyance at figuring as the libeller and satirist of private persons. I painted the distress of Gratarol, and the sympathy which I felt for him. 'The kindness of your heart is worthy of all honour,' she answered; 'but if you knew the whole facts, you would not take compassion on that man. He has not merely let himself be bamboozled by an actress, fomented the scandal from which he is now suffering, set himself up against the decrees of the tribunals, calumniated people who deserve respect,

[1] Gratarol intimates that Gozzi acted with bad faith in this negotiation.—*Narrazione*, i. 111 f. (S)

pretended that the prima donna's leg was broken, and floundered from stupidity to stupidity until the Government itself is enraged against him. He has not merely committed all these follies. He has done more, of which you are not yet aware.'

'I am quite prepared to believe you,' I replied; 'but in a case like his, any honest man might be excused for losing his head and acting with imprudence. Do not let us think of him. I come to beg you to save me from what I regard as an odious source of humiliation to myself. Signor Gratarol persists in saying that I can and ought to stop the performance of my play.' The noble lady looked laughing in my face and said: 'Any blind man can see that you have no power over your comedy. You made a gift of it to certain actors. It has been twice revised and licensed by the censors of the State. It belongs to the public, and the public have the right to profit by it. You will only get yourself into a scrape if you insist on championing the cause of that presumptuous, conceited, and unruly man. If I cannot persuade you, there are senators in that room' (pointing to her drawing-room) 'who will tell you plainly that you are impotent—your comedy no longer yours, but the property of the public and the magistrates of State.' 'All this I know quite well,' I answered; 'and I have repeated it a hundred times. I cannot stir a finger. This is the very reason why I come to you. I know that you can settle matters if you like. Intelligent people will perhaps understand how helpless I am in the whole matter. But the vulgar and the populace are sure to think otherwise, and I shall be prejudiced in the opinion of my countrymen. It is to your feeling heart that I make this last appeal, beseeching you to liberate me from the purgatory I am in of hearing all these scandals daily, and seeing the unfortunate Gratarol exposed to scorn in a base and cruel pillory.' At the end of this speech I bent down, and stooped to the, for me, unwonted abasement of kissing a woman's hand five or six times.

All my entreaties, and even this last act of submission, were of no avail. Madame told me in conclusion that, for reasons which I did not know, the official decree was irreversible.

Signora Ricci would be conducted by an officer of the Council of Ten to the theatre next evening. After that, the comedy might cease to run; and my protégé Gratarol ought to be well contented with the result of the whole matter. She rose to rejoin her company, and I took my departure with my witness, Benedetti.

This was not, however, the last act for me of that long trying day. I met my best of friends, Maffei, and reported the ill success of my efforts. He undertook to go at once to Gratarol, and tell him that the performance on the 17th was inevitable. He must try to endure his humiliation in silence. On the 18th, and from that night forward, my comedy should never more be seen upon the stage.[1]

45

Gratarol's case against me, which had no foundation in fact or verity—His chivalrous way of meeting the difficulty, which had arisen between us through his own bad management

On the evening of 17 January, the *Love-Potions* was given again, as strict orders from the Government made necessary. I kept away from the theatre, and passed my time at S. Giovanni Grisostomo, where I heard, to my vexation, that S. Salvatore was thronged with spectators. However, I contented myself with thinking that this was the last night of the notorious comedy.

When my servant came to call me next morning, he

---

[1] On the same evening (16 January) Gozzi tried again to persuade Gratarol to accept the compromise proposal put forward by him at their interview in the morning. Gratarol's uncle, Francesco Contarini, was chosen to act as intermediary. Gozzi's account of these conversations, which accomplished nothing, has been omitted.

volunteered this information, much to my astonishment :
'Your comedy, sir, is going to be played again tonight at S.
Salvatore.' 'How do you know that?' I asked. 'I read the
posters just now set up at the Rialto.'

While putting on my clothes in haste to see if this had not
been some blunder of the bill-stickers, I was interrupted by the
visit of two friends, the patrician Paolo Balbi and Signor
Raffaello Todeschini, a young *cittadino* of the highest probity.
They came to congratulate me on the repetition of my play,
which had been called for last evening by an overwhelming
and irresistible vote of the audience. On hearing this news,
which admitted of no doubt, I felt the blood freeze in my
veins.

'You do not know,' I said to Signor Balbi, 'what sort of fish
are stewing in my kettle. I gave my word yesterday that the
play should not be repeated. How was I to imagine that my
blameless reputation would have to suffer by an actor's
breach of faith?' My friends tried to comfort me and soothe
me down, while I, oblivious of all the laws of politeness, kept
fastening my shoe-buckles, washing my hands, and busying
myself about my toilet. I was desperately impatient to get
out, and do the utmost in my power to remedy the mischief.

This was my one thought, as the above-named gentlemen
can bear me witness, when a new turn was given to affairs by
a fresh act of Signor Gratarol's imprudence and vindictive rancour. My servant entered and announced that a footman was
waiting outside with a letter which he had orders to deliver
into my hands. I left my room, and found the man there
at the top of the staircase. He handed me the letter, and stood
waiting for my answer. I saw at a glance, before I opened it,
from whom it came, broke the seal, and read the following
missive : [1]

SIR COUNT—Pursuant to the arguments I maintained in
your house two mornings ago, the playbill published yester-

[1] This letter is reported in the *Narrazione*, i. 123. (S)

day entitles me to say that in the whole course of my life I have never met with hypocrisy and imposture equal to yours; and the playbill published this morning proclaims you on the face of it to be no gentleman and a liar.

Go on, I pray. Satiate your vengeance—vengeance begotten by an amorous passion, in part concealed from the public gaze, possibly not credited by some folk, and which is known to only me in all its real extent. Continue I say, to rear your masked forehead in the front rank of all those foes who envy, calumniate, persecute, and hate me. Today it is your turn to laugh. Perhaps this will not always be so. Perhaps the vicissitudes of human life will one day reverse your unworthy triumph and my unmerited oppression.

From my house, 18 January 1777.

PIETRO ANTONIO GRATAROL.

Having perused this fine flower of Pietro Antonio Gratarol, nobleman of Padua, his eloquence, I folded up the paper, and told the footman, with a smile which concealed my boiling indignation, and saved him from being kicked down the staircase at the risk of his neck, that he might go back to his master and say that I fully understood the contents of his note.

Returning to the room where I had left Balbi and Todeschini, I put Gratarol's letter into the hands of the former, and said: 'Your Excellency will learn from this to what annoyances I am exposed by the recall of my comedy.' He turned pale, and so did Todeschini, when they gathered the contents of the cowardly, disgusting document.

Balbi asked me what I meant to do. I replied, putting the last touches to my toilet, that the right thing for me to do would be to compel Sacchi at once to play my comedy every night until the end of the Carnival. 'Gratarol's letter has certainly been spread broadcast before now over Venice. I do not mean to give him an answer. What I propose would be the best means of punishing Sacchi for his want of faith—since the theatre will certainly be empty—and Gratarol for his delirious importunity. But, if your Excellency permits me, I shall walk abroad. I should like to let a certain lady, who bolstered up my comedy against my will, and who protected a reckless avaricious comedian—I should like her to see and read in this letter to what she has condemned my peaceable nature, incapable of injuring a fly, by her wrong-headed, whimsical, unbecoming pique against a madman.'

While I spoke thus to my friend Balbi, the blood was boiling in my veins. Concealed from him, I had quite other plans in preparation. They were not consistent with philosophy; they were not in agreement with the Gospel. Some time later, but not till many days had passed and these heats had cooled, I recognized and condemned them as wrong and reckless, begotten by the blindness of the natural man deprived of reason for the moment.[1]

Signor Balbi offered to accompany me to the noble lady, Signora Caterina Dolfin Tron; and I was rejoiced to have so excellent a witness of our interview. On presenting ourselves, and being received with her customary gaiety, I contented myself with these few words: 'Your Excellencies have been amusing yourselves with the *Love-Potions,* and its recall to the stage. The amusements which fall to my poor share are these.' I handed her the letter.

She cast her eyes over the page, and I could read upon her countenance and by the trembling of her hands, how deeply she was moved. It is right for me to add that, strongly as I condemned the revengeful caprice against Signor Gratarol which caused this lady to involve me in a series of revolting annoyances, I felt a thrill of gratitude for the cordial emotions expressed at that moment by her every gesture. I saw that she felt for me. I saw that, although her judgment had been spoiled by a course of unwholesome reading, and by conversation

---

[1] It is amusing to read Gozzi's *Memorie* and Gratarol's *Narrazione* side by side. Gratarol exclaims: 'Count, you owe your life to some guardian angel, whose blessing enabled me to curb my blind fury,' etc. He meditates 'open revenge', and so forth (i. 115–117). And yet these two swelling turkey-cocks did not think of fighting a duel. (S)

with the vaunted *esprits forts* of our 'unprejudiced' age, her heart remained in the right place and uncontaminated.[1]

When she had finished reading, she only said: 'Leave this paper in my hands.' I obeyed, and took my departure.

It is needless to add that innumerable copies of the precious letter flew about the city. There was not a house, a shop, in which Signor Gratarol's chivalrous proclamation of his rights and wrongs did not form the theme of conversation.

Perhaps I ought to have used circumspection while taking my walks alone about the city, according to my wont. I ought perhaps to have reflected that my antagonist was a man who showed his prowess mainly in ambuscades.[2] But it was never in my nature to know what fear is; and the perils to which I exposed myself while serving in Dalmatia had inured me to ignore it. Therefore, returning to what I hinted some few pages back, I confess that my one burning desire, concealed from every friend, was to find myself face to face with the author of that brutal cartel.[3] Day and night, alone and unattended, I prowled around his casino at S. Moisè, nursing this condemnable desire within my breast. Of a truth, I should have been forced to set fire to the house before I drew him from its shelter. That I shall prove; but I was not an incendiary.

Doctor Andrea Comparetti, professor of medicine now in the University of Padua, expressed astonishment when he met me pacing the darkest and the most perilous alleys on the night of that famous 18 January. He lectured me upon my want of prudence, and reminded me of the circumstances in which I was placed. I laughed the matter off, and he had to leave me with a smile. Let no one imagine, however, that I am boasting of the desire which burned my blood, or that I record my nocturnal wanderings as a sign of heroism. I have

[1] Though this is told to his own advantage, Gozzi must have known that he was placing a new weapon in the hands of Gratarol's worst enemy when he consigned to Caterina Tron the letter of defiance. (S)

[2] Gozzi here alludes, I think, to the attack on the actor Vitalba at Milan, which will be related farther on. (S)

[3] Why did he not call Gratarol out? This is very comedian-like. (S)

never been a gasconading braggart. From a man who could pen a letter like Gratarol's I had to expect some stab in the dark. It was only a blind human weakness which prompted this temerity. I know well enough how to distinguish reckless-ness from courage.

46

The sequel to Gratarol's missive of defiance—My personal relations with him cease

On the morning of the 19th I rose from sleep with a calm mind, and recovered my natural risibility. My antechamber was thronged with gentlemen, relatives, and friends, who thought it their duty to pay me respects after the event of yesterday. They were not a little eager to learn how I had been dragged into a mess so much at variance with the well-known tenor of my life. While I was gratifying their excusable curiosity with a candid and humorous account of the whole matter, my brother Gasparo appeared. He took me with him to the Senator Paolo Renier, afterwards Doge of Venice,[1] whom I had not hitherto the privilege of knowing.

[1] Paolo Renier was one of the most striking figures in the last years of the Republic. A man of brilliant and versatile abilities, widely read and profoundly instructed by experience of the world, he possessed eloquence so weighty and persuasive that one speech from his lips had power to sway conflicting parties in the State and bring their heated leaders to his lure. (See Romanin, op. cit., vol. viii. chap. 7, for an extra-ordinary instance of his oratory.) Yet Renier's character does not in-spire respect. Before he became Doge, he had pursued a tortuous course in politics, and had only escaped serious entanglements by his extraordinary intellectual finesse. He married a woman off the stage, who impaired his social credit; and when he appeared as candidate for the ducal cap, he lavished bribes with cynical shamelessness. Grata-rol has penned two pungent pages upon Renier's character, which are worth attention. 'Talent and art,' he says, 'both fail me in describing this man of a hundred colours. An intellect of the highest, a heart of the proudest, a face of the most deceptive; such are his component parts. A more fraudulent plausible orator, a more turbulent politician, I have

In compliance with this nobleman's request, I told the whole tale over again. 'So then,' he said, 'make a plain and brief statement in writing of the facts you have described to me. Put it in the form of a memorial to the Supreme Tribunal. Petition to have your honour vindicated. Enclose Gratarol's defamatory letter. Name your witnesses. Add anything you think of use, and bring the whole to me.'

I obeyed him blindly; and I do not suppose that anyone will be so foolish as to imagine that I departed in one hair's breadth from the truth while appealing to those awful Three, before the very name of whom the whole town trembles.[1]

The difficulty of narrating a long series of closely connected incidents prevented me from making my memorial as short as I could have wished. Such as it was, I took it, with its appended documents, to Senator Renier. When he had read it through, he said: 'I must confess that the tribunal before which this document will appear is not accustomed to peruse compositions of such length. Yet I can find no superfluities which could be omitted. So it will serve its purpose.'

What happened to my supplication is utterly unknown to me. I can only say that on the morning of 23 January, while I was still in bed, the same footman who had brought me the letter of the 18th was introduced into my chamber. He handed me a sealed missive, saying: 'My master bade me give this note into your hands.' I took it, and read what follows:

SIR COUNT, my most revered friend—In complete contradiction of the sentiments expressed by me in a letter of some days ago, I beg you to understand by these present, which are in no way different from the sincere esteem and good-will I have entertained for you through many years, that I never

---

never known. Whether fortune or some charm defends him, he always escapes unhurt from the mortal perils into which he wilfully plunges.' —*Narrazione*, i. 77 f. (S)

[1] Gozzi publishes a copy of his memorial to the Inquisitors of State. Since the document is long, and repeats what is already known to the readers of his Memoirs, I have not judged it necessary to translate it. (S) See *Memorie inutili*, ii. 126–9.

T

meant to offend you; and that, forgetting bygones,[1] I shall continue to profess towards you the same regard and friendship, in the hope of receiving from you a reciprocation of feeling commensurate with the candour of my declaration.

From my house, 23 January 1777.

Your most devoted servant and friend,

PIETRO ANTONIO GRATAROL

Folding the paper, I bade the servant carry my respects to his master.

Visitors arrived, and Gratarol's letter of retractation circulated through the city in a score of copies. There was the usual result of tittle-tattle, especially among the idlest and most numerous members of the community.

I repaired to the senator who had espoused my cause, in order to express my thanks and to report what had occurred. On hearing that I had received the letter, he replied with

[1] Gratarol reports this letter, but expressly states that he was obliged by Signor Zon, secretary to the Inquisitors of State, to omit the words 'forgetting bygones'. His account of how he was compelled to sit down and scribble off the apology, while Zon stood over him, is very amusing. He taught his servant, on delivering the letter into Gozzi's hands, to repeat these words: 'el mio paron xe stà comanda de scriverghe sto viglietto.' ('My master has been ordered to write you this note.') In fact, Gratarol was forced by the supreme authority in Venice to send this apology, and refusal to do so would have involved his immediate imprisonment. According to his own confession, Gratarol, after hearing the ultimatum of the Supreme Tribunal, went to his writing-table and penned the above letter, expressing at the same time his readiness to kiss Count Gozzi's . . . . on the piazza, or to do anything else ridiculous which the Inquisitors might impose upon him. The Republic of St. Mark had reached the last stage of decrepitude, and well deserved to be swept into the lumber-room of bygone greatness, when Gratarol's and Gozzi's squabble about a woman and a play brought the machinery of state thus into action. Venice, always an artificial power (in the same sense as the Greek cities of antiquity were artificial), subsisting mainly upon commerce and on the tribute levied from dependencies, had in the eighteenth century dwindled into dotage, through lack of natural resources and revolutions in the world-trade. The rulers of Venice, reduced to insignificance among the powers of Europe, occupied their brains with parochial affairs and the contests of comedians.—*Narrazione*, i. 130–134. (S)

gravity: 'I am well aware of it.' 'I was thinking,' I continued, 'of paying that gentleman a visit. He has been twice to my house; and as I harbour no ill-will against him, and can excuse the errors into which his heated temper drove him, I should like to assure him of my cordiality by a friendly embrace.' Signor Renier dissuaded me from taking this course. 'You have ability and penetration,' he observed, 'but you do not sufficiently understand the nature of men puffed up with pride. In case you meet Gratarol, and only if he should be the first to raise his hat, you may return the salute with reserved politeness. Do not extend your civility to words or any inconsiderate demonstrations. A man so perversely proud as he is may stir up new mischief and involve you in further embarrassments. I take it that now the actors will continue to perform your comedy.' 'I do not know,' I answered, 'but from what I have heard, the piece has been withdrawn.' 'Wrong, very wrong!' he rejoined; 'that arrogant fellow will try to make it be believed that his retractation was given as an equivalent for the suspension of the performance. They ought at least to put your comedy once more upon the boards, letting the public know that people of importance have bespoken it.' I could only answer that, so far as I was concerned, the production, repetition, continued presentations, and suspension of the play had taken place without my interference. Comedians, I added, only looked to their own pecuniary interests. The senator proceeded to deliver an eloquent and singularly penetrative discourse upon the corruption of the age, and the ill-regulated ways of thinking which had been introduced and widely diffused amongst us. I have never heard this matter handled with more acumen, learning, precision of judgment, logical clearness, breadth of view, and pungent truth. I am speaking only of an elevated mind and ready tongue. I do not pretend to see into the inmost hearts of men.[1]

[1] This reads like a satire upon Renier, whose elevation to the Dogeship was attended with a pomp and profligate expenditure, not to mention a lavish use of bribes, pernicious to all public and private morals. Compare Gratarol's account of an interview he had with

When I took my leave, I resolved to carry out the recommendations of Signor Renier to the letter. In obedience to this determination, I told Sacchi what he had said about the repetition of my comedy. He replied that he should not have withdrawn it except for the behaviour of Signora Ricci. During the last two evenings she mumbled and gabbled out her part in a way to provoke the audience. Cat-calls from the pit and gallery and opprobrious epithets from the boxes were showered upon her; all of which, together with the reproaches of her comrades, she bore with stolid indifference. 'Verily,' cried I, 'Gratarol owes a great deal to that poor woman. For his sake she fell down a staircase, and now she bears the brunt of public outrage! You have done well to stop a comedy which ought to have been damned beyond redemption on the first night.'

To wind up the episode of Signor Gratarol, I may say, in conclusion, that I often met him both in Venice and at Padua. To his credit let it be spoken, that he never stooped one inch from the high perch of his incorrigible haughtiness. His hat stuck to that cage of cockchafers he called his head, as though it had been nailed there. Mindful of the advice I had received, and which amounted to a command, I refrained from bowing. I should have liked to be on good terms with him, and felt uncomfortable at the rudeness I was bound to display. Had he drawn his sword upon me, I could have understood that his retractation had been forced. But there was nothing in his stupid inurbanity to justify this supposition. Who could have divined that he was planning a flight to Stockholm, and that he would draw his sword upon me there and stab me with words, while I remained at Venice?[1]

Renier (*Narrazione*, i. 79). The man made on Gratarol exactly the same sort of impression by his eloquence, philosophy, urbanity, and learning, mixed with a sense of untrustworthiness, that he did on Gozzi. (S)

[1] The chapter that follows this in the *Memorie inutili* describes Gasparo Gozzi's attempt to commit suicide by throwing himself into the Brenta from the window of a house at Padua. It throws no new light on the personality of the author and has been omitted.

47

Once more about the Love-Potions—*I leave my readers to decide upon the truth of my narration—Final dissolution of Sacchi's company—Sacchi leaves Venice for ever*

In this chapter I shall wind up the history of my comedy *The Love-Potions*, and relate the termination of my long connexion with Sacchi's company of actors.

Sacchi, who had proceeded on his summer tour to Milan, thought fit to exhibit the notorious play in that city. Although it could not win the *succès de scandale* which made it so profitable to his pocket at Venice, the performance gave rise to fresh prepossessions against Signor Gratarol.

News reached Venice that the actor Giovanni Vitalba, who played the too famous part of Don Adone, had been assaulted by a ruffian one night, going to or returning from the theatre. The fellow flung a huge bottle of ink full in his face, with the object of spoiling his beauty. Fortunately for Vitalba, the bottle, which was hurled with force enough to smash his skull, hit him on the thickly-wadded collar of his coat. To this circumstance he owed his escape from injury or death, designed by the abominable malice of some unknown ill-wisher.

The peaceable character of this poor comedian, who lived retired and economically, earning his bread upon the stage, and implicitly obeying Sacchi's orders, was so well known that no one suspected the hand of a private enemy. Suspicion fell not unnaturally upon Gratarol. For myself, I may say with candour that I did not lend my mind to the gossip which disturbed the town; but it is certain that this act of violence inflamed Gratarol's political adversaries, and made them remorseless when he applied for the ratification of his appointment to the embassy at Naples.[1]

On my brother's return to Venice, I begged him to speak as warmly as he could in Gratarol's behalf to the Procuratore Tron and his all-powerful lady. Everybody knew that Gratarol was expecting a decree of the Senate granting him some thousands of ducats for the expenses of his outfit; it was also asserted that, having received the usual allowance for an embassy to Turin, which he had not been able to employ upon that mission, his enemies intended to make this a reason for cancelling his appointment to Naples. I thought it therefore worth while to engage Gasparo's influence with that noble couple for the benefit of my would-be foe and rival in his present difficulty. What Gratarol may think about my intervention, it is impossible for me to imagine. Not improbably he will stigmatize it as an act of officious hypocrisy. Yet I am certain that it was sincerely and cordially meant to serve him.

My brother punctually discharged his mission, and returned with a verbal answer from the Procuratessa and her husband, to the effect that 'insuperable obstacles lay in the way of sending the Secretary to the Court of Naples; Pietro Antonio Gratarol cannot and will not go; the best course for him to take is to send in his resignation.' That was the ostensible pith of their reply; but the gist, if gist it was, lurked from sight in a cloud of political and economical considerations, anecdotes about Gratarol's ways of life and fortune, personalities, piques, private spites, and evidences of an unbecoming and vulgar will to trample on him. I do not intend to expose myself to the charge of evil intentions by setting down Signora Dolfin Tron's malicious ultimatum in full here. I wrote it out, however, and have kept the memorandum among the papers locked up in my desk, whence I hope that no one will have the wish to drag it forth and read it.

Gratarol, at the close of these transactions, finding himself

[1] Gratarol indignantly denies that he had anything to do with this attack upon Vitalba, and says he was at Vienna when it happened. *Narrazione*, i. 178. (S)

disfavoured by the Senate, did not take the prudent course of sending in his resignation and lying by for a better turn of affairs, such as is always to be looked for in a government like ours of Venice. On the contrary, he flung out with all the violence of his headstrong and indomitable temper. He left the country in a rage, exposing himself and his relatives to the thunderbolts which were hurled upon him, partly by the mechanical operation of our laws, but also by the force of a rapacious and inhuman tyranny.

I shall not enlarge upon what followed after Gratarol's flight to foreign lands. These circumstances, disastrous to himself and prejudicial to the enemies he left behind him, are only too fresh in the memory of men. But I may indulge in one philosopher's reflection. The man was said to be, in spite of his many profligacies and excesses, gifted with exuberant health and physical vigour. Considering his mental parts and moral qualities, it is a pity that he did not suffer from a tertian or a quartan fever, the headache, the colic, or peradventure piles. Handicapped in this salutary way, he might have continued to be a prosperous and able servant of the State. So true is it that men often find the faculty on which they most pride themselves their worst stumbling-block in life!

After Signor Gratarol's departure to the frozen North, I felt strongly inclined to have done, at once and for ever, with my lucubrations for the stage. Friends, however, pointed out that a sudden retirement from the pastime of many previous years would expose me to malignant comments. Accordingly, I completed two plays which I had already planned—*The Metaphysician* and *Bianca, Countess of Melfi*—giving them to Sacchi in exchange for the autograph and all the copies of my now too notorious *Love-Potions*. Those manuscripts I locked up in my escritoire, vowing that the comedy should never see the footlights of a theatre again.

It will not be impertinent, as I have touched upon these stage-affairs, to relate the dissolution of Sacchi's company in detail.

I had patronized my friends with heroico-comical perseverance for a quarter of a century. The time now came for me
to part with them. Sacchi himself, aged in years, was falling
rapidly to pieces. Absurd octogenarian love-affairs completed
the ruin of his dotage. His daughter, who not unreasonably
expected to inherit money, plate, and jewels of considerable
value, never ceased inveighing against her father's anachro-
nistic fondnesses. These invectives reached his ears, and exasperated a naturally irritable temper. Meanwhile, his partners in the company resented the despotism with which he
claimed to rule the roast and use their common purse for
benefactions to his mistresses. Detected in these private
foibles, yet far from being taught the error of his ways, old
Sacchi became a kind of demon. He never opened his lips
without insulting his daughter, his partners, and the whole
troupe. I do not expect my reader to imagine that their replies
were sweetmeats. Discord ruled in every hall and chamber of
this house of actors. It came to drawing swords and knives;
and bloodshed was only obviated by the bodily intervention of
bystanders.

I felt that the moment had come to take my leave. With
this in view, I packed up a bundle of Spanish books lent to me
by Sacchi and returned them. But things had gone too far to
be remedied by hints and intimations. Petronio Zanerini, the
best actor of Italy; Domenico Barsanti, a very able artist; Luigi
Benedetti and his wife, both of them useful for all ordinary
purposes; Agostino Fiorilli, stupendous in the rôle of Tartaglia;
each and every one of these retired in disgust and took engagements with rival companies. Sacchi's eccentricities had
reduced his troupe to a mere skeleton. Finally, the patrician
who owned S. Salvatore, scenting disaster in the air, gave the
lease of his theatre to another set of players.

I took certain steps at this juncture to keep what remained
of the company together and to heal its breaches. Through my
mediation Atanagio Zannoni, a splendid actor, an excellent
fellow, and Sacchi's brother-in-law, consented to hold on upon

the understanding that Sacchi should execute a deed according his partners their just share in the management. The document was drawn up and signed. Sacchi cursed and swore while signing; and Zannoni told me that it would prove waste paper, as indeed it did.

Patched up in this way, the company removed to the theatre of S. Angelo, which had been their old quarters before I succeeded in transferring them to S. Salvatore. They were scarce of money, scarce of actors, and the few actors they had were people of no talent. Two pieces I composed for them, *Cimene Pardo* and *The Daughter of the Air*,[1] could not be put upon the stage for want of funds and proper players to sustain the parts. I had eventually to give these dramas to two different companies. The history of one of them, *Cimene Pardo*, brings my old friend and gossip Teodora Ricci, once more upon the scene; but I do not think that I should interest my readers by relating it.[2]

Suffice it to say, that everything went daily from bad to worse with Sacchi's troupe. He did not improve in temper. Receipts dwindled. The paid actors had to recover their salaries by suits at law, and left the company. Nothing was heard but outcries, lamentations, mutual reproaches, threats, complaints, demands for money, talks about executions, writs, and stamped papers from the courts. At last, after two years of this infernal squabbling, a troupe which had been the terror of its rivals and the delight of our theatres broke up in pitiable confusion.

Sacchi, on the point of setting out for Genoa, came to visit me, and spoke as follows, shedding tears thereby. I remember his precise words: 'You are the only friend on whom I mean to call before I leave Venice secretly and with sorrow for ever. I shall never forget the benefits you have heaped upon me.

---

[1] *La figlia dell'aria.*

[2] Teodora Ricci spent two seasons with the Italian players in Paris. After their suppression in 1779, she returned to Venice to join the troupe at the theatre of S. Giovanni Grisostomo (*Memorie inutili*, Pt. III, chap. 3).

You alone have told the truth with candour. Do not deny me the favour of a kiss at parting, the favour of your pardon, and of your compassion.'

I gave him the kiss he asked for. He left me weeping; and I—I am bound to say it—remained not less affected at the closing of this long and once so happy chapter in my life.[1]

After that moment I laid my pen down, and never again resumed it for dramatic composition.

48

We cannot always go on laughing—Deaths of friends —Dissolution of the old Republic of St. Mark—I lay my pen down on 18 March 1798

As years advanced, it came to me, as it comes to all, to be reminded that we cannot go on always laughing. One Sunday I was hearing mass in the Church of S. Moisè, when a friend came up and whispered whether I had heard of the fatal accident to the patrician Paolo Balbi. 'What accident?' I said with consternation. 'Last night he died,' was the reply. 'What!' exclaimed I, still more terrified: 'why, I was with him three hours yesterday evening; he was in perfect health and spirits.' 'Nevertheless,' said my informant, 'the poor gentleman is dead. Excuse me if I have been the bearer of disastrous news.' When the mass, to which I listened without listening, was over, I ran to the patrician's house. I cherished warm affection for this friend of many years, and hoped against hope that the news might be false. Alas! the house resounded with funeral lamentations; the widow and children had already left it for the palace of their relatives, the Malipieri.

---

[1] Sacchi, the last great representative of the *Commedia dell'arte*, was a Ferrarese, born at Vienna in 1708. After leaving Venice he sank into poverty, and died at sea in 1788 between Genoa and Marseilles. His body was committed to the waters. (S)

Not many days afterwards I received the sad announcement that my brother Francesco was seriously ill of a kind of cachexy on his estate in Friuli. A few days later I learned that he had breathed his last. The poor fellow left his wife and three sons well provided for; but when the salutary restraint of his authority was removed by death, they showed every inclination to dissipate what he had brought together for their comfort.

One morning my friend Raffaello Todeschini was announced. His countenance wore an expression of alarm, while he began: 'I come to bring you painful news. Last evening, in the coffee-house at Ponte dell'Angelo, that honourable gentleman, Carlo Maffei, died suddenly.' The blow fell heavy on my heart; for I have enjoyed few friendships equal to that of this most excellent gentleman. In his will he mentioned me in terms of the highest and most unmerited praise, bequeathing me his gold snuff-box by way of remembrance. That was the one and only legacy which fell to my share in the course of my whole life.

In a short period of time I lost successively several other relatives and friends. My brother Gasparo expired at Padua, recommending his second wife, the Mme Cenet who had nursed him through his long illness, to my care. A sudden stroke of apoplexy robbed me of the first and faithfullest friend I ever had, Innocenzo Massimo. My sister Laura, who was married and lived at Adria, passed away while yet in the prime of womanhood. I could add other names to this funereal catalogue, if I were not unwilling to detain my readers longer in the graveyard.

Meanwhile, a terrible attack of fever laid me low in my turn. The physician, Giorgio Cornaro, a man of the highest probity and candour, who showed a vigilant affection for his patients, came at once to visit me. The intense pains I suffered during the following night, and the excessive fierceness with which the fever renewed its assaults, made me feel that I was about to follow my relatives and friends to the tomb. I waited through those sombre hours; but when I heard my servant stirring, I sent him for a confessor. The man refused at first, and had to be dispatched upon his errand by a voice more worthy of a cut-throat than a penitent. While I was confessing, Dr. Cornaro entered. He inquired what I had been about, and I replied that I did not think it amiss to be prepared beforehand. 'I felt sufficiently ill to fulfil the duties of a Catholic upon his death-bed, and have saved you the trouble of breaking the news to me in case of necessity.' 'Very well,' said he, feeling my pulse and frowning. 'We must cut short this fever with quinine, before it reaches the third assault. It is a violent attack of the sort we call pernicious.' How many pounds of the drug I swallowed is unknown to me. I only remember that they brought me a large glassful every two hours. The fever abated; but I had to drag through three months of a slow and painful convalescence.

But now it is time to close these Memoirs. The publisher, Palese, informs me that the third volume will be more than large enough. I lay my pen aside just at the moment when I should have had to describe that vast undulation called the French Revolution, which swept over Europe, upsetting kingdoms and drowning the landmarks of immemorial history. This awful typhoon caught Venice in its gyration, affording a splendidly hideous field for philosophical reflection. 'Splendidly hideous' is a contradiction in terms; but at the period in which we are living paradoxes have become classical.

The sweet delusive dream of a democracy, organized and based on irremovable foundations—the expectation of a moral impossibility—made men howl and laugh and dance and weep together. The ululations of the dreamers, yelling out *Liberty*, *Equality*, *Fraternity*, deafened our ears; and those of us who still remained awake were forced to feign themselves dreamers, in order to protect their honour, their property, their lives. People who are not accustomed to trace the inevitable effects of doctrines propagated through the centuries see only mysteries and prodigies in convulsions of this kind. The whole tenor of my writings, on the other hand, and particularly my poem *Marfisa the Bizarre*, which conceals philosophy beneath the mantle of burlesque humour, proved that I was keenly alive to the disastrous results which had to be expected from revolutionary science sown broadcast during the past age. I always dreaded and predicted a cataclysm as the natural consequence of those pernicious doctrines. Yet my Cassandra warnings were doomed to remain as useless as these Memoirs will certainly be—as ineffectual as a doctor's prescriptions for a man whose lungs are rotten. The sweet delusive dream of our physically impossible democracy will end in the evolution of . . .

But Palese calls on me to staunch this flow of ink upon the paper. Let us leave to serious and candid historians the task of relating what we are sure, if we live, to see.

Today is 18 March in the year 1798; and here I lay my pen down, lest I injure my good publisher. Farewell, patient and benign readers of my useless Memoirs!